Ethical Economy. Studies in Economic Ethics and Philosophy

Volume 55

Ethical Economy describes the theory of the ethical preconditions of the economy and of business as well as the theory of the ethical foundations of economic systems. It analyzes the impact of rules, virtues, and goods or values on economic action and management. *Ethical Economy* understands ethics as a means to increase trust and to reduce transaction costs. It forms a foundational theory for business ethics and business culture.

The Series *Ethical Economy. Studies in Economic Ethics and Philosophy* is devoted to the investigation of interdisciplinary issues concerning economics, management, ethics, and philosophy. These issues fall in the categories of economic ethics, business ethics, management theory, economic culture, and economic philosophy, the latter including the epistemology and ontology of economics. Economic culture comprises cultural and hermeneutic studies of the economy.

One goal of the series is to extend the discussion of the philosophical, ethical, and cultural foundations of economics and economic systems. The series is intended to serve as an international forum for scholarly publications, such as monographs, conference proceedings, and collections of essays. Primary emphasis is placed on originality, clarity, and interdisciplinary synthesis of elements from economics, management theory, ethics, and philosophy.

More information about this series at http://www.springer.com/series/2881

Patrici Calvo

The Cordial Economy - Ethics, Recognition and Reciprocity

 Springer

Patrici Calvo
Universitat Jaume I
Castellón de la Plana, Spain

ISSN 2211-2707 ISSN 2211-2723 (electronic)
Ethical Economy
ISBN 978-3-319-90783-3 ISBN 978-3-319-90784-0 (eBook)
https://doi.org/10.1007/978-3-319-90784-0

Library of Congress Control Number: 2018940436

Printed on acid-free paper

This Springer imprint is published by the registered company Springer International Publishing AG part of Springer Nature.
The registered company address is: Gewerbestrasse 11, 6330 Cham, Switzerland

Acknowledgements

The research work presented in this book forms part of a wider study of the role of reciprocity in economics from an ethical perspective carried out over the last 10 years. During this time, I have received the support and advice of many people and help and finance from many public institutions. Firstly, I would particularly like to thank Dr. Domingo García-Marzá, Dr. Elsa González-Esteban, Dr. Sonia Reverter, Dr. Ramón A. Feenstra, Dr. Carmen Ferrete-Sarria, Dr. Daniel Pallarés, Dr. Maria Medina-Vicent, Dr. Joaquín Gil, Ms. Martha M. Rodríguez and Mr. José L. López of the Universitat Jaume I in Castellón; Dr. Stefano Zamagni and Dr. Pierpaolo Donati of the Università di Bologna; and Dr. Adela Cortina and Dr. Jesús Conill of the Universitat de Valencia for their advice and contributions. Secondly, I would like to thank the Universitat Jaume I for its institutional assistance and all its support; the Spanish Ministry of Science and Innovation for a pre-doctoral grant from the University Lecturer Training scheme (FPU/AP2007/20534); the Valencian Regional Government Department of Education, Culture and Sport for the VALi+d postdoctoral grant (APOSTD/2013/048); the Uehiro Centre for Practical Ethics at the University of Oxford; the Dipartimento di Sociologia e Diritto dell'Economia at the Università di Bologna; the ÉTNOR Foundation and the Instituto de Filosofía CSIC-Madrid for giving me the opportunity to extend my studies in ethics, economics and neuroscience via research trips; the Spanish Ministry of Economy, Industry and Competitiveness for financing the Research and Technological Development Project FFI2016-76753-C2-2-P, and the Universitat Jaume I for financing Research and Technological Development Project A2016-04. Finaly, I would like to thank Diana Nijenhuijzen (Springer) her help and kindness and Miriam Rodríguez, Octavi Calvo and Cristóbal Calvo your love and encouragement.

Contents

Prologue

Ethics and Economic Rationality: The Cordiality Horizon

We live in times made tense by aspirations, which we now consider to be our goals – just as humanity as a whole does in the form of Millennium Goals or Human Rights – and constantly clashing political, economic and cultural realities. In the last two decades, reality has plunged us into several crises. To mention only the three with the strongest media impact and effect on people, there was first the economic crisis linked to financial markets, then the humanitarian crisis arising from war and political conflict, leading to international migration and finally the political crisis linked to corruption and a discredited democratic system offering no voice, participation or response to public demands. Nor should we forget the cultural crisis, with political and economic institutions failing to help and washing their hands of the issue. It is also worth highlighting the education crisis that began some time ago with a system that has not yet, in practice, managed to achieve intercultural, critical and all-round guidance at all stages of education focusing on society rather than exclusively on the market.

Amongst these tensions between what we aspire to as a society and the realities we shape and weave every day, the scope of applied ethics has been extended as it attempts to blaze plausible normative trails we can use to help cope with the crises we have already mentioned.

By investigating the area of economics, this book aims to find the precise rationality models dominant during the economic crisis we have been through, and proposes an ethical rationality model offering a new normative and practical ethical horizon.

This study is, then, highly pertinent for the times we live in, which lack suggestions to shape and model normative proposals and then put them into in practice. Basically, philosophical rigour and profound interdisciplinary debate are combined with practical guidance for human activity. In short, they originate as genuine applied ethics intended to reduce the gap between what we wish for or value and everyday actions and decisions.

The main thesis sustained throughout this work is about the cooperation that appears and develops in economic activity, not only through self-interest or for strategic reasons, but also through the cordial recognition that already exists, *in fact,* when we establish relationships with one another. Along these lines, cordial reciprocity is proposed as a basis for cooperation. In other words, emphasis is placed on this exclusively human capacity to reciprocate, to be committed and to deal with a common objective from the perspective of *us* and not just *I*: an *us* that must be cordially acknowledged.

The cordial economics proposed in this book deals rigorously and in depth with the difference between altruism and reciprocity by introducing readers to the main debates and discussions that have arisen on cooperation in neuroscience, applied ethics, economics, anthropology, psychology, sociology and sociobiology. Reading this study therefore allows us to discover the elements required for the cooperative process, such as rules and prosocial feelings, from first principles and to identify the moral resources required for ethical economic cooperation. This is recognised by the author as cordial goods.

If rigour and depth are two features of the study of rationality models and the ethical rationale of the cordial economics model, the third main virtue of this book is that it moves this ethical horizon of economics as far as possible into the applied terrain, towards institutions, organisations, businesses and civil society. In other words, the author already offers the possibility of applying the implications in practice.

The effort comes in the context of a much more ambitious project that has been continuously developed since the end of the 1990s in Spain, led by the Professors of Moral Philosophy, Adela Cortina and Domingo García-Marzá, who have attempted to show the potential and results of discourse ethics to provide guidance in practical areas, including economics, and a full dialogue with current advances in other sciences, such as neurosciences. For this reason, the Cordial Economics proposal has been supported by the research project "Moral Neuroeducation for the Applied Ethics" (FFI 2016-76753-C2-2-P), financed by the Spanish Ministry of Economy, Industry and Competitiveness.

The move from theory to practice by allowing theoretical models to be developed and improved is one of the circularities demanding the presence of applied ethics. This book guides specialised and non-specialised readers in an area like economics, which undoubtedly affects us all, and where ethical horizons need to be established to lead us closer to the ethical economic aspirations we so badly need.

Tenured University Lecturer in Moral Philosophy   Elsa González-Esteban
Universitat Jaume I
Castellón de la Plana, Spain

Introduction

Towards a Cordial Economy

In *Metropolis* (Lang 1927), the ultimate work of film expressionism also considered by UNESCO as 'Memory of the World', Thea Gabriele von Harbou and Fritz Lang offered a critical reflection on the possible consequences deriving from acritically following the rational model promoted by modern economic theory. Amongst other things, von Harbou and Lang show how twentieth century society had become a highly unequal two-tier system governed by a privileged intellectual elite living in an external world surrounded by opulence, majestic buildings and Gardens of Eden and sustained by a marginalised working class subsisting in a subterranean world surrounded by poverty, dismal buildings and inhuman factories. The aim of the privileged class is to live well and to do that they try to imagine the best possible world and implement the mechanisms necessary to actually recreate it. For example, the re-creation and management of an underground world to maintain the standard of living of citizens outside it will hide any indication of pollution, dirt, ugliness or noise deriving from manufacturing industry, as well as the inequality, inhumanity, cruelty and alienation underlying an unequal social order where the majority of the population is obliged to live in poverty and work without rest to safeguard the welfare of a few.

With *Metropolis,* von Harbou and Lang attempted to call attention to the drama, or even tragedy, involved in any attempt to rationalise the economy based on merely technical and strategic aspects, ignoring the underlying communicative and emotional dimension that gives a meaning to existence and allows the proper implementation of the rational aspects. This is, amongst other things, because the struggle for the communicative recognition and fulfilment of the excluded – those who yearn to live well, with dignity, in equal conditions – seems inevitable, generating greater instability and uncertainty and less cohesion, development and happiness. To prevent such extremes being reached, von Harbou and Lang propose the reconciliation of the two subsystems, the world of reason and the world of strength, through the mediation of another world, that of the heart. This is the domain of those who feel and know they are connected, whether or not they have a function or market value. From this point of view, a society worthy of the name would be one forged and developed based on cordiality; on people who reciprocally recognise in one another the cumulative capacity to come to an understanding about matters in this world; the emotional competences to feel for oneself and for others, either openly or in private; the absolute value and respect they deserve as human beings; and the *ligato* that *obliges* them to be connected, whether they want to or not.

Aesthetically and practically, the modern world is a long way from being like the one dreamed up by von Harbou and Lang during the 1920s. However, it does maintain certain similarities on some far-reaching issues inviting critical reflection. For example, the lack of a moral horizon capable of guiding the different spheres of activity, the unsustainability of the current market system and the incapacity of the dominant economic model to extend the benefits of its application to all societies have led to certain negative aspects, like lack of recognition, the difficulties of the most disadvantaged classes in accessing the economic world, increasing inequalities, the degradation of ecosystems and the problems of personal fulfilment, which limit economic, as well as social and human, development.

Firstly, the crisis of the first decade of the twenty-first century which we have already mentioned reveals the lack of an appropriate moral horizon in areas as important for human and social development as politics and economics. In contrast with the way most governments of developed countries adopted measures to rescue financial institutions and large companies, some of which are socially, institutionally and judicially notorious for their bad professional practices, they show a clear lack of interest in designing and implementing effective policies to fight corruption, fraud, business cartels, tax evasion, tax havens, the misuse of public funds and accountability, amongst other things. However, the lack of government action intended to mitigate the negative effects on the most disadvantaged population, such as the high level of unemployment, energy poverty, evictions, the exodus of young people, the increase of inequalities and the retreat of the welfare state, is particularly surprising. Considering these issues, it is not surprising that Angus Deaton, winner of the Nobel Prize for Economics in 2015 for his analysis of consumption, poverty and welfare, should have publicly stated that the cyclical crises affecting the system are designed to benefit the rich. Amongst other factors, this is because they make it easier for them to rewrite the rules in their favour.

Meanwhile, the environmental problems affecting the twenty-first century show the unsustainability of the current economic development model. Climate change represents one of the greatest threats to the progress and subsistence of society, and this is intrinsically related to irresponsible patterns and behaviour connected with the economic sphere, such as the encouragement of acritical consumption, the indiscriminate use of natural resources, planned or perceived obsolescence strategies, the delocalisation of waste and the application of severely polluting industrial processes, amongst other things. All this leads to the degradation of natural ecosystems, the increase and effects of diseases caused by pollution, rising poverty, the persistence of inequalities and the extinction of many animal species. As Stefano Zamagni has stressed, ecology is a common good which is neither private nor public but is currently being managed privately or publicly. The main problem, therefore, lies in the need to find the right system for managing it – a global management system we do not have at the moment.

Finally, the poor results obtained by the Millennium Development Goals (2000–2015) reflect the lack of political and business will and commitment to meeting the great challenges of the twenty-first century and, above all, the failure of the dominant economic model to extend the supposed benefits of its implementation to society as a whole. A two-tier world still exists: one capable of wasting the same quantity of consumer goods the rest of the world needs every day, and the other underdeveloped but essential for maintaining the current level of consumer demand in the former. The eradication of the great inequalities that separate the two worlds is therefore hampered by the need to maintain their current status. This is, amongst other things, because the so-called underdeveloped countries not only provide raw materials and cheap labour to produce goods for the consumer world, they also serve as sinks and dumps for waste whose recycling is currently expensive, such as technological waste, or impossible, like atomic waste. This has led Amartya Sen, winner of the Nobel Prize for Economics in 1998 for his contribution to the analysis of economic welfare, to propose a change of perspective on development, moving from the economic growth model – based on the possibility of having the means necessary to achieve a given objective – to focus on capacities, based on the people's freedom to achieve the ends they have good reasons to value.

As in *Metropolis*, after the modern economic process promoted first by marginalism and then by neoclassicism there is a considerable underlying deficit of reasons of the head and the heart, particularly because this is a line of thought based on the assumed motivational and behavioural homogeneity of economic agents. Selfish by nature, their rational behaviour in economic contexts is conditioned by their propensity to constantly maximise their own welfare. And, despite the fact that nowadays the influence of moral values and prosocial emotions is acknowledged in the different decision-making processes, they are still considered as irrational elements to be avoided. However, this deficiency prevents, hampers and conditions the generation and promotion of the goods necessary for proper economic development, such as reciprocity, reputation and trust. In particular, this is because, behind these goods, there is an underlying dimensions which is not merely strategic but above all a communicative and affective dimension that needs to be properly clarified, justified and managed so they can be used and promoted.

Along these lines, from a cordial perspective like the one developed by Adela Cortina and the relational one developed by Zamagni, guidelines can be found for creating a deeper economic model that is fairer, more efficient and provides greater happiness for all the parties in the relationship. Amongst other things, this comes from encouraging institutions, organisations and companies to include in their designs aspects as important for carrying out their activities as cordial reciprocity, mutual recognition of the communicative and affective capacities of the linked or linkable parties, public commitment and the active participation of civil society. A cordial economy which, structured around cordial institutions, organisations and business, matches both what is observed empirically in laboratory experiments and field studies and the expectations and desires of a plural society with a post-conventional level of moral development and emotional maturity. In other words, one that is capable of giving reasons for its actions and decisions and properly managing its underlying motivational and behavioural heterogeneity.

To this end, the book will first show the conceptualisation of the process of self-interest as operating for one's own benefit and its inclusion in the orthodox economic model. Secondly, it will show some of the logical/formal and experimental limits of the axiomatic economics model to discover the possibility of building bridges between theoretical modelling and factual validation. Thirdly, it will demonstrate the fragility of a rationality model based on the paradigmatic figure of *homo oeconomicus*, a naturally avaricious being who simulates civic behaviour as a strategy for achieving maximum personal benefit. Fourthly, it will reflect on the critical process that has identified reciprocity as a determining factor for human cooperation, turning this behaviour into a paradox in which the lack of a reasonable explanation from the selfish perspective becomes inconsistent in the predominant economic theory. Fifthly, from a moral point of view it describes and criticises the different approaches to reciprocity observed by sociologists, biologists, psychologists and economists in laboratory experiments and field studies, detecting structure, functionality, weaknesses and basic characteristics. Sixthly, it analyses three mutual recognition proposals as possible foundations for human cooperation, highlighting one of them – cordial recognition, developed by Cortina – because it is more closely related to studies of reciprocity, particularly the most recent contributions from the neurosciences. Seventhly, it proposes cordial reciprocity as a horizon of meaning for the various approaches to reciprocity observed – the type of reciprocity underlying Cortina's proposal of *ethica cordis*, which allows approaches worthy of empirical observable and both demanded and desired by a society with a post-conventional level of moral development. Eighthly, it explores the possible emergence and development of cordial goods, a type of relational and communicative good that enables joint actions to take place in different contexts of human activity. Ninthly, it analyses the application and implementation of cordial reciprocity at the macro, meso and micro levels of the economy. And finally, it proposes guidelines for designing a monitoring system which, based on the communication, storage and processing of big data and the committed participation of stakeholders, offers businesses the possibility of inspecting their underlying dimensions of morality, emotions and responsibility.

Chapter 1
Economic Selfishness: The Architecture of *Homo Oeconomicus*

Abstract Self-interest is one of the fundamental aspects of the traditional theory of economics. Interpreted today as the constant search for one's own maximum benefit, it is a perspective that is rooted in the *psychological selfishness* of the seventeenth century, opening into economic thought through the works of authors like Bernard Mandeville and Joseph Butler in the eighteenth century. It found its place in economic science with the marginalist revolution and the subsequent appearance of the Neoclassical School in the second half of the nineteenth century. This chapter aims to show the self-interest conceptualisation process of operating for one's own benefit and its inclusion in the orthodox economic model as a fundamental assumption of the rational behaviour of economic agents.

Self-interest has been one of the fundamental concepts of the traditional economic model since Adam Smith proposed it in *Inquiry into the Nature and Causes of the Wealth of Nations* (1776) as a disruptive element with respect to medieval economic ideas. However, the self-interest concept currently dealt with in economic theory is extremely restrictive and has very little to do with Adam Smith's proposal. Whereas Smith begins with reciprocity as the mid-point between benevolence and selfishness, and is concerned about well-being for oneself and for others within a framework of minimum levels of justice, the self-interest concept used by economic theory is related to selfishness as the natural propensity of economic agents to constantly maximise their own benefit.

This idea of self-interest forms part of the legacy of modernity, but not part of the thought of a single author or movement.[1] It began to be shaped between the

---

[1] It must be borne in mind that the reflective comprehension of human behaviour included in the in-depth study and discussion made of selfish individual inclinations are not an exclusively modern phenomenon. Throughout history, other currents of thought have contributed to theorising it. These included, for example, the Aristotelian-Thomist current, whose comprehension of human rationality and social impulses contains the type of general and particular justice this study is trying to promote through the concept of cordial reciprocity, especially through the commutive justice governing interpersonal relations. Platonic-Augustinian thought is also relevant in this sense. Its arguments had a decisive influence on the construction of the critical thought of Corneille Janssens (Jansenius), a leading figure in the Jansenism championed by François de La Rochefoucauld.

© Springer International Publishing AG, part of Springer Nature 2018
P. Calvo, *The Cordial Economy - Ethics, Recognition and Reciprocity*,
Ethical Economy 55, https://doi.org/10.1007/978-3-319-90784-0_1

sixteenth and seventeeth centuries through the works of many different authors who formed part of the Hispanic line of thought, such as Francisco Suárez, Luis de Molina, Diego de Saavedra-Fajardo or Baltasar Gracián; or the English-speaking current of Thomas Hobbes or David Hume; or the French line of thought of Michel de Montaigne and François de La Rochefoucauld. It was introduced into the economic sphere in the eighteenth-century thanks to thinkers like Bernard Mandeville and Joseph Butler, and was formalised in the nineteenth century by marginalist theorists, for example Stanley Jevons with his reinterpretation of utilitarianism.

For this purpose, the seed of selfishness as a single action guiding human behaviour will first be analysed through the thinkers of the sixteenth and seventeeth centuries before showing the introduction of selfishness in the eighteenth century as a driver of economic practice directly enabling agents' particular requirements and indirectly allowing the development of societies. Thirdly and finally, the use of selfishness as a single source of motivation for economic behaviour in the nineteenth century will be shown.

1.1 Psychological Selfishness: Self-Interest as a Guide for Human Behaviour

The cultivation of virtues provided one of the principal court debates in the seventeenth century. Kings and queens, princes and princesses, and nobility in general, sought to legitimise their power, justify their political role, magnify their prestige or promote their sanctification by linking their image to characters from ancient times who were outstanding for their virtuous and moral behaviour. These included, for example, Solomon's wisdom, Alexander the Great's magnanimity, Lucretia's chastity, Zenobia's *amour-propre* and David's honesty (Rodríguez-Moya 2015; Moriarty 2011). So it was that virtue became an efficient means of maintaining social order and traditions.

The propagandistic use of virtue, however, led to rejection among those who sought feasible and original solutions to the problems arising in the eighteenth-century society. These problems were closely related to an order, established by an absolutist style, that worked on restricting or limiting the possibilities of developing various areas of human activity linked to social and human progress and enrichment. Harsh criticism of the discourse on the social role of virtue therefore began to be heard from certain sectors, which focused their reflections on antagonistic yet observable elements like selfishness and the vices of the human spirit. Along these lines, Thomas Hobbes (1588–1679) and François de La Rochefoucauld (1613–1680) particularly[2] promoted –from a socio-political or courtly viewpoint depending

---

[2] These ideas were neither original nor exclusive to Hobbes and La Rochefoucauld. They were presented by many other contemporary and previous authors; for example see the interesting study about the similarities between the ideas of Hobbes and some Spanish Jesuits like Francisco Suarez, Luis de Molina and Baltasar Gracián by Victoriano Martín and Nieves San Emeterio (2015: 67–82).

on the case, and via certain sporadic ideas – psychological selfishness, a theory about motivation that conceives self-interest as the ultimate criterion for any human conduct. As Elliott Sober explains, this school of thought understands that: "Whenever we want others to do well (or ill), we have these other-directed desires only instrumentally; we care about others only because we think that the welfare of others will have ramifications for our own welfare" (Sober 2013: 129).

Firstly, Thomas Hobbes described the human being as a rational animal capable of dealing with its endless anxieties for power and appropriation by making pacts with other people (1651). For Hobbes, and for many other thinkers of his time,[3] *homo homini lupus est.* (1642). Based on the perspective that all human beings are born equal in body and spirit, he understood that this equality was the basis of all human beings' problems, as it breeds mistrust when human beings recognise their capacity to desire, but not to enjoy purposes and goods at the same time. Such mistrust produces competition for available resources, which induces a constant state of war of everyone against everyone to obtain benefits. This, in turn, stimulates a search for anticipated security by dominating others through force (1651: 60–61). Human conduct is, therefore, motivated by the desire for survival or the thirst to fulfil merely personal objectives because, as Hobbes argues, "(…) men have no pleasure (but on the contrary a great deal of grief) in keeping company, where there is no power able to over-awe them all" (Hobbes 1651: 61).

Based on these premises and the fourth law of nature –*gratitude*– Hobbes (1651) proposed direct and merely self-interested reciprocity as a condition for the possibility of people's peace, prosperity and well-being. A state of war is simply a breach of the restitution principle: a suitable response to help that has been received. In other words, war is a logical consequence of all exchange processes where some related parties either intentionally or unintentionally ignore their responsibility. This law of nature, based on perpetually self-interested motivation for the related parties, warns:

> (…) That a man which receiveth Benefit from another of meer Grace, Endeavour that he which giveth it, have no reasonable cause to repent him of his good will. For no man giveth, but with intention of Good to himselfe; because Gift is Voluntary; and of all Voluntary Acts, the Object is to every man his own Good; of which if men see they shall be frustrated, there

---

[3]Although the famous *homo homini lupus est.* citation is commonly attributed to Hobbes, who included it in the "Epistle" of his work *Elementorum Philosophiae. De cive* (1642: ij), it is actually a quotation from Maccius Plautus (254–184 BC), who used it in one of his dialogues in *Asinaria*: "Fortassis! Sed me tamen Numquam hodie induces, ut tibi credam hoc argentum ignoto. Lupus est. homo homini, non homo; quom qualis sit non novit (Plautus, Act II, Scene IV [Levée, J.-B 1820: 385]). However, it is worth stating that this idea was highlighted by many seventeeth–century thinkers, such as Diego de Saavedra-Fajardo who, a year before Hobbes published *De cive*, stated in *Idea de un príncipe político christiano, representada en cien empresas* (1641), and indicated that there is "(…) no greater enemy of man than man. An eagle does not eat an eagle or an asp another asp, but Man is always plotting against his own species" (Saavedra-Fajardo 1658 [1641]: 395). Or as Baltasar Gracián, who, as Martín and San Emeterio indicated (2015: 76), in the same year that Hobbes published *Leviathan* (1651), in *El Criticón* that "You grew up among wild beasts and here I am among men, as each is a wolf to the other, but is not worse than a human being" (Gracián 1651: 51).

will be no beginning of benevolence, or trust; nor consequently of mutuall help; nor of reconciliation of one man to another; and therefore they are to remain still in the condition of War; which is contrary to the first and Fundamental Law of Nature, which commandeth men to Seek Peace. The breach of this Law, is called Ingratitude; and hath the same relation to Grace, that Injustice hath to Obligation by Covenant (Hobbes 1651: 75).

So, for Hobbes, reciprocity was merely a social mechanism to satisfy the personal passions and desires of the individuals of a society through mutual exploitation. Thus, any benevolent action must fall within the limits of seeking personal objectives. Any other feasible interpretation of this generates the unease and anger of those who do not feel they have been repaid, plus disagreement and a struggle to fully repay any help received. Peace therefore depends only on accurate knowledge not only of human nature, but also of the expected and fitting correspondence among peers.

François de La Rochefoucauld, on the other hand, influenced by Jansenism and the moral thinking of both Michel de Montaigne[4] and Baltasar Gracián,[5] was much more drastic than Hobbes in his interpretation of the human soul. He attacked the falseness of the discourse about the virtuous spirit as a source of personal and social prosperity (1665). Virtues, that "(…) are lost in Interest, as Rivers in the Sea"[6] (La Rochefoucauld 2003: 162), are merely tricks that human beings use to cover up their true nature, full of passion and vice. As La Rochefoucauld argued, "What the world calls virtue is usually only an image inspired by our passions, and we give it a good name in order to cloak any shady conduct we wish to porsue"[7] (La Rochefoucauld 2003: 201). No rectitude, honesty, chastity, temperance, courage or friendship exists in human beings; only vices that are covered up with false, gallant appearances. For instance, friendship, (…) is only a partnership; a reciprocal regard for one another's interests and an exchange of good offices; in a word 'tis a mere traffic, wherein self-love always proposes to be a gainer"[8] (La Rochefoucauld 2003: 90).

---

[4] La Rochefoucauld mentioned Montaigne in his work *Reflections and moral maxims* (1784: 43). To learn more about Montaigne's impression of La Rochefoucauld's thinking, see the work by Louis Hippeau "Montaigne et La Rochefoucauld" (1967b).

[5] Gracián's influence was controversial to say the least (Hidalgo-Serna 1993). In general terms, other than his incipient pessimism and the atomised analysis made of human beings – methodological individualism – it is not easy to find similarities between the two thinkers. This is particularly true in the main theme of this study, as virtue for Gracián was the most valuable asset that human beings possess, along with its praiseworthy cultivation in both life and death. Therefore: "(…) there is no more pleasant thing than virtue nor more abhorrent thing than vice: virtue is a thing of truth, the rest is mockery: capability and greatness must be measured by virtue, not be fortune, it only feeds itself: the man who becomes kind in life is memorable in death" (Gracián 1659 [1647]: 200).

[6] "(…) se perdent dans l'intérêt, comme les fleuves se perdent dans la mer (La Rochefoucauld 1665: 332, M.171)

[7] "Ce que le monde nomme vertu, n'est. d'ordinaire qu'un fantôme formé par nos passions, à qui on donne un nom honnête, pour faire impunément ce qu'onveut" (1665: 179).

[8] (…) n'est. qu'une société, qu'un ménagement réciproque d'intérêts, et qu'un échange de bons offices; ce n'est. enfin qu'un commerce, où l'amour-propre se propose toujours quelque chose à gagner" (1665: 315, M.83).

Thus, as with Hobbesian theory, La Rochefoucauld's reciprocity concept did not transcend mere self-interest. This appeared fundamental to his theory, as it was used to justify the exploitation of human beings and their relationships, even those based on friendship or love. Hence La Rochefoucauld, like Hobbes, prevented unrest and its negative consequences stemming from misunderstandings and misinterpretations of reality. If everyone clearly sees that human nature predisposes individuals to use anything they have to hand to achieve their own purposes, including people and relationships, no-one will feel offended or annoyed when they find out that professed love or friendship is merely a strategy to maximise usefulness. Consequently, for La Rochefoucauld, seeking virtue was an illusion – a waste of time – from which people and societies would receive nothing good or beneficial.

> But admitting our Author believed, that there was no truly perfect Vertue in Man, yet, confidering him in the pure State of Nature, he is not the first that advanced this Opinion. If I were not afraid to lie under the Scandal of amighty Man in Quotation with you, I could cite you several Authors, nay Fathers of the Church, and celebrated Saints, who were Opinion, that Self-Love, and Pride, were the very Soul of the most Heroical Actions the Pagans can boast of. I could make it appear, that some of them have not even pardoned the Chastity of Lucretia, whom all the World believed to be virtuous, till they discover'd the falsity of the Vertue, which produced the Liberty of Rome, and has drawn the Admiration of so many Ages after it[9] (La Rochefoucauld 1706: xiii).

Thus, based on the assumed virtuousness of the chaste and honest Lucretia, who was a reference for behaviour among the high nobility in the seventeenth century (Rodríguez-Moya 2015: 423–437; Rodríguez-Moya and Mínguez 2017), La Rochefoucauld showed how vice, and not virtue, generated prosperity and enriched society. As Rodríguez-Moya argued, "Lucretia represents better than anyone the strong woman in the world of the Romans" (2015: 431). Wife of nobleman Collatinus, Lucretia's chastity was known by everyone and she was idolised by her husband. Yet everything changed when the son of King Tarquinius (Tarquin the Proud) or Sextus Tarquinius, fell in love with her and decided to seduce her. When she refused him, he coerced her into making love with him. La Rochefoucauld understood that Lucretia's virtuosness was merely for appearances' sake, because otherwise she would not have given into Sextus Tarquinius' blackmail, even if the price had been dishonour or death. But it was Sextus' vice, and not Lucretia's virtue, that allowed Roman society to advance as "(…) Lucius Junius Brutus, a relative of the family, swore that he would end the Tarquinius monarchy and his abuses and would, therefore, end the monarchy to set up the Republic" (Rodríguez-Moya 2015: 431).

---

[9] "Mais quand il seroit vrai qu'il croiroit qu'il n'y en auroit aucune de véritable dans l'homme, il ne seroit pas le premier qui auroit eu cette opinion. Si je ne craignois pas de m'ériger trop en docteur, je vous citerois bien des auteurs, et même des Pères de l'Eglise et de grands saints, qui ont pensé que l'amour-propre et l'orgueil étoient l'âme des plus belles actions des payens; je vous ferois voir Sue quelques uns d'entre eux n'ont pas même paronné à la chasteté de Lucrèce, que tout le monde avoit crue vertueuse, jusqu'a qu'uils eussent découvert la fausseté de cette vertu, qui avoit produit la liberté de Rome et qui s'étoit attiré l'admiration de tant de siècles" (La Rochefoucauld 1853: 243).

So, for La Rochefoucauld,[10] the only true driver behind human behaviour lay in the interest in meeting one's own desires and passions, while society's prosperity depended particularly on all the proposed impetus and success of its citizens in achieving their personal aims. As La Rochefoucauld argued, hypocrisy "(…) is the Homage of Vice to Virtue"(1706: 105)[11] because, what human beings call virtues are merely unseemliness and disgraceful behaviour which, concealed behind a socially accepted but artificial and empty label, allow humans to fulfil and maximise their greatest pleasure without fearing rejection or reprisal.[12] The result of all this is that only one virtue exists – the art of deceit – and only one kind of virtuous person exists – the individuals who manage to skilfully, elegantly and expertly disguise all their vices from themselves and for others and, in this way, express their true nature to the maximum, thereby obtaining prosperity and wealth for society.

1.2   Selfish Economics: Vice as the Driving Force for Human Progress and Social Welfare

Partially published in 1705 and entitled *The Grumbling Hive: or Knaves Turn'd Honest,* and clearly influenced by the Hobbesian view of human nature and, above all, by Rochefoucauldian ideas about the falseness of virtue, and vice as a source and driver of human and social progress,[13] *The Fable of the Bees: or, Private Vices, Public Benefits* (1714), by Bernard Mandeville, metaphorically describes human beings as insatiable, possessive animals using reason for the sole purpose of constantly fulfilling their passions and desires.

> That noble sin; whilst luxury
> Employ'd a million of the poor,
> And odious pride a million more:
> Envy itself, and vanity,
> Were ministers of industry;
> Their darling folly, fickleness,
> In diet, furniture, and dress,
> That strange ridic'lous vice, was made
> The very wheel that turn'd the trade.
> Their laws and clothes were equally
> Objects of mutability!

---

[10]To examine La Rochefoucauld's thinking closely, see the works by Jonathan Culler (1973), Francisco Diez del Corral (2012), Donald Furber (1969), Louis Hippeau (1956, 1967a, 1967b), Jean Lafond (1986), Raquel Lazaro (2003), Michael Moriarty (1988, 2011), Richard G. Hodgson (1995), Jean Starobinski (1966) and Vivien Thweatt (1980).

[11]"(…) est. un hommage que le vice rend à la vertu" (1675, M. 218).

[12]The most relevant maxims in this sense are: M. 1, M. 17, M. 215, M. 219, M. 224, M. 226, M. 228, M. 230, M. 234, M. 240, M. 243, M.262, M. 421 (1824). However, the "Discurso sobre las reflexiones ó sentencias y máximas morales" –Discourse on reflections or sentences, and moral maxims– (1824: vii–xliij) is particularly relevant.

[13]Mandeville openly admitted being influenced by La Rochefoucauld. See "Index to Commentary" (Mandeville 1724).

Thus vice nurs'd ingenuity,
Which join'd with time and industry,
Had carry'd life's conveniences,
Its real pleasures, comforts, ease,
To such a height, the very poor.
Liv'd better than the rich before.
And nothing could be added more. (Mandeville 1724: 10–11)

For Mandeville, virtues, among other relevant concepts, were invented by politicians to tame citizens. Virtues, expressed as honesty, value, honour and chastity, managed to reduce, or even inhibit, people's natural appetites and impulses, which were the true drivers of their actions thanks to their capacity to satisfy what humans yearn for more than anything else: the esteem of others. As Mandeville argued, this was particularly because "(...) the Raptures we enjoy in the Thoughts of being liked, and perhaps admired, are equivalents that over-pay the Conquest of the strongest Passions" (Mandeville 1724: 40). Just as in La Rochefoucauld, excellence of character is thus not found by seeking virtue, but selfishness,[14] and, indeed, the "(...) nearer we search into human Nature, the more we shall be convinc'd, that the Moral Virtues are the Political Offspring which Flattery begot upon Pride" (Mandeville 1724: 37).

Mandeville's thinking consequently deduced that a society's prosperity is not related to virtue and moral maturity, or to the degree of benevolence and honesty achieved, but rather to the sum of all the personal interests pursued and fully satisfied. So, in contrast to Hobbes, for Mandeville, what was required for the construction and achievement of the maximum potential of society was not a political contract, but a mechanism capable of satisfying the personal desires and interests of all the individuals making it up – a place where equivalents were exchanged, based on individual freedom and competitiveness.

Thus every part was full of vice,
Yet the whole mass a paradise;
Flatter'd in peace, and fear'd in wars.
They were th' esteem of foreigners,
And lavish of their wealth and lives,
The balance of all other hives.

Such were the blessings of that state;
Their crimes conspir'd to make them great:
And virtue, who from politics.
Has learn'd a thousand cunning tricks,
Was, by their happy influence,
Made friends with vice: And ever since,
The worst of all the multitude.
Did something for the common good. (Mandeville 1724: 9)

When *The Fable of the Bees* was published, the concepts of both perfect and complete rationality and methodological individualism were beginning to appear, providing the fundamental pillars of modern economic theory. Perfect or complete

---

[14] Mandeville also uses the example of Lucretia to reveal the selfishness underlying virtue (1724: 231–232).

rationality stems from the idea that people are, by nature, selfish animals – calculating beings who use reason for the sole aim of maximising their personal benefit. In this way, cooperation between agents, especially in an economic context, is perceived as tautology – a nonsense not supported by empirical reality – and any efforts made to implement it are futile. The favourable method for studying the economic situation is therefore one that pays attention to individuals rather than to groups or societies, particularly non-self-interested groups set up to meet commonly desired objectives.

Mandeville's pronouncements on the self-interested nature of humans were absorbed and sustained by the theologist Joseph Butler in *The Analogy of Religion Natural and Revealed to the Constitution and Course of Nature* (1736) and in *Fifteen Sermons Preached at the Rolls Chapel* (1726). Described by Adam Smith as an "(…) ingenious and subtle philosopher" who sought "(…) to prove, by arguments, thet we had a real simpathy with jopy, and thet congratulation was a principle of human nature" (1774: 71), Butler[15] recognised and promoted the human and social benefits of allowing oneself to be led by self-interested behaviour:

> Men daily, hourly sacrifice the greatest known interest, to fancy, inquisitiveness, love or hatred, any vagrant inclination. The thing to be lamented is, not that men have to great regard to their own good or interest in the present world, for they have not enough (Butler 1749: xxx).

Butler's view focused on the idea that humans' natural tendency to constantly satisfy their own interests could not differ from God's will so allowing oneself to be led by this tendency would lead to something good, and not to something bad, both for oneself and the rest of society. Thus, self-interest was not only legitimised as the main driving force behind the progress made by society, but it also became the main ally of its citizens' moral and spiritual development, giving rise to a new expression of the psychological selfishness announced by Hobbes and La Rochefoucauld, among others, in the seventeenth century: moral selfishness.

All these ideas left their impression on the construction and development of modern economic thought.[16] Adam Smith, who is considered the precursor of economics as a scientific and autonomous discipline (Etxezarreta 2015: 15), strongly criticised most of the theses by Mandeville and La Rochefoucauld (1774: 373–374),[17] but not those of Butler (1774: 298), and he only partially and elegantly

---

[15] Butler did not appear explicitly in any of the six editions of this work. His name appeared much later in the twentieth century, when it was found either in inverted commas (Smith 1997: 113) or footnotes (Smith 2002: 53).

[16] For a study of the impression made by La Rochefoucauld and Mandeville noted in Adam Smith's thinking, see the interesting works by Raquel Lazaro (2003: 619–631; 2002).

[17] Adam Smith stated that most of these authors' ideas were mistaken, especially when they attempted to eliminate any possible difference between vice and virtue: "There are, however, some other systems which seems to take away altogether the distinction between vice and virtue, and of which the tendency is, upon that account, wholly pernicious: I mean the systems of the duke of Rochefoucauld and Dr. Mandeville. Though the notions of bouth these authors are in almost every respect erroneous (…)" (Smith 1774: 415). However, the name of La Rochefoucauld no longer appears in this passage in the book. This must be due to the current use of the sixth and last edition of the work, published in 1790, where Adam Smith removed the name of La Rochefoucauld, as

criticised Hobbes (1774: 393–399). In particular, the idea that both upheld about virtues being nothing more than vices covered up with a touch of apparent, but deceitful, morality and civility[18] meant that vanity and other private vices were converted into public goods, "(...) without them no society could prosper or flourish" (Adam Smith 1774: 385). Yet Adam Smith recognised a certain degree of truth in the Rochefoucauldian and Mandevillean idea of a society that progresses thanks to the indirect action of those who seek and satisfy their personal interest in the market. This is explicitly recognised in the *Theory of Moral Sentiments* (1774: 383–384), and indirectly in *Inquiry into the Nature and Causes of the Wealth of Nations* (1776), through certain key ideas that were clearly influenced by *The Fable of the Bees*: the intrinsic relationship between self-interest and the division of labour, and between social progress and indirect actions.

> The rich only select from the heap what is most precious and agreeable. They consume little more than the poor, and in spite of their natural selfishness and rapacity, though they mean only their own conveniency, though the sole end which they propose from the labours of all the thousands whom they employ, be the gratification of their own vain and insatiable desires, they divide with the poor the produce of all their improvements. They are led by an invisible hand to make nearly the same distribution of the necessaries of life, which would have been made, had the earth been divided into equal portions among all its inhabitants, and thus without intending it, without knowing it, advance the interest of the society, and afford means to the multiplication of the species (Adam Smith 1774: 273–274).

However, Adam Smith took one step further and recognised, on one hand, that others' well-being also forms part of personal interest as it "(...) is connected with the prosperity of society" and with "(...) happiness, perhaps the preservation of his existence, depends upon its preservation" (1774: 151); on the other hand, he criticised the anthropologically negative position adopted by Hobbes: that society "(...) cannot subsist among those who are at all times ready to hurt and injure one another" (1774: 147); and finally, that reciprocity, rather than mere selfishness or benevolence, was key in the division of labour and in achieving one's own interests and those of others. Indeed, a full reading of the paragraph containing the famous *butcher, brewer* and *baker* passage (Smith 1793: 21–22), used widely by neoclassical theorists to justify the paradigmatic *homo oeconomicus* figure and its perfect and complete rationality, reveals how Adam Smith's idea was not to sustain universal selfishness, nor even selfishness itself, but to show reciprocity as a key element of economics and, thus, of society's development.

Benevolence is good provided it is used to set up exchange processes that generate wealth directly for oneself and indirectly for society. It is an acceptable and necessary behaviour that serves to empower someone else, and to promote exchange-

---

requested by his grandson, and as seen in *The Correspondence of Adam Smith* (Campbell-Mossner and Simpson-Ross 1987: 233). So, in the year when Adam Smith died, the passage was amended and focused exclusively on Mandeville: "There is, however, another system which seems to take away altogether the distinction between vice and virtue, and of which the tendency is, upon that account, wholly pernicious: I mean the system of Dr. Mandeville. Though the notions of this author are in almost every respect erroneous (...) (Smith 1790: 305).

[18] Adam Smith argued that Mandeville's fallacy was based on its attempt "(...) to represent every passion as wholly visious, which is so in any degree and in any direction" (Smith 1774: 382).

type relationships between people, because "(…) nobody but a beggar chooses to depend chiefly upon the benevolence of his fellow citizens (Smith 1793: 22). So what worried Adam Smith were not only the attitudes of solidarity of those who showed benevolence to fellow citizens, but the unfruitful behaviours of those who gave without expecting anything in return or reacted passively to any help received; i.e., lack of reciprocity.[19] In the context of reciprocal relationships, benevolence for Smith acted as a mechanism for economic inclusion and therefore had an impact on society's wealth and development.

In this way, Adam Smith broke away from the intrinsic conceptual relation between selfishness and self-interest, stated during the modern period by Hobbes, La Rochefoucauld and Mandeville, among others. As Butler argued, being interested in oneself is not necessarily bad or immoral. It is related, among other aspects, with the survival instinct, the search for happiness and the need to avoid pain. What is selfish is allowing oneself to be led only by self-interested preferences, which is immoral, as such behaviour ends up exploiting everything, even animals which, rather like people, have an absolute value and deserve respect. Adam Smith, however, maintained interests that were necessarily supplementary: interest in one's own well-being, interest in others' well-being and interest in fair outcomes. However, the famous and decontextualised passage about the *butcher, brewer* and *baker* was enough to have Adam Smith labelled as the main promoter of economic selfishness and the process of reducing human beings to the status of mere selfish animals (Sen 1977: 322–323; 2000: 325; 2003: 41).

Economic selfishness, which was studied and developed in the seventeenth and eighteenth centuries, influenced both the marginalist school of thought between 1830 and 1871 and the Neoclassical School between 1871 and 1874. This school of thought sought to provide the discipline with behavioural predictability and theoretical consistency to convert it into an exact, rigorous and autonomous science through axiomatisation and mathematisation.

1.3 Marginal Selfishness: Utility as the Maximisation of Economic Profit

In the first half of the nineteenth century, economic science abandoned its intention to become an autonomous discipline and its concern to justify the intrinsic relationship between modern economics and the wealth of nations and socio-human development. In these themes, which were backed by classical sources, what really began

---

[19] Adam Smith seemed to suggest one kind of transitive reciprocal behaviour —*inclusive reciprosity*, which was strikingly similar to that developed by Zamagni in the first decade of the twenty-first century (2006). Help is given for one purpose, to empower, and an active attitude is expected from whoever receives. What Smith attempted to warn about with this passage was how unfruitful it was for society to both give without expecting and receive without acting. Benevolence is positive, as long as it is used within the frame of relations controlled by the logic of reciprocity.

to interest the theorists of that time was providing the discipline with scientific rigour and the necessary theoretical consistency to make it not only productive, but also predictive, knowledge. From such efforts, what was first known as the marginalist movement emerged, and, once this was consolidated, the result was the Neoclassical School.

The marginalist movement emerged mainly from the ideas of Hermann H. Gossen, and was consolidated thanks to the works of Williams S. Jevons, Carl Menger and Léon Walras between 1871 and 1874. This school of thought was characterised by the use of both marginal calculus and social atomism or methodological individualism as a source for studying and analysing economic facts. It incorporated the notion of marginal value and the maximisation of utility, both concepts based particularly on psychological and subjective elements, such as the individual need or desire that naturalises selfishness and converts it into both the basis and the only reason for the actions of a rational economic agent (Etxezarreta 2015: 29–36; Roncaglia 2005: 278).

In *The Theory of Political Economy* (1871), Jevons presented his idea of what the economy should be like, which he did in accordance with two basic postulates. He considered utility to be the pleasure that arises from using a product, and the tendency of human beings to "(…) satiety as the most relevant law for the economy" (Borgucci 2006: 24). In line with this, Jevons pointed out that these ideas involved the hedonistic selfishness proposed by Jeremy Bentham halfway through the eighteenth century (1998: 81–84), which was a version of psychological selfishness based on the idea that "(…) whatever is interest or importance to us must be the cause of pleasure or of pain; and when terms are used with a sufficiently wide meaning, pleasure and pain include all the forces which drive us to action. They are explicitly or implicitly the object of all our calculations, and form the ultimate quantities to be treated in all the moral sciences" (Jevons 1871: 28). Jevons, therefore, accepted the utilitarian doctrine, but adapted its discourse to economic language. Along these lines, pleasure would be the motivation that attracts a certain course of conduct, and pain would be all motivation that dissuades such conduct. Nonetheless, the possibility of inhibiting an appealing or dissuasive motivation for a given behaviour exists not because these motivations do not have a horizontal and symmetrical relationship, but because they are arranged in two levels or degrees depending on their capacity to influence people's will. This basis would therefore include all the feelings stemming from physical pleasures and pains – those originating from bodily requirements and sensitivities. All the feelings resulting from mental and moral pleasures and pains would be on a higher level. This second level was, in turn, arranged as several internal sublevels, which were placed in order according to their power and authority; i.e., according to their capacity. Thus, for Jevons, people's natural inclinations were found, for example, to be based on obtaining food or satisfying their individual desires. At this point, the maxim of the best product comes into play for more people in order to offer an order of preference. The feelings that stem from satisfying, for instance, a family's requirements are placed in a higher order than those linked to an individual's needs, and those of society are placed above those of the family.

This hierarchical order of feelings allowed Jevons to determine the place the economy occupied and the role corresponding to it. By starting with the postulate that no motivation stemming from a higher level prohibits an individual's wealth from being maximised, economics deals with the feelings and motivations stemming from first-order pleasures and pain; i.e., the order of bodily requirements and sensitivities. Consequently, it is a morally aseptic and neutral level due to a lack of precision and care concerning what is, and what is not, morally valid.

> The calculus of utility aims at supplying the ordinary wants of man at the least cost of labour. Each labourer, in the absence of other motives, is supposed to devote his energy to the accumulation of wealth. A higher calculus of moral right and wrong would be needed to show how he may best employ that wealth for the good of others as well as himself. But when that higher calculus gives no prohibition, we need the lower calculus to gain us the utmost good in matters of moral indifference (Jevons 1871: 32).

Jevons therefore understood that economics "(…) is entirely based on a calculus of pleasure and pain; and the object of economy is to maximise happiness by purchasing pleasures, as it were, at the lowest cost of pain" (Jevons 1871: 27). In line with this, for Jevons, the philosophical debate opened up by Mandeville and Adam Smith about whether virtues or vices enable modern society's prosperity and development made no sense. If humans are interested in satisfying requirements as much as possible, then they must properly account for everything they can do to achieve this, regardless of whether they are virtues or vices, and exchange equivalents.[20]

We now move on to Carl Menger, the founder of the Austrian School, who in *Grundsätze der Volkswirtschaftslehre* (1871) developed some of the basis for neoclassicism. Like Jevons, he based his ideas on individualism and self-interest, but remained sceptical about the predictive capacity of mathematics. He also shaped a radical idea of the consumer as a sovereign (Roncaglia 2005: 297–302).

Menger, however, established a logical order of economic goods to justify this: first-order goods, which encompass the series of consumer goods that meet the requirements and desires of economic agents; and second-order goods, which encompass the mechanisms that enable consumer goods to be produced. From this dual goods perspective and his logical order, Menger understood "(…) economic activity as a research for knowledge and power" (Roncaglia 2005: 299), where "(…) the wealth of economising individuals is nothing but the sum of these goods" (Menger 2007: 111).

Menger introduced two elements into his analysis, which was to become a dominant factor for the economic theory of that time: shortage of resources and competitiveness. For Menger, economic goods were the source of the personal progress made by the individuals of a society as their consumption allowed optimum states of individual well-being. Unlike non-economic goods, economic ones were scarce and their appropriation was restricted. They could therefore never meet existing demand (if they did, they would not be economic goods). Thus, agents must com-

---

[20] By paraphrasing Francis Bacon (2002: 716), Jevons stated that "(…) while philosophers are disputing whether virtue or pleasure be the proper aim of life, do you provide yourself with the instruments of either?" (Jevons 1871: 32).

pete with one another to appropriate them and to satisfy their requirements and desires, which is precisely the basis for their development. Along these lines, Menger argued:

> Needs arise from our drives and the drives are imbedded in our nature. An imperfect satisfaction of needs leads to the stunting of our nature. Failure to satisfy them brings about our destruction. But to satisfy our needs is to live and prosper. Thus, the attempt to provide for the satisfaction of our needs is synonymous with the attempt to provide for our lives and well-being. It is the most important of all human endeavors, since it is the prerequisite and foundation of all others (2007: 77).

Finally, Menger justified economic selfishness by seeking support in three existing ideas: humans' natural tendency to completely satisfy their needs and desires, which is the basis of their wealth and development; the scarcity of resources, which prevents everyone being able to reach the optimum point of satisfaction, and the competitiveness that stems from the impossibility of everyone being able to completely satisfy their requirements. This entailed having to think about oneself and forget about everyone else:

> (...) nothing is more certain than that the needs of members of this society will be satisfied either not at all or, at any rate, only in an incomplete fashion. Here human self-interest finds an incentive to make itself felt, and where the available quantity does not suffice for all, every individual will attempt to secure his own requirements as completely as possible to the exclusion of others (Menger 2007: 96–97).

So, he focused his study on analysing the scarcity of consumer goods, the appropriation of the best mechanisms to satisfy them and the underlying competitiveness. Menger laid the basis for the modern economics concept as a "(...) science that studies human behaviour as a relationship between given ends and scarce means which have alternative uses" (Robbins 1932: 15). He also raised two issues that were to become fundamental for the neoclassical economic theory of the time: the use of the *Atomistic Method of Analysis* to study the economic situation (Hayek 2007: 24) and, above all, its influence on the subsequent axiomatisation of selfishness through assumed monotony, greed or insatiability, and the paradigmatic *homo oeconomicus* figure.

To conclude, although Adam Smith has been classified as a promoter of the process of boiling down human beings to the status of selfish animals, self-interest as the pure maximisation of one's own benefit is fed by a school of thought that emerged in the 16th and 17th centuries. This was introduced into economic thought in the early decades of the eighteenth century through thinkers like Mandeville, taking its place in the economic model in the second half of the nineteenth century with the works by marginalist theorists like Menger, and, above all, Jevons.

Firstly, this chapter analyses how the behavioural homogeneity of human beings began to take shape in the seventeenth century as a plausible alternative in the search for solutions to the social and political problems and conflicts of the Ancien Regime. The concern for tradition and collective morality of that time proved insufficient or inappropriate to deal with the challenges of the new modernity. Thus, authors like Hobbes and La Rochefoucauld focused their concerns on finding out about human nature and, with this knowledge, suggesting conflict-free relational structures. In this way, a school of thought emerged, reducing all human relationships to a mere game of individual interests in which people appropriate everything that comes their way to satisfy their own selfish impulses.

Secondly, the chapter explains how these ideas were taken and adapted to the economic domain by Mandeville in the eighteenth century to shape *economic selfishness*. For Mandeville, society's prosperity was intrinsically related to the prioritisation of selfish impulses and satisfying the pleasures of the different individuals who made up that society. This depended on generating a place of suitable exchange –the market– which is free of the impositions or restrictions deriving from traditional institutions and from social/moral norms. In this way, economic relationships based on the logics of selfishness became the main source of society's prosperity.

Thirdly, this chapter indicates how the consolidation of the marginalist movement, which took place in the second half of the nineteenth century, moved away from Adam Smith's idea of self-interest and turned selfishness, defined as maximising marginal utility first and personal benefit next, into one of the fundamental concepts of the modern economic model, mainly through the ideas of Jevons and Menger.

This concept of interest was strengthened during the axiomatisation process of economics throughout the 1950s, considering *greed* or *insatiability* to clearly refer to the idea of self-interest as maximising one's own benefit. However, in that decade and in later ones, assumed greed ran into certain limitations that robbed it of meaning, and led to criticism from most economists. Nor was it possible for an axiomatised theory to be both consistent and complete at the same time. There was also the considerable problem of the complete lack of realism implied by assumed greed or insatiability.

Bibliography

Bacon, Francis. 2002. *The major works*. Oxford: Oxford University Press.
Borgucci, Emmanuel. 2006. William Stanley Jevons: Precursor del pensamiento económico neoconservador. *Telos. Revista de Estudios Interdisciplinarios en Ciencias Sociales* 8 (1): 13–33.
Butler, Joseph. 1726. *Fifteen sermons preached at the rolls chapel*. London: W. Botham.
———. 1736. *The analogy of religion natural and revealed to the constitution and course of nature*. Dublin: J. Jones.
———. 1749 [1729]. The preface. In *Fifteen sermons preached at the rolls chapel*, i–xxxiv. London: John and Paul Knapton Botham.
Campbell-Mossner, Ernest, and Ian Simpson-Ross, eds. 1987 [1977]. *Correspondence of Adam Smith*. Oxford: Clarendon Press.
Culler, Jonathan. 1973. Paradox and the language of morals in La Rochefoucauld. *Modern Language Review* 68 (1): 28–39.
de La Rochefoucauld, François. 1665. *Reflexions ou sentences et Maximes morales* [The Firts Edition]. Paris.
———. 1706. Moral maxims and reflections Morales. In *London*. Richard Sare: Daniel Browne. Richard Wellington and William Gilliflower.
———. 1784. *Reflexiones ó sentencias y máximas morales*. Cádiz: Imprenta del Traductor.

————. 1824. *Reflexiones, sentencias y máximas morales*. Paris: Casa de Masón e hijos.

————. 1853. *Reflexions, sentences et Maximes morales*. Paris: P. Jannet.

————. 2003. *Moral Maxims [a dual language edition with an introduction and futher notes by Irwin primer]*. London: Rosemont Publishing.

de Saavedra Faxardo, Diego. 1658 [1641]. *Idea de Un Príncipe Político Christiano. Representada Por Cien Empresas*. Amsterdam: Ioh. IanBonium Iuniorem.

Diez del Corral Francisco. 2012. El rostro de la máscara. In *Máximas*. François de La Rochefoucauld, 163–165. Madrid: Akal.

Etxezarreta, Miren. 2015. *¿Para qué sirve realmente la economía?* Barcelona: Paidós.

Furber, Donald. 1969. The myth of amour-propre in La Rochefoucauld. *The French Review* 43: 227–239.

Gracián, Baltasar. 1651. *El Criticón. Primera parte, En la primavera de la niñez, y En el estilo de la iuventud*. Zaragoza: Juan Nogués.

————. 1659 [1647]. *Oráculo manual, y arte de prudencia*. Amsterdam: Ivan Blaev.

Hayek, Friedrich A. 2007. Introduction: Carl Menger. In Carl Menger, *Principles of economy* (Introduction by Friedrich A. Hayek), 15–45. Auburn: Ludwig von Mises Institute.

Hidalgo-Serna, Emilio. 1993. *El pensamiento ingenioso en Baltasar Gracián: el "concepto" y su función lógica*. Barcelona: Antropos.

Hippeau, Louis. 1956. La vertu épicurienne selon les Maximes de La Rochefoucauld. In *La Lable ronde*, 204–207. Paris: A.G. Nizet.

————. 1967a. *Essai sur la morale de La Rochefoucauld* Paris: A.G. In *Nizet*.

————. 1967b. Montaigne et La Rochefoucauld. *Bolletin de la societé dels amics de Montaigne* 11: 41–50.

Hobbes, Thomas. 1642. *Elementorum Philosophiae: De cive*, Paris.

————. 1651. *Leviathan*, ed. C. B. Macpherson. Harmondsworth: Penguin.

Hodgson, Richard G. 1995. *Falsehood disguised: Unmasking the truth in La Rochefoucauld*. West Lafayette: Perdue University Press.

Jevons, W. Stanley. 1871. *The theory of political economy*. London: McMillan and Co..

Lafond, Jean. 1986. *La Rochefoucauld*. Editions Klincksieck: Augustinisme et Literature. Paris.

Lázaro, Raquel. 2002. *La Sociedad Comercial de Adam Smith. Método, moral, religión*. Eunsa: Pamplona.

————. 2003. Un apunte sobre el pensamiento moderno: La Rochefoucauld, B. Mandeville y A. Smith. *Anuario Filosófico* XXXVI/3:619–631.

Mandeville, Bernard. 1705. *The grumbling hive, or knaves Turn'd honest*. London: Sam Ballard.

————. 1724 [1714]. *The fable of the bees: Or, private vices, public benefits [third edition]*. London: J. Tonson.

Martín, Victoriano, and San Emeterio Nieves. 2015. Baltasar Gracián: el concepto de interés propio como guía de la acción humana. *Estudios de Economía Aplicada* 32 (1): 67–82.

Menger, Carl. 1871. *Grundsätze der Volkswirtschaftslehre*. Vienna: Wilhelm Braumüller.

————. 2007. *Principles of economy* (Introduction by Friedrich A. Hayek). Auburn: Ludwig von Mises Institute.

Moriarty, Michael. 1988. La Rochefoucauld: tastes and their vicissitudes. In *Taste & ideology in seventeenth-century France*, 120–140. Cambridge: Cambridge University Press.

————. 2011. *Disguised vices: Theories of virtue in early modern French thought*. Oxford: Oxford University Press.

Plauto, Tito M. 1820. *Asinaria*. In *Theatre Complet des Latins*, ed. J.-B. Levée. Paris: Chez A. Chasseriau.

Robbins, Lionel. 1932. *An essay on the nature and significance of economic science*. London: MacMillan & Co.

Rodríguez-Moya, Inmaculada. 2015. Heroínas suicidas: la mujer fuerte y la muerte como modelo iconográfico en el Barroco. In *Valor discursivo del cuerpo en el barroco hispánico*, ed. Rafael García-Mahíques and Sergi Doménech García, 423–437. Valencia: Universidad de Valencia.

Rodríguez-Moya, Inmaculada, and Víctor Mínguez. 2017. *The seven ancient wonders in the early modern world*. New York: Routledge.

Roncaglia, Alessandro. 2005. *The wealth of ideas a history of economic thought*. Cambridge: Cambridge University Press.

Sen, Amartya. 1977. Rational fools. A critique of the behavioral foundations of economic theory. In Frank Hahn and Martin Hollis, ed. Philosophy and public affairs 6 (4): 317–344. Oxford: Blackwell Publishing.

———. 2000. *Development as freedom*. New York: Anchor.

———. 2003. Ética de la empresa y desarrollo económico. In *Construir confianza*, ed. Adela Cortina, 39–54. Madrid: Trotta.

Smith, Adam. 1774 [1759]. *Theory of Moral Sentiments, or An Essay towards An Analysis of the Principles by which Men naturally judge concerning the Conduct and Character, first of their Neighbours, and afterwards of themselves, to which is added a Dissertation on the Origin of Languages* (4th edn.). London: W. Strahan; and J. & F. Johnston; and T. Logman; and T. Cadell in the Strand; and W. Creech at Edinburgh.

———. 1790 [1759]. *Theory of Moral Sentiments, or An Essay towards An Analysis of the Principles by which Men naturally judge concerning the Conduct and Character, first of their Neighbours, and afterwards of themselves, to which is added a Dissertation on the Origin of Languages*. I & II (sixth edition). London: A. Strahan; and T. Cadell in the Strand; and T. Creech and J. Bell & Co. at Edinburgh.

———. 1793 [1776]. *An inquiry into the nature and causes of the wealth of nations*. London: A. Strahan and T. Cadell.

———. 1997. *La Teoría de los sentimientos morales*. Madrid: Alianza.

———. 2002. *Theory of moral sentiments*. Cambridge, MA: Cambridge University Press.

Sober, Elliott. 2013. Psychological selfishness. In *The Blackwell guide to ethical theory*, ed. Hugh LaFollette and Ingmar Persson, 129–148. Oxford: Wiley.

Starobinski, Jean. 1966. La Rochefoucauld et les morales substitutives. *Nouvelle Revue Française* 163: 16–34.

Thweatt, Vivien. 1980. *La Rochefoucauld and the seventeenth-century concept of the self*. Ginebra: Libraidie Droz.

Zamagni, Stefano. 2006. *Heterogeneidad motivacional y comportamiento económico. La perspectiva de la economía civil*. Madrid: Unión Editorial.

Chapter 2
Economic Theory. The Axiomatisation of *Homo Oeconomicus*

Abstract One of the main aspirations of the science of economics throughout history has been the formal modelling of its theories. This desire has led to approaches including William Petty's political arithmetic, William Jevons' marginal calculus and the general equilibrium of Leon Walras. The greatest achievements in this field, however, occurred during the second half of the twentieth century, largely thanks to the work of mathematicians like Kenneth J. Arrow and Gérard Debreu. The pair of them formalised the Walrasian general equilibrium and the rational behaviour of economic agents via certain self-evident axioms and assumptions from which all their theorems followed by deduction. During this modelling process, selfishness was axiomatised largely through the assumption of greed. However, logical/formal limits to the axiomatisation of economics emerged, together with a considerable deficit with regard to empirical reality. The aim of this chapter is to show some of the formal and empirical limits of axiomatised economics to discern the possibility of building bridges between theoretical modelling and validation with facts.

Currently, as the 2014 Nobel laureate for economics Jean Tirole argued in *Economics for the common good* (2017: 104–108) there is nothing to compare with the use of mathematical language by economic science in any other branch of social sciences. Steps have also been take to formalise political science, law, evolutionary biology, psychology and sociology, but not to the same degree as economics, which has applied mathematics to a great extent in theoretical modelling, experimentation and empirical validation.

However, the formalisation of economics is quite recent. Interest in it goes back to the consolidation of the marginalist revolution and the constitution of the Neoclassical School at the end of the nineteenth century, when Williams Stanley Jevons at University College, London, and Leon Walras, in Lausanne, used and promoted the use of mathematics as a suitable method for specifying and developing a theoretical model, and for its practical application. As Jevons, stated, the "(…) *economy*, scientifically speaking, is a very contracted science; it is in fact a sort of vague mathematics which calculates the causes and effects of man's industry, and shows how it may best be applied" (Jevons 1886: 101).

© Springer International Publishing AG, part of Springer Nature 2018   17
P. Calvo, *The Cordial Economy - Ethics, Recognition and Reciprocity*,
Ethical Economy 55, https://doi.org/10.1007/978-3-319-90784-0_2

Marginal calculus, designed by the marginalists and developed by the neoclassicists to study the economic situation, proved insufficient almost as soon as its application began. This involved the application of the differential or infinitesimal calculus that had been successfully used by theoretical physics since the seventeenth century, so there were considerable problems of adaptability. Because of this, the formalisation of economics did not begin to reap relevant results until the use of topology and the axiomatic method for the theoretical modelling and invention of econometrics for empirical validation between the 1930s and 1950s. In particular, this came with the works of Kenneth J. Arrow —winner of the Nobel Prize for economics in 1972— and Gérard Debreu —winner of the Nobel Prize for economics in 1983— on Walras's general equilibrium and of Paul A. Samuelson —winner of the Nobel Prize for economics in 1970— and Arrow on the theory of the rational choice of economic agents.

This formalisation process for the theoretical model absorbed the selfishness introduced by Mandeville in the eighteenth century and developed by the marginalist movement in the nineteenth century and neoclassicism in the twentieth century. Through the *assumption of greed* and *insatiability,* self-interest, understood as the constant maximisation of individual benefit, became one of the fundamental axioms of economics.

But, despite the progress brought for economics by formalisation, the underlying model has attracted strong internal and external criticism since it first began to be established. Its high degree of abstraction, its increasing distancing from reality and its formal and empirical limitations have led to a widening gap between theoretical modelling and empirical validation –between formal truth and factual reality– which mean it is not accepted by large numbers of economists.

The aim of this chapter is to show some of the formal and empirical limits of axiomatic economics through Kurt Gödel's theorem of incompleteness and Neuronal Game Theory in order to reflect on the possibility of building bridges between theoretical modelling and factual validation. To do this, we will firstly show the way in which marginalist theorists like Jevons and Walras promoted the formalisation of economics based on marginal calculation and the conceptualisation of the fundamental assumptions of the model. Secondly, the axiomatisation process in economics will be described. This was carried out during the 1950s by Arrow and Debreu, paying special attention to the *assumption of greed and insatiability* as a fundamental element of the rational behaviour of economic agents. Finally, the formal limits of the axiomatisation of the model will be examined through the theorem of incompleteness and its empirical limits, using the latest advances from the neurosciences along with the debate among economists arising from these issues, especially about whether or not there is a possibility of building bridges between theory and reality.

2.1   Economic Mathematisation: Marginal Calculus and General Equilibrium

The interest of economics in formalisation goes back to the early theorists. From a materialistic-mechanical perspective, in his work *Political arithmetick,* published in 1690, William Petty proposed that the method of economics must be descriptive, based on mathematics and on the formula "Number, Weight, and Measure" (Petty 1690: xv). However, the marginalists Jevons and Walras designed and promoted theoretical modelling based on mathematics between 1871 and 1874. Although it is true that many of their ideas subsequently required thorough revision and their methods were revised, discarded and/or replaced by others, their works were a reference for a good number of the economists who undertook the formalisation of the theoretical model.

A fundamental work in this process of formalising economics was *The Theory of Political Economy* (1871) by Jevons. In it, Jevons argued about the need and possibility of building an exact economic theory from mathematics: "It seems perfectly clear that Economy, if it is to be a science at all, must be a mathematical science" (Jevons 1871: 3). Accordingly, Jevons proposed applying *marginal calculus*, a model based on differential calculus or on infinitesimal calculus, which was deliberated in the seventeenth century by Gottfried Leibniz and Isaac Newton for theoretical physics, and the hedonist selfishness, as proposed by Jeremy Bentham in the second half of the eighteenth century, by means of which everything related with the economic domain was rigorously and objectively analysed.

> The theory consists of applying differential calculus to the familiar notions of wealth, utility, value, demand, supply, capital, interest, labour, and all the other quantitative notions belonging to the daily operations of industry. As the complete theory of almost every other science involves the use of that calculus, so we cannot have a true theory of Economics without its aid (Jevons 1871: 4).

In this sense, as Jevons argued in this economic theory "(…) is entirely based on a calculus of pleasure and pain; and the object of Economy is to maximise happiness by purchasing pleasures, as it were, at the lowest cost of pain" (Jevons 1871: 27). It is, therefore, a normative economic proposal shaped by seeking individual happiness, like the appropriation and use of subjective pleasures, and the motivation of economic agents is always the same, based on pure self-interest.

Another fundamental work in the process of formalising economics was *Éléments d'économie politique pure, ou théorie de la richesse sociale* (*Elements of Pure Economics, or the theory of social wealth*) by Léon Walras. Published in two volumes in 1874 and 1877, its author defined social wealth as the set of assets that are useful, but scarce. In other words, they are assets which, if acquired, satisfy subjective desires, but their use is limited, so they cannot be used as much as one would like to fully satisfy one's desires: "By social wealth I mean all things, material or immaterial (it does not matter which in this context), that are scarce, that is to say, on the one hand, useful to us and, on the other hand, only available to us in limited quantity"[1] (2013 [1874]: 213).

Walras consequently understood economic as the sphere of social wealth, related to usefulness and shortage. Everything that is useful, but, according to Walras,

---

[1] "J'appelle richesse sociale l'ensemble des choses matérielles o u immatérielles (car la matérialité ou l'immatérialité des choses n'importeicien aucune manière) qui sont rares, c'est-à-dire qui, d'une part, nous sont utiles, et qui, d'autre part, n'existent à notre disposition qu'en quantité limitée" (Walras 1874: 23).

unlimited, such as air or light, does not form part of the set of social wealth and does not, therefore, have a market value. Nor does it form part of the concerns of modern economic science (Walras 1874: 159–160).

Walras also put forward the General Equilibrium Theory, which tried to explain mathematically how prices performed in macro-economic terms based on different interactions to exchange goods between individuals motivated by different interests at a microeconomic level (Etxezarreta 2015: 35). This equilibrium revealed economics as an overall system where all products were interrelated and, therefore, fluctuations in the price of one affected the price of all the others. In other words, if the supply of a given product exceeds demand, its price falls and the income of the individual who produces it also falls. This producer's weaker purchasing power negatively affects the demand for other useful products, so their price also falls, as there is excess supply. So, if a market exists with perfect competition – where no operation takes place unless its conditions are announced and known, and without sellers having the chance to lower their prices or buyers the chance to increase them (Walras 1874: 48) – prices are determined when, after removing any surplus, supply and demand balance: $[\Sigma\ pD-\Sigma\ pS = 0]$.

With his General Equilibrium Theory, Walras managed to extend and mathematise the partial equilibrium worked on by Marshall and Antoine Agustin Carnout, and introduced into the theory concepts like competition and perfect information, where the exchange value, left to itself, spontaneously appears under the dominance of competition: "Value in exchange, when left to itself, arises spontaneously in the market as the result of competition"[2] (Walras 2013: 83).

With their ideas and methods, Jevons and Walras managed to consolidate the *marginalist revolution* and to found the Neoclassical School, a strand of economic thought whose main ideas were the basis for the conventional economic theory which currently dominates the discipline around the world. Among other items, we find: an analysis method based on marginality, individuality and the rigorous mathematisation of all its postulates and theorems; an anthropologically negative notion of the human being, used as a fundamental axiom of the whole theory; and a perfect conception of both available information and underlying competition. Moreover, the Neoclassical School also included other fundamental concepts and ideas in its development process throughout the twentieth century. These include Adam Smith's *invisible hand* and his *unintended consequences*, free trade, moving capital and products, market deregulation, and the minimal state or eradication of the public sector, among many other things (Etxezarreta 2015).

Marginal calculation and general equilibrium, however, proved insufficient for the difficult task of formalising economic theory. Firstly, Jevonsian marginal calculation turned out to be of very limited use for economic analysis. As has been mentioned, it involved adapting the infinitesimal calculus that had given such good results in theoretical physics since the seventeenth century. But economics is a social science and analysis of its content turned out to be much more complicated

---

[2] "La valeur d'échange laissée à elle-même se produit naturelle ment sur le marché sous l'empire de la *concurrence*" (Walras 1874: 48).

than the study of factual physics because of the quantity and diversity of variables involved. Meanwhile, Walras's works did not manage to mathematically demonstrate the existence, uniqueness and stability of general equilibrium. Based on this, many economists, particularly those interested in formalising the Walrasian general equilibrium, began to become interested in methods such as topology, axiomatisation and praxeology, allowing the logical-formal development of economic theory.

2.2 Economic Axiomatisation: The Topological-Axiomatic Method and Praxeology

With set theory, developed by Georg Cantor between 1874 and 1897, the branch of mathematics studying the properties and relations of sets, both the logicians and mathematicians of the period assumed it was possible to base both arithmetic and the other branches of mathematics on logic (Huertas and Manzano 2005: 4). However, in 1902, Bertrand Russell suggested that, based on the definition of set given by Cantor as the set of elements not including itself, the theory inevitably led to certain logical contradictions that made it inconsistent (Russell 1902: 124–125 [Heijenoort 1967]).[3] Formulating his idea through the *barber's paradox*, Russell showed that the set of all sets that does not have itself as a member simultaneously does and does not have itself as a member. In other words, there is no way of proving whether the set of all sets is a set, as proving that it does not form part of its own content automatically makes it part of that content and, therefore, means that it cannot be considered a set (José 2006: 84).

To deal with the challenge posed by the paradox of set theory to any attempt to provide a logical formalisation of arithmetic and the other branches of mathematics, in 1908 Ernst Zermelo (1908) proposed a solution that would later be refined and perfected by Abraham Fraenkel (1922), Thoralf Skolem (1923) and John von Neumann (1925) among others: to determine some propositions – axioms so clear and obvious that they are accepted without prior proof. From these it would be possible to consistently derive a whole theoremic structure of theory exclusively using the principles of logic (Murawski 2010, Nagel and Newman 1970: 19). So, axiomatic set theory establishes that only groups of elements meeting the conditions imposed by its elementary axioms – Extensionality, Foundation, Schema of specification, Pairing, Union, Schema of replacement, Infinity, Power set and Choice – can be accepted as sets (Vialar 2015: 17; Cameron 1999: 114–118).

The solution provided by Zermelo for set theory, clearly influenced by Euclidian geometry,[4] was enthusiastically received by large numbers of logicians and mathematicians of the time. In 1920, the leading mathematician David Hilbert even suggested to the scientific community a programme later known as the *Hilbert*

---

[3] A contradiction is a "(…) set of two statements, one of which is the negation of the other" (Mosterín and Torreti 2002: 132).

[4] Euclid systemised geometry based on five self-evident axioms.

programme (Franks 2009) to provide all branches of mathematics with a logical basis, thereby avoiding the dreaded inconsistency. In other words, the programme prevented the coexistence of theorems generating contradictions within the system (where proving one negated the other).

> The goal of finding a secure foundation of mathematics is also my own. I should like to regain for mathematics the old reputation for incontestable truth, which it appears to have lost as a result of the paradoxes of set theory; but I believe that this can be done while fully preserving its accomplishments. The method that I follow is none other than the axiomatic (Hilbert 1998 [1922]: 200).

To achieve this aim, to draw up a fully formalised deductive system, the Hilbert programme established two basic objectives: to fully and accurately axiomatise all mathematical theories and to prove the consistency of the underlying axiomatic system (Torres 1995). To do this, Hilbert proposed starting with elementary arithmetic, the most basic of all mathematical theories and extending it from there to other much more complex theories (Mosterín 2013: 118).

The *Hilbert programme* began to make considerably progress when, in 1928, Hilbert and Wilhelm Ackermann managed to precisely delimit first-order logic in *Grundzüge der Theoretischen Logik* (*Principles of Mathematical Logic*), although they did not specify whether the deductive calculation they presented was semantically complete and repeatedly confused semantic and syntactic ideas. Both issues were resolved by a young member of the *Vienna Circle* called Kurt Gödel in his doctoral thesis *Die Vollständigkeit der Axiome des logischen Funktoinenkalküls* (1930), deposited in 1929 and defended in 1930 (Mosterín 2000: 226–228). In it, Gödel demonstrated that the deductive calculus proposed by Hibert and Akermann was semantically complete, and he precisely differentiated semantic notions from syntactic ones, an encouraging first success for the *Hilbert programme*. It seemed that finally the attempt to find a complete formalisation of all mathematical theory was close to success.

The progress of the *Hilbert programme* influenced the economists of the time, particularly those seeking a mathematical solution to prove the existence, uniqueness and stability of Walras's general equilibrium. So, at the end of the twenties and beginning of the thirties, economists began to abandon the differential calculus used by Jevons and Walras in their work. It gradually came to be replaced by the mathematical tool of topology (Roncaglia 2005: 345–346), the branch of mathematics concerning itself with the properties of figures that remain invariable (Macho 2002: ix), and the method of axiomatic theorisation consisting of formulating a rigorous set of basic assumptions expressed in formal terms. Both tools – topology and axiomatisation – were simultaneously used by Arrow and Debreu in *Social choice and Individual values* (Arrow 1951), "Existence of an Equilibrium for a Competitive Economy" (Arrow and Debreu 1954) and *Theory of Value. An axiomatic analysis of economic equilibrium* (Debreu 1959) to offer a solution to general equilibrium based on certain initial axioms (Roncaglia 2005; Franco de los Ríos 2005): convex preference, perfect competition and independent demand.[5] Based on this, as Roncaglia argues, the analysis of the general economic equilibrium is considered to be the starting point to reduce economic theory to "(...) a precise set of axioms from which, with the addition of further assumptions which could change from case to case, we can deduct a series of theorems constituting a 'complete' representation of economic reality or at least, according to the famous thesis of the early Wittgenstein, of everything in economic reality which is capable of scientific expression" (Roncaglia 2005: 348).

But the topological-axiomatic method was not reduced to the Walrasian general equilibrium. Just as neoclassicism had reduced economic science to the study of rational conduct,[6] some mathematicians and economists involved in developing revealed preference theory, particularly Arrow, were concerned to axiomatise the behaviour of economic agents in order to ensure their rationality (Brunet and Pastor 2001: 167).

Revealed preference theory, introduced by Giovanni B. Antonelli in 1886 in his work *Sulla teoria matemática della economia pura*, fixed by Samuelson (1938, 1947, 1948) and subsequently developed by John Green (1957), Arrow (1950, 1951, 1959), James Henderson and Richard Quandt (1971), Hal Varian (1978) and Mas-Colell et al. (1995), among others, understands that it is possible to pick out the best possible response of each individual by observing his or her purchasing habits (Celaya 1962: 7–61). It means that, if a set of goods is available and if it is observed that an agent chooses [A] ahead of [B], and [B] ahead of [C], by applying transitive criteria, [A] is shown to be preferred to [C] (Mas-Colell et al. 1995: 10). In this way, the utility of the agent is predetermined and ordered ordinally under the numerical representation of its observable internal preferences. There can be no doubt about this if one does not wish to be inconsistent and, therefore, irrational.

From this point of view, the rational conduct of the economic agent requires the internal consistency of its order of preferences and this, in turn, requires scrupulously following the natural human propensity to constantly maximise one's own personal welfare (Sen 1977, 1987, 2000). So, based on these premises, any deviation from the maximisation of one's own interest results in decision-making that may not correspond to the correct natural order of the observable preferences. This proves internal inconsistency and, therefore, irrationality in the agent. For this reason, orthodox economic theory assumes that, when faced with different options, human beings

---

[5] By axiom, the Oxford English Dictionary (2017) understands "A statement or proposition which is regarded as being established, accepted, or self-evidently true, and, in mathematics "A statement or proposition on which an abstractly defined structure is based". And the *Diccionario de la Lengua Española* (2017) understands a "Proposition so clear and obvious that is accepted without proof" and, in mathematics "Each fundamental and unprovable principle on which a theory is constructed".

[6] As Ludwig von Mises, one of the leading representatives of the Austrian School stated, in this sense, "The transformation of thought which the classical economists had initiated was brought to its consummation only by modern subjectivist economics, which converted the theory of market prices into a general theory of human choice" (Mises 1998: 3).

tend to choose the goods that allow them not only to satisfy their internal preferences but also to maximise them.

Arrow suggested in *A Difficulty in the Concept of Social Welfare* (1950) and *Social Choice and Individual Values* (1951) that the notion of rational behaviour as "(...) a choice among a given set of alternative actions maximising a target function (more specifically, the expected value of a given utility function) taking account of the expected outcome of each course of action" (Roncaglia 2005: 501), required three principal axioms to be followed: *completeness* – the agent knows its preferences and can compare and order them; *transitivity* – the agent is consistent with its internal order of preferences, so if it prefers A to B and B to C it will also prefer A to C; and *reflexivity* – the agent makes decisions which are at least as good at meeting its aims as the other possible choices (García-Lapresta 1992: 249; Pearce 1999: 31–32). Based on these three basic axioms, other axioms, or assumptions about the rational behaviour of economic agents were formulated, such as *continuity* – if there are identical or similar goods the order of preference will be the same; *monotonicity*[7] – as goods are scarce and cannot fully meet the maximising expectations of the agent, utility is directly proportional to the quantity of each of them bought; *convexity* – if one good is preferred to another, intermediate goods will be too; *independence* – if two goods are equal in some respects, the preference will be determined by what differentiates them; *greed* – faced with two groups of available goods, the agent will prefer the one that has the largest quantity of them; *insatiability* – in as far as resources are scarce and desires unlimited, the agent will never feel satisfied with the goods he or she possesses and will therefore always try to seek a better result, and so on.

Underlying this set of axioms, especially *monotonicity*, *greed* and *insatiability*, is a rather stylised, radically subjective and relatively abstract view of the concept of human being – *homo oeconomicus* – a long way from the Smithian anthropological view.

From the Austrian School, Ludwig von Mises also worked on axiomatising economics in *Human Action: A Treatise on Economics* (1949). However, unlike Arrow, Debreu and others, von Mises rejected positivism and the methods of natural scientists because he considered them inappropriate[8] (von Mises 1998: 31). For him, human action is too complex for it to be understood through observation and quantification. The number of variables underlying it is so high it is impossible to find universal constants and statistical parameters. On this basis, for von Mises, the

---

[7]This axiom is also known by other names such as *greed, non-satiation* or *dominion*. It is the axiom most clearly related to economic selfishness. However, although the assumption of *monotonicity* includes that of *greed*, that of *greed* does not include that of *monotonicity*.

[8]As von Mises argues in this respect, "The postulates of positivism and kindred schools of metaphysics are therefore illusory. It is impossible to reform the sciences of human action according to the pattern of physics and the other natural sciences. There is no means to establish an *a posteriori* theory of human conduct and social events. History can neither prove nor disprove any general statement in the manner in which the natural sciences accept or reject a hypothesis on the ground of laboratory experiments. Neither experimental verification nor experimental falsification of a general proposition is possible in its field" (von Mises 1998: 31).

method of economics is not mathematics but rather terminological conceptualisation and logical argument through praxeology, an aprioristic and deductive method based on analytical judgements whose main aim is to clarify, through argument, the conceptual root of economics to spell out the mental structure of human behaviour (von Mises 1998: 38–42). In other words, to find, in reason and through reason, the absolute and self-evident truths of human action which nothing and no-one can doubt or deny without falling into a pragmatic contradiction.[9]

> However, the sciences of human action differ radically from the natural sciences. All authors eager to construct an epistemological system of the sciences of human action according to the pattern of the natural sciences err lamentably. (…) The theorems attained by correct praxeological reasoning are not only perfectly certain and incontestable, like the correct mathematical theorems. They refer, moreover, with the full rigidity of their apodictic certainty and incontestability to the reality of action as it appears in life and history. Praxeology conveys exact and precise knowledge of real things (von Mises 1998: 39).

Through the application of the praxeological method, von Mises established the different axioms that make up the mental structure of individuals. To do this, von Mises began with the idea that all the theorems of economics follow deductively from a self-evident statement whose truth is determined aprioristically[10]: the axiom of action (von Mises 1998: 11). This axiom establishes that all human beings act consciously with a purpose, end or objective: to move from a specific situation to another more satisfactory one.[11] This is precisely the fundamental characteristic of the human being: carrying out conscious actions. It is why humans must be seen as homo sapiens, but also, and above all, as homo agens (von Mises 1962:4; 1998: 14). Based on this self-evident idea, von Mises proposed the four theorems that follow deductively and constitute, *a priori*, the mental structure of human action: the law of decreasing marginal utility; the law of variable proportions; the law of temporary preference; and Ricardo's law of association.

The various attempts to axiomatise the economic model, based either on mathematics or praxeology, have proved to be limited. Firstly, the publication of the Incompleteness Theorem in 1931 demonstrated that no arithmetical theory can be axiomatic, consistent and complete all at the same time. In other words, all axiomatic methods contain certain intrinsic constraints that exclude the possibility that not even the ordinary arithmetic of integers is completely axiomatised (Nagel and Newman 1970: 3). Meanwhile, the emergence of Evolutionary Game Theory in 1982 and, above all, Neuronal Game Theory in 2001 is providing data on the deficit of empirical realism in the predominant economic model suggesting the need to reflect on the possibility of changing and/or reviewing its fundamental concepts, axioms and assumptions.

---

[9] Human beings have the capacity to know the necessary truth from what is *a priori* self-evident "The starting point of all praxeological thinking is not arbitrarily chosen axioms, but a self-evident proposition, fully, clearly and necessarily present in every human mind" (von Mises 1962: 4).

[10] In this way, for von Mises, action precedes experience.

[11] Trying to refute the axiom of action creates contradiction, according to von Mises, as it requires the statement of its truth.

2.3   Economic Theorisation: Limits and Consequences of the Deductive Model

Keen to continue contributing to the *Hilbert programme* by "(…) finding finite evidence of the consistency of the axioms of the analysis" (Mosterín 2000: 231), in the end Gödel found that this was unachievable. His proof of the theorem of incompleteness in *Über formal unentscheidbare Sätze der Principia Mathematica und verwandter Systeme* (Gödel 1931) involved, among other things, the fact that any axiomatic theory with claims to completeness is inconsistent – it will have undeterminable propositions it cannot prove (Mosterín 2000: 226–228). Similarly, Gödel's work noted two determining aspects for the axiomatic method:

> He offered mathematicians the astonishingly melancholy conclusion that the axiomatic method has certain intrinsic limitations which rule out the possibility of even ordinary arithmetic with whole numbers every being fully axiomatised. Moreover, he showed that it is impossible to establish the internal logical consistency of a broad class of deductive systems (Nagel and Newman 1970: 20).

An axiomatic theory like the proposal based on neoclassical economics with the works by Arrow, Debreu, von Mises and others cannot therefore be consistent and complete at the same time. It is necessary to choose whether to it should consider all reality or concern itself only with internal coherence. If it chooses to be complete it must accept coexistence with theorems which, although they are true, cannot be proved based on the theory itself. If internal consistency is chosen, it can only take account of the specific reality within the limits imposed by its axioms. Economics as axiomatised by the neoclassicists, for example, can only take account of the behavioural reality relating to merely selfish beings.

With his work, Gödel established an alternative thought current, which began in the nineteenth century with the works by Carl Friedrich Gauss, János Bolyai, Nikolái Ivánovich Lobachevsky and, above all, Bernhard Riemann, on the axiom of parallels in Euclidian geometry. These authors had managed to demonstrate that, on the one hand, this fundamental proposal was neither so evident and clear as believed, nor could it be deduced from the other axioms in the theory. On the other hand, it was possible to deliberate new geometrical theories from axioms that differed from Euclidian ones.[12] Similarly, the Incompleteness Theorem does not attack the axiomatisation or mathematisation of theories, but rather the absolutist and monopolist ambition for them to account for all reality: the belief that there is, or can be, a theory that explains all the statements in the world based on certain self-evident proposals. In addition, according to Xavier Zubiri's (1982, 1983) interpretation, the theorem of incompleteness proposes "(…) "what was constructed by postulation takes 'in its own right' more properties than those formally postulated, expressed as,

---

[12] Riemann's study about the axiom of parallels in classical geometry led to a new theory, one applicable to curved spaces and not only flat ones, like those described by Euclid (1854). This new theory was crucial in formalising the General Theory of Relativity put forward by Albert Einstein in November 1915.

in my view, that what is postulated as reality more than it is truth" (1982: 146). In other words, it displays "(…) the previousness of what is real over what is true in mathematics" (1982: 146). In this way, Zubiri emphasises the importance of the empirical basis of theories and the need for their postulates to concern themselves not only with finding the truth through their internal consistency but also staying up to date with respect to the reality of the world.[13]

As for this reality, before Zubiri's "truth", the emergence of disciplines such as Game Theory and, above all, Evolutionary Game Theory from 1982 and Neuronal Game Theory from 2001, called into question the empirical basis of axiomatised economic theory (Bowles 2016; Camerer et al. 2005; Glimcher et al. 2008; Fehr and Rockenbach 2004). Among other things, through laboratory experiments and field studies, they empirically show that neoclassical axioms describe only the behavioural reality of a small set of agents: those exclusively guided by self-interested rationality in the Jevonsian sense. The other behaviours observable in the economic sphere, such as reciprocal and altruistic conduct, generate paradoxes and contradictions: true statements that cannot be proved based on conventional theory. For example, noting that economic agents seek and establish relationships that are not merely self-interested to meet mutually beneficial objectives (Cárdenas and Ostrom 2004); the motivational heterogeneity shown by economic agents in the different economic decision-making processes (Calvo 2013, 2017; Calvo and González-Esteban 2013; González-Esteban and Calvo 2019); the involvement of moral judgements concerning fairness and unfairness (Fehr and Rockenbach 2003, 2004); affective factors (feelings and prosocial emotions) in decision-making which therefore affect the possibility of maximum benefit (Glimcher et al. 2008); and the cognitive basis behind the emotions and their relationship with and influence on feelings (Damasio 2003).

In fact, there were already interesting results from the first experiment carried out with a strategy game, designed and applied in 1950 by Melvin Dresher and Merrill Flood of the RAND corporation. Later known as the *Prisoner's Dilemma* thanks to

---

[13] Zubiri states that "Mathematical objects have their "in its own right" properties; that is, they are real. Indeed, the real object postulatedly made according to the concepts that have, by being made, more notes or properties than those defined in their postulation. Therefore, and only for this reason, it considers problems that cannot be solved with the finite system of axioms and postulates that have defined their fulfilment. What has been constructed in "the" reality is, as it has been fulfilled, of somewhat greater value than that postulated to be fulfilled. This how I see the scope of Gödel's theorem. It is not a matter of an intrinsic limitation to axiomatic and postulated statements as far as statements are concerned – this is the usual interpretation of this theorem. Instead, before intelligence, it reveals the real nature of what is constructed according to the axioms and postulates in question. So, it is not the intrinsic insufficiency of a system of postulates, but the radical originality of that constructed as being real; a reality that is not exhausted by what has been postulated in it. This object is no real thing in itself and for itself, just as this stone is here. But neither is it only what 'the real thing'would be, but that which is postulatedly and constructively 'real'. This is, in my view, the interpretation of Gödel's theorem. Mathematical judgements are, therefore, judgements of something real, as they are judgements of 'postulated reality'. They are not judgements about 'whether something is possible', but about 'postulated reality' itself" (Zubiri 1982: 138).

Albert Tucker,[14] it pointed out an important anomaly in the axiomatic theory of rational choice: after 100 games were played, the results showed that reciprocity and not self-interest had come out on top. Despite the fact that one player showed a strong tendency to act guided by his own interests, the predisposition of his opponent both to cooperate in seeking optimum benefits for all the related parties and to punish non-cooperative attitudes meant that, in the end, both preferred cooperation over desertion in most cases (60%). The result of the game called into question both the paradigm of *homo oeconomicus* and the thesis of equilibriums put forward that year by the mathematician John F. Nash[15] (Flood 1952). Based on this, it was initially thought necessary to revise the theory to include new axioms that would make it possible to better explain the behavioural reality of economic agents. As Flood points out (1952: 1):

> The non-constant-sum case of the theory of games remains incomplete. Several authors have considered the problem of extending the initial theory. Some very interesting contributions have been made recently [2, 4, 5]. The approach has been to add new axioms, and to modify old ones, in an effort to obtain a set that is at once quite acceptable on *a priori* grounds of reasonableness and also strong enough to determine each player's moves. This effort has not yet been very successful.

Despite this, the predominant theory has chosen to ignore the axioms and assumptions of the theory and base responsibility for its lack of empirical reality on the refutable hypotheses and its internal inconsistency on the irrational behaviour of economic agents; in other words, not on the validity of its fundamental concepts but rather on the predictability of the consequences and psychological issues involved. It involves two models, a formal model and an experimental one, attempting to explain the same fact, but its results are not binding because there is no causality between the two of them, although there is correlation (Tirole 2017: 105). As Robert M. Solow argues in *A Contribution to the Theory of Economic Growth* (1956):

> All theory depends on assumptions which are not quite true. That is what makes it theory. The art of successful theorising is to make the inevitable simplifying assumptions in such a way that the final results are not very sensitive. A "crucial" assumption is one on which the conclusions do depend sensitively, and it is important that crucial assumptions be reasonably realistic. When the results of a theory seem to flow specifically from a special crucial assumption, then if the assumption is dubious, the results are suspect (Solow 1956: 65).

Debreu expressed himself along the same lines in *The Mathematization of Economic Theory* (1991) when, doubting the existence of a measurable experimen-

---

[14] Albert Tucker, a Princeton mathematician, transformed Dresher's and Flood's game into a story about two prisoners facing a dilemma for a lecture on Game Theory in the Department of Psychology at Stanford University, coining the term the "Prisoner's Dilemma" (Poundstone 2005: 202–203).

[15] The players opted for non-equilibrium strategies in 78% and 68% of cases (Poundstone 2005: 192).

tal basis for economics, he committed himself to mathematical/deductive reasoning, in clear allusion to the contributions and criticisms from experimental economics (Rubiano 2009: 283):

> The experimental results and the factual observations that are at the basis of physics, and which provide a constant check on its theoretical constructions, occasionally led its bold reasonings to violate knowingly the canons of mathematical deduction. (...) In these directions, economic theory could not follow the role model offered by physical theory. (...) Being denied a sufficiently secure experimental base, economic theory has to adhere to the rules of logical discourse and must renounce the facility of internal inconsistency. A deductive structure that tolerates a contradiction does so under the penalty of being useless, since any statement can be derived flawlessly and immediately from that contradiction (Debreu 1991: 2–3).

As has been mentioned, von Mises was also reluctant to accept that the theoretical model could be influenced in any way by the results of experimental studies. Declaring the primacy of pure reason over experience and analytical judgement over synthetics, although these merely provide knowledge,[16] von Mises suggested that the validity of the proposed theoretical models does not depend on comparing them with reality or the level of correspondence between the theoretical model and empirical reality (von Mises 1998: 31). It is reason itself that extracts, clarifies and validates the universal categories and concepts behind the mental structure of human action. The empirical dimension is not universal, as it is influenced by an indefinite number of variables. This means it cannot be used as a tool to verify or refute aprioristic and deductive theoretical models such as those drawn from mathematics, logic or *praxeology*.[17]

> It is not a deficiency of the system of aprioristic science that it does not convey to us full cognition of reality. Its concepts and theorems are mental tools opening the approach to a complete grasp of reality (...). Theory and the comprehension of living and changing reality are not in opposition to one another. Without theory, the general aprioristic science of human action, there is no comprehension of the reality of human action (von Mises 1998: 38–39).

Based on this reasoning, in *Essays in Positive Economics* (1953) Milton Friedman —winner of the Nobel Prize for economics in 1976— argues that economists have licence to ignore evidence that economic agents violate axiom-based predictions because the theories' validity does not depend on the degree of correspondence with the behavioural reality of economic agents but rather on their

---

[16] As Kant showed in *Critik der reinen Vernunft* [*Critique of Pure Reason*] (1781), synthetic judgement describes universal, necessary and non-extendable statements where the predicate is contained within the subject. They therefore do not provide greater information.

[17] As von Mises states, although mathematics is also aprioristic, its method of knowledge differs from the praxeological: "The *a priori* knowledge of praxeology is entirely different – categorially different – from the *a priori* knowledge of mathematics or, more precisely, from mathematical *a priori* knowledge as interpreted by logical positivism" (von Mises 1962: 4).

capacity, in comparison with any other alternative theory, to predict the present or future of the phenomena they are attempting to explain (Friedman 1953: 19).[18]

> (…) the relevant question to ask about the "assumptions" of a theory is not whether they are descriptively "realistic," for they never are, but whether they are sufficiently good approximations for the purpose in hand. And this question can be answered only by seeing whether the theory works, which means whether it yields sufficiently accurate predictions. The two supposedly independent tests thus reduce to one test.

Based on this, for Friedman the criticism poured on orthodox theory based on its lack of realism is unfounded, as "(…) theory must be judged for its power of prediction for the class of phenomena it is trying to explain" and not for its strict correspondence with reality (Brunet and Pastor 2001: 167). So, although many economic agents do not behave as they should according to the axioms, the theory will continue to be valid if a large group shows that it predicts their behaviour. As Friedman argues,

> The abstract methodological issues we have been discussing have a direct bearing on the perennial criticism of "orthodox" economic theory as "unrealistic" as well as on the attempts that have been made to reformulate theory to meet this charge. Economics is a "dismal" science because it assumes man to be selfish and money-grubbing, "a lightning calculator of pleasures and pains, who oscillates like a homogeneous globule of desire of happiness under the impulse of stimuli that shift him about the area, but leave him intact". (...) criticism of this type is largely beside the point unless supplemented by evidence that a hypothesis differing in one or another of these respects from the theory being criticised yields better predictions for as wide a range of phenomena. Yet most such criticism is not so supplemented; it is based almost entirely on supposedly directly perceived discrepancies between the "assumptions" and the "real world." (...) A theory or its "assumptions" cannot possibly be thoroughly "realistic" in the immediate descriptive sense so often assigned to this term. (...) Any attempt to move very far in achieving this kind of "realism" is certain to render a theory utterly useless (Friedman 1953: 19–20).

In this way, economic theory can be understood as true by appealing to its internal coherence concerning strict compliance with logical rules and not with empirical evidence (Rubiano 2009: 283); and it is valid considering the predictive potential of the hypothesis put forward, or its level of correspondence with reality. For Friedman, therefore, theories are no more than devices or instruments used by economists to make causal predictions of reality and to draw conclusions. For this reason, it does not matter whether the assumptions of the theory correspond to reality or not. What is really important about a theory is its functionality, in other words the level of its predictive capacity. There is therefore no relationship between theory and reality. Its assumptions may be false, but if they constitute the framework for a theory making it possible to predict the observable facts better than any other, it is still valid.

However, criticism of these ideas came from both theoretical and experimental sides. From an operationalist perspective, for example, Samuelson strongly criticised Friedman's ideas in *Problems of Methodology* (1962), with the well-known *F-Twist* argument. Among other things, Samuelson argues that when the conse-

---

[18] This thought comes within the instrumental proposal of rational choice. For a comparison of the different proposals of rational choice, see Martínez-García (2004).

quences of a theory are compared with observable reality, what is being evaluated is its descriptive capacity, not its predictive capacity. Samuelson, recognises that the axioms of theory do not allow a complete prediction of economic reality but that does not mean, as Friedman thinks, that "(...) the (empirical) unrealism of the theory 'itself', or of its 'assumptions', is quite irrelevant to its validity and worth" (Samuelson 1962: 232). For Samuelson, "The fact that nothing is perfectly accurate should not be an excuse to relax our standards of scrutiny of the empirical validity that the propositions of economics do or do not possess" (Samuelson 1962: 232, 236). Because of this, Samuelson proposes theoretical modelling concerned with a) specifying the axioms and logical/formal assumptions that best describe reality; b) formulating the rules of correspondence that relate true axioms and assumptions with the conditions of empirical reality; c) comparing the consequences deriving from the underlying hypotheses in order to empirically compare the proposed model; and d) calculating the qualitative and quantitative variables to assess how suitable the theory is (Samuelson 1962). From this point of view, whether the theory is appropriate depends on the set of all propositions, not just the empirically refutable hypotheses as in Friedman's case (Munt and Barrionuevo 2010).

Amartya Sen expressed himself in the same critical line in *Rational Fools. A Critique of the Behavioral Foundations of Economic Theory* (1977) and *On Ethics and Economy* (1987) when he attacked excessive abstraction and the lack of an empirical basis for the theory of rational choice. Firstly, following the previous reflection by Samuelson, for Sen, this rational behaviour approach *leads to a mute theory*, as the behaviour is explained in terms of preferences or utilities defined through the behaviour itself and validated by actual observation. Secondly, the model has a slight or weak basic structure, as it assigns the agent an ordinal order of preferences and assumes that, through this, it is possible to see its interests, personal welfare, criteria for what it should do and behaviour all represented. Finally, the *assumption of greed* is called into question because of its lack of precision and relative consistency, as it relates preferences with the set of economic goods just because these are the only ones over which the agent could have real direct control and not because selfishness is its only behavioural motivation (Sen 1977).

For Sen, the issues he notes are worthy of in-depth reflection concerning the assumptions on which the theory is based. Firstly, concerning whether this stylised, abstract and simplified view of human beings is the best possible approach to the real behaviour of the economic agent (Sen 2000). Secondly, concerning whether there are foundations and sufficient empirical evidence to be able to make such a radical restrictive statement like the *assumption of greed*. And, finally, about whether behaving in a purely selfish way brings greater benefits than not doing so (Sen 1987).

The response to the issues noted by Sen has shown that the attempts to axiomatise economic theory have been proved to be limited (Sen 1977, 1987, 2000, 2002). Evolutionary Game Theory and Neuronal Game Theory not only call into question the possibility of reducing the whole behavioural reality of an economic agent to perfect, complete rationality from which it is possible to predict its movements; they also suggest the probability that the axioms of the theory are *sufficiently good* to prevent them being refuted any longer. For example, the restrictive axiom of monotonicity, greed or non-satiation, clearly related to the assumed selfishness of the economic agent, does not correspond at all well to empirical reality, as shown by both the mere observation of cases and a good number of the different laboratory experiments carried out, and nor does it prove to have greater predictive power. Other behaviours, like reciprocal conduct, which curiously combine self-interested attitudes with altruistic behaviour, moral conduct and prosocial emotions, have been empirically tested and can provide interesting guidance for a possible revision and/or expansion of this axiom or the set of axioms of the theory of rational choice. Or the model of perfect rationality on which orthodox theory is based, which does not appear to correspond to reality and which also turns out not to be more beneficial or predictive than other models.

Along the same critical lines as Samuelson and Sen on the reality deficit of the economic model, John Kenneth Galbraith, one of the leading figures of the institutionalist school, spoke out. In *The Affluent Society* (1958), he stated that economic cannot be subordinated to certain self-evident and inviolable laws – the conventional wisdom – because it is strongly influenced by the cultural and political medium in which it emerges and develops. For this reason, Galbraith criticises the lack of interest of neoclassical economics in the factors that have the power to transform economic reality but are not susceptible to axiomatic descriptions, for example, formal and informal institutions, demand manipulation techniques, oligopolies, technostructures and the interference of the military sector in politics and economics, among other things (Screpanti and Zamagni 2005; Roncaglia 2005: 479–480).

> The enemy of the conventional wisdom is not ideas but the march of events. As I have noted, the conventional wisdom accommodates itself not to the world that it is meant to interpret, but to the audience's view of the world. Since the latter remains with the comfortable and the familiar while the world moves on, the conventional wisdom is always in danger of obsolescence. This is not immediately fatal. The fatal blow to conventional wisdom comes when the conventional ideas fail signally to deal with some contingency to which some contingency to which obsolescence has made them palpably inapplicable. This, sooner or later, must be the fate of ideas which have lost their relation to the world. At this stage, the irrelevance will often be dramatized by some individual. To him will accrue the credit for overthrowing the conventional wisdom and for installing the new ideas. In fact, he will have only crystallized in words what the events have made clear, although this function is not a minor one. Meanwhile, like the Old Guard, the conventional wisdom dies but does not surrender. Society with intransigent cruelty may transfer its exponents from the category of wise man to that of old fogy or even stuffed shirt (Galbraith 1958: 21–22).

In conclusion, as Tirole argues (2017: 106–107), despite its defects, the economic model has a significant value and is indispensable, for many reasons. This is especially because it establishes a framework of meaning for experimental studies; because it offers guidance on specifying and developing economic policies; because it demands the verification of the logic of the arguments set out to prevent any possible deception of the intuition; because it promotes reflection on the possibility of new ideas and hypotheses, and so on. However, beyond the degree to which it corresponds to the behavioural reality of the economic agent, the principal criticism aroused by the predominant theoretical model is its conservatism and lack of criticism, as well as its promotion of an unbridgeable gap between truth and reality that makes it a meaningless tautology. Because of this, as Roncaglia argues,

(…) the link between specific theory and general view is an aspect that we are bound to address if we wish to clarify the foundations upon which the specific theory rests. On the other hand, the idea of representing all aspects of economic reality with a single, general model is considered excessively far-fetched – an aspiration reminiscent of the ideas in early Wittgenstein and, significantly, abandoned in the face of Sraffa's criticisms (Roncaglia 2005: 513).

So, a way of building bridges between the two conceptual and real dimensions should be sought to provide the model with greater meaning through constant fact-based approach work, making it possible to improve its potential and, in that way, generate greater benefits and possibilities for experimental theory. This issue is essential because, among other factors, economic policies are not based on information from experimental studies but rather general models increasingly divorced from reality. For this reason, we cannot leave such an important issue in the hands of abstract/conceptual models that are barely realistic, or not at all, however formally true they may be.[19] It is necessary to work on a true model, but also a more precise and realistic one generating meaning and providing a solid basis for the different theories.

Concerning the adoption of selfishness as a fundamental axiom of the rational behaviour of economic agents, largely through the adoption of the assumption of monotonicity, greed and non-satiation, a possible criticism focuses on why the Jevonsian notion of self-interested rationality, based on his interpretation of utilitarianism, is predominant despite the fact that empirical evidence shows that Adam Smith's proposal of self-interested rationality, based on reciprocity, is broader, more flexible, more enriching and much closer to the behavioural reality of economic agents.

As Sen (1977, 1987) explains, Adam Smith's rationality combines three levels of application and implementation in which self-interest plays an important part: interest in one's own welfare (self-interest); interest in the welfare of others (prosocial emotions); and interest in everyone's welfare (moral commitment). Curiously, as will be seen in the next chapter, these are the same three levels are currently promoted by field studies and laboratory experiments with strategy games. Should we, therefore, revise the general model of rational choice based on a less restrictive and more realistic assumption of interest, like Adam Smith's?

Bibliography

Antonelli, Giovanni B. 1886. *Sulla teoria matemática della economia pura*. Pisa.
Arrow, Kenneth J. 1950. A difficulty in the concept of social welfare. *Journal of Political Economy* 58 (4): 328–346.
———. 1951. *Social choice and individual values*. New York: Wiley.
———. 1959. Rational choice functions and orderings. *Economica. New Series* 26 (102): 121–127.

---

[19] For a constructive, critical reflection on these issues, see Roncaglia (2005: 500–504).

Arrow, Kenneth J., and Gérard Debreu. 1954. Existence of an equilibrium for a competitive economy. *Econometrica* 22 (3): 265–290.

Bowles, Samuel. 2016. *The moral economy: Why good incentives are no substitute for good citizens.* New Haven/London: Yale University Press.

Brunet, Ignasi, and Inma Pastor. 2001. La axiomática de la ciencia económica convencional. *Política y Sociedad* 37: 161–179.

Calvo, Patrici. 2013. Neuro-racionalidad económica: heterogeneidad motivacional y compromise moral. *Daimon. Revista Internacional de Filosofía* 59: 157–170.

———. 2017. Reciprocidad cordial: el fundamento ético de la cooperación. *Ideas y Valores* 265.

Calvo, Patrici y González-Esteban, Elsa. 2013. Neuroeconomía, ¿un saber práctico? In *Ética y neurociencias: la aportación a la política, la economía y la educación*, ed. Domingo García-Marzá and Ramón A. Feenstra. Castellón: Servei de Publicacions de la Universitat Jaume I

Camerer, Colin, George Loewenstein, and Drazen Prelec. 2005. Neuroeconomics: How neuroscience can inform economics. *Journal of Economic Literature* 43 (1): 9–64.

Cameron, Peter J. 1999. *Set, logic and categories.* New York: Springer.

Cárdenas, Juan-Camilo, and Elinor Ostrom. 2004. What do people bring into the game? Experiments in the field about cooperation in the commons. *Agricultural Systems* 82: 307–326.

Celaya, Francisco. 1962. La Teoría de la Preferencia Revelada. *Revista de Economía Política* 32: 7–61.

Damasio, Antonio R. 2003. *Looking for Spinoza: Joy, sorrow and the feeling brain.* New York: Harvest Book Harcourt, INC..

de los Ríos Camilo-Andrés, Franco. 2005. El formalismo axiomático en economía. *Cuadernos de Economía* XXIV (43): 35–63.

Debreu, Gerand. 1959. Theory of value. In *An axiomatic analysis of economics equilibrium.* New Haven/London: Yale University Press.

———. 1991. The mathematization of economic theory. *The American Economic Review* 81 (1): 1–7.

Diccionario de la Lengua Española. 2017. Axioma. http://dle.rae.es/srv/fetch?id=4bO6PH0. Accessed 25 Sept 2017.

Etxezarreta, Miren. 2015. *¿Para qué sirve realmente la economía?* Barcelona: Paidós.

Fehr, Ernst, and Bettina Rockenbach. 2003. Detrimental effects of sanctions on human altruism. *Nature* 422 (6928): 137–140.

———. 2004. Human altruism: Economic, neural, and evolutionary perspectives. *Current Opinion in Neurobiology* 14: 784–790.

Flood, Merrill M. 1952. *Some experimental games*, Research MemorandumRM-789- 1. Santa Monica: RAND Corporation.

Fraenkel, Abraham. 1922. Zu den Grundlagen der Cantor-Zermeloschen Mengenlehre. *Mathematische Annalen* 86: 230–237.

Franks, Curtis. 2009. *The autonomy of mathematical knowledge: Hilbert's program revisited.* Cambridge: Cambridge University Press.

Friedman, Milton. 1953. *Essays in positive economics.* Chicago: University of Chicago Press.

Galbraith, John Kenneth. 1958. *The affluent society.* Boston: Houghton Mifflin.

García-Lapresta, José L. 1992. Preferencia e indiferencia en la teoría de la elección racional. *Anales de Estudios Económicos y Empresariales* 7: 247–254.

Glimcher, Paul W., Ernst Fehr, Colin F. Camerer, and Russell A. Poldrack, eds. 2008. *Neuroeconomics. Decision making and the brain.* Amsterdam: Elsevier Academic Press.

Gödel, Kurt. 1930. *Die Vollständigkeit der Axiome des logischen Funktoinenkalküls/The completeness of axioms of the functional calculus of logic*, Doctoral thesis [English version: 1986. *Kurt Gödel Collected Works. Volume I. Publications 1929–1936*, ed. Feferman Sólomon, 102–123. Oxford: Clarendon Press].

———. 1931. Über formal unentscheidbare Sätze der Principia Mathematica und verwandter Systeme I. *Monatshefte für Mathematik und Physik* 38 (1): 173–198 [English version: 1986.

Kurt Gödel Collected Works. Volume I. Publications 1929–1936, ed. Feferman Sólomon, 144–195. Oxford: Clarendon Press].

González-Esteban, Elsa, and Patrici Calvo. 2019. *Homo reciprocans* from the neuroscientific literature: Limited reciprocity. Criticism from neuroethics (in press). *Anuario Filosófico*.

Green, H.A. John. 1957. Some logical relations in revealed preference theory. *Economica* 24 (96): 315–323.

Henderson, James M., and Richard D. Quandt. 1971. *Microeconomic theory*. New York: McGraw-Hill.

Hilbert, David. 1922. Neubergründung der Mathematik. Erste Mitteilung. Abhandlungen aus dem Mathematischen Seminar der Hamburgischen Universität 1, 57–177.

———. 1998. The New Grounding of Mathematics. First Report. In *From Brouwer to Hilbert. The debate on the foundations of mathematics in the 1920s*, ed. Paolo Mancosu, 198–214. Oxford: Oxford University Press.

Hilbert, David, and Wilhelm Ackermann. 1928. *Grundzüge der Theoretischen Logik*. New York: Springer.

Huertas, Antonia, and María Manzano. 2005. *El universo matemático*. Madrid: Summa Logicae.

Jevons, W. Stanley. 1871. *The theory of political economy*. London: McMillan & Co.

———. 1886. *Letters & Journal of W. Stanley Jevons*. London: Macmillan & Co.

José, Elena T. 2006. *Conocimiento, pensamiento y lenguaje: una introducción a la lógica y al pensamiento científico*. Buenos Aires: Biblos.

Kant, Immanuel. 1781. *Critik der reinen Vernunft*. Riga: Johann Friedrich Harknoch.

Macho, Marta-Stadler. 2002. *Topología general*. Universidad del País Vasco.

Martínez-García, José S. 2004. Distintas aproximaciones a la elección racional. *Revista Internacional de Sociología (RIS)* 37: 139–173.

Mas-Colell, Andreu, Michael Whinston, and Jerry R. Green. 1995. *Microeconomic theory*. New York: Oxford University Press.

Mosterín, Jesús. 2000. *Los Lógicos*. Madrid: Espasa-Calpe.

———. 2013. *Ciencia, filosofía y racionalidad*. Barcelona: Gedisa Editorial.

Mosterín, Jesús, and Roberto Torretti. 2002. *Diccionario de Lógica y Filosofía de la ciencia*. Madrid: Alianza editorial.

Munt, Juan, and Gisela Barrionuevo. 2010. Reflexiones sobre la ontología de la economía. La vision tradicional vs. la heterodoxia moderna. *Kairos. Revista de Temas Sociales* 26: 1–20.

Murawski, Roman. 2010. *Essays in the philosophy and history of logic and mathematics*. Brill Publisher.

Nagel, Ernest, and James R. Newman. 1970. *El teorema de Gödel*. Tecmos: Madrid.

Oxford English Dictionary. 2017. *Axiomy*. https://en.oxforddictionaries.com/definition/axiom. Accessed 25 Sept 2017.

Pearce, David W., ed. 1999. *Diccionario Akal de Economía Moderna*. Madrid: Akal.

Petty, William. 1690. *Political arithmetic*. London: Robert Clavel & Henry Mortlock.

Poundstone, William. 2005. El dilema del prisionero. John von Neumann, la teoría de juegos y la bomba, Madrid: Alianza [English version]: Poundstone, William. 1992. *Prisoner's dilema: John von Neumann, Game theory and the puzzle of the bomb*. Doubleday: New York.

Riemann, Bernhard. 1854. *Ueber die Hypothesen, Welche der Geometrie zu Grunde liegen* [Habilitationsschrift]. In *1868. Abhandlungen der Königlichen Gesellschaft der Wissenschaften zu Göttingen*, vol. 13, 133–150.

Roncaglia, Alessandro. 2005. *The wealth of ideas a history of economic thought*. Cambridge: Cambridge University Press.

Rubiano, Néstor. 2009. ¿Axiomática o empirismo? Sobre el uso de las matemáticas en economía. *Revista de Economía Institucional* 11 (20): 271–286.

Russell, Bertrand. 1902. From Frege to Gödel. A source book in mathematical logic, 1879–1931. In Jean van Heijenoort, ed. 1967. *Letter to Frege*, 124–125. Cambridge, MA: Harvard University Press.

Samuelson, Paul A. 1938. A note on the pure theory of consumers. *Behaviour Economica* 5: 61–71.

————. 1938/1947. *Foundation of economic analysis*. Cambridge, MA: Massachusetts Institute of Technology

————. 1938/1948. Consumption theory in terms of revealed preference. *Economica. New Series* 15 (60): 248–253.

————. 1938/1962. Problems of methodology. *The American Economic Review* 53 (2), 231-236. In Archibald, G. Christopher; Herbert A. Simon and Paul A. Samuelson. 1962. Problems of methodology. *The American Economic Review* 53(2):227–236.

Screpanti, Ernesto, and Stefano Zamagni. 2005. *An outline of the history of economic thought*. Oxford: Oxford University Press.

Sen, Amartya. 1977. Rational fools. A critique of the behavioral foundations of economic theory. In Frank Hahn and Martin Hollis, ed. *Philosophy and public affairs* 6 (4): 317–344. Oxford: Blackwell Publishing.

————. 1987. *On ethics and economy*. Oxford: Blackwell Publishing.

————. 2000. *Development as freedom*. New York: Anchor.

————. 2002. *Rationality and freedom*. Harvard: Harvard Belknap Press.

Skolem, Thoralf A. 1923. The foundations of elementary arithmetic established by means of the recursive mode of thought, without the use of apparent variables ranging over infinite domains. In Heijenoort, Jean Van, ed. 1967. *From Frege to Gödel. A source book in mathematical logic, 1879–1931*, 302–333. Cambridge, MA: Harvard University Press.

Solow, Robert M. 1956. A contribution to the theory of economic growth. *The Quarterly Journal of Economics* 70 (1): 65–94.

Tirole, Jean. 2017. *Economics for the common good* (Trans. Rendall, S.). Princeton: Princeton University Press.

Torres, Carlos. 1995. The philosophy and the program of Hilbert. *Mexican Studies in the History and Philosophy of Science* 172: 151–172.

van Heijenoort, Jean, ed. 1967. *From Frege to Gödel. A source book in mathematical logic*. Vol. 1879-1931. Cambridge, MA: Harvard University Press.

Varian, Hal R. 1978. *Microeconomic analysis*. New York: Norton & Co.

Vialar, Thierry. 2015. *Handbook of mathematics*. Paris: BoD.

von Mises, Ludwig. 1949. *Human action: A treatise on economics*. New Haven: Yale University Press.

————. 1962. *The ultimate foundation of economic science. An assay on method*. Princeton: D. Van Noastrand Company.

————. 1998. *Human action: A treatise on economics*. Auburg: Ludwig von Mises Institute.

von Neumann, John. 1925. Eine Axiomatisierung der Mengenlehre. *Journal für die reine und angewandte Mathematik* 154: 219–240.

Walras, Léon. 1874. *Éléments d'économie politique pure, ou théorie de la richesse sociale*. Lausanne: L. Corbaz & Cie.

————. 2013. *Elements of pure economics, Or the theory of social wealth*. New York: Routledge.

Zermelo, Ernst. 1908. Untersuchungen über die Grundlagen der Mengenlehre I. *Mathematische Annalen* 65: 261–281.

Zubiri, Xabier. 1982. *Inteligencia y Logos*. Madrid: Alianza editorial.

————. 1983. *Inteligencia y Razón*. Madrid: Alianza editorial.

Chapter 3
Economic Racionality. The Reciprocity Paradox

Abstract Self-interest, as the constant maximisation of personal benefit, is one of the fundamental concepts of rational choice theory. Axiomatised through certain assumptions, like those corresponding to greed and insatiability, it has managed to confine the economic agent within the paradigmatic *homo oeconomicus* figure, a motivationally homogeneous and behaviourally predictable animal, whose only reason for relating with others is because it might improve its own well-being. Nonetheless, the traditional, evolutionary and neuronal version of Game Theory has, over decades, shown that *homo oeconomicus* has no empirical basis. In highly competitive contexts like economic ones, most agents' behaviour is influenced by emotional heterogeneity and a moral commitment to what they have good reasons to value, far removed from the vision promoted by neoclassicism. The aim of this chapter is to show the behavioural perspective that underlies different laboratory experiments and field studies conducted with strategy games, especially those resulting from recent neuroeconomic studies, where the role of reciprocity in the field of economics is made clear, along with the emotional and moral aspects making it possible.

The logic-formal assumptions of greed and insatiability introduced the paradigmatic *homo oeconomicus* figure from among the fundamental concepts of the predominant economic model. Promoted by marginalists like Jevons and Menger and supported by very different currents of thought, such as American institutionalism or German historicism, among others, *homo oeconomicus* personifies economic agents' natural tendency to constantly increase their own benefit. This is a simplifying hypothesis, according to which those who make decisions are rational and, therefore, act to promote their interests depending on the information they have available (Tirole 2017: 106–108).

As Tirole explains (2017), economic science came up with the idea of the fictitious *homo oeconomicus'* to shape its own identity at the expense of doing away with any connection to other human and social sciences. In this way, economic science conceived the economic agent as an emotionally homogeneous and behaviourally limited creature whose only reason to relate to other economic agents is the chance to improve its own well-being at the expense of others. From this time onwards, most recommendations about political economics have been based on

© Springer International Publishing AG, part of Springer Nature 2018

P. Calvo, *The Cordial Economy - Ethics, Recognition and Reciprocity*,
Ethical Economy 55, https://doi.org/10.1007/978-3-319-90784-0_3

externalities or failures in the market; in other words, the difference between individual rationality and collective rationality.

One of the most widely used arguments on this issue has been Arrow's Impossibility Theorem, as demonstrated in *Social Choice and Individual Values* (1951), which states that the combination of individual preferences – individual rationality – cannot produce social choice – collective rationality. Initially, through the application of the axiomatic theorising method and the mathematical topology instrument, Arrow's proposal states that individual preferences must comply with two essential rules –comparability and transitivity– and a social choice system must meet four basic conditions: freedom of choice of individual preferences; unanimity of adding individual preferences; independence of irrelevant alternatives; and no dictatorship. Secondly, according to these two essential rules of individual rationality, and also the five basic conditions of collective rationality, Arrow demonstrated that a democratic social choice system capable of guaranteeing the transitivity of more than two individual preferences without breaking the system's basic conditions does not, or cannot, exist.

However, *homo oeconomicus* has been strongly criticised for its unjustified conceptual narrow-mindedness. One of the strongest attacks on this conceptually stylised version of the human being was by von Mises. He considered it wrong that orthodox economics had focused on the study of an imaginary being whose only motivation was to obtain maximum material and monetary benefits. He also stated: "Such a being does not have, and never did have, a counterpart in reality; it is a phantom of a spurious arm chair philosophy. No man is exclusively motivated by the desire to become as rich as possible; many are not at all influenced by this mean craving" (von Mises 1998: 62). Thus, for von Mises, *homo oeconomicus* is not an idealised prototype of the human being, but a mere abstraction of one of its many hopes.

Yet, in particular, the *homo oeconomicus* paradigm is being strongly criticised by experimental and behavioural economics for it lacking empirical realism. Firstly, Game Theory and Evolutionary Game Theory are providing proof for the economic agent's motivational and behavioural heterogeneity by means of field studies and laboratory experiments with strategy games. Secondly, by capturing brain images, Neuronal Game Theory is demonstrating some cerebral basis for the economic agent's behaviour where selfishness does not appear to occupy such an outstanding place as the traditional theoretical model assumes.

The aim of this chapter is to show the role played by reciprocity in economics and by prosocial feelings in all rational decision-making processes. For this purpose, we will first show the initial and successive laboratory experiments with strategy games as of 1950. These began to reveal the cooperative capacity of economic agents, which, based on reciprocity, began to question the empirical basis of assumed cases of greed and insatiability. Secondly, we will look in-depth at the motivational heterogeneity underlying human behaviour and the role played by the *prosocial emotions* resulting from the commitments and moral judgements about what is fair and unfair through the contributions made by the Evolutionary Game Theory from 1984 onwards. Thirdly and finally, there are the latest contributions made by neuroscientific studies of the implications of reciprocity, and their implications for the economy, will be analysed.

3.1 Game Theory: Strategic Rationality and Cooperation

Game Theory was proposed by mathematician Émile Borel in "La theorie du jeu et les equations integrales ä noyau symetrique" (1921) as a possible source and method of studying human behaviour in highly competitive fields like politics and economics. However, its application to economics was made possible thanks to the works of John von Neumann, Oskar Morgenstern and John Forbes Nash. First the Minimax Theorem mathematically demonstrated von Neumann's theorem in "Zur Theorie der Gesellschaftsspiele" (1928); secondly, the potential of strategic games for science economics was clarified and the specific mathematical body for the economic science was defined by von Neumann and Morgenstern with their work *Theory of Game and Economic Behavior* (1944). Finally, Nash confirmed that the theory could cover positive-sum cooperative game types with n-players and n-strategies, in the articles entitled "Equilibrium Points in n-Person Games" (1950a) and "The Bargaining Problem" (1950b).

Theory of Games and Economic Behavior was the beginning of modern microeconomics. For von Neumann, one of the main problems for fully developing economic science was that it lacked its own mathematical model (Poundstone 2005). Differential calculus corresponded to physics, but was unsuitable for analysing such a complex domain as economics, with so many variables of such diversity that it is impossible to provide a universal model. So, beginning from the idea that all economic agents seek to optimise the final outcome[1] – maximising profits or minimising losses – and by using the strategic Game Theory methodology proposed by Borel in 1921 as a tool, von Neumann, along with economist Oskar Morgenstern, came up with a specific mathematical corpus for microeconomic studies that allowed the conceptualisation of the strategic decisions made by related rational agents with clashing interests (Tirole 2017: 109–110). As Morgenstern explains in this sense:

> As for its methods, the Game Theory strongly contrasts with the practice of the physical analogies that dominated in economic science, irrespectively of it using common language or mathematical formulae. This contrast is due not only to the different way of conceiving things, but also to the typical economic problems in which situations arise with nothing to do with physics in general, or with mathematics in particular. This also counts for branches of mathematics that apply to physics, and also, therefore, to mathematical economics. The mathematics employed in the Game Theory completely differ as they consider unknown problems and theorems in classic mathematics or in physics (Morgenstern 1955: 346)

From this viewpoint, the Game Theory of von Neumann and Morgenstern is characterised by games of the zero-sum type with complete information, where two players should find the strategy that suits their interests by considering the opponent's expected response: maximising profits or minimising losses. Consequently,

---

[1] The *Games Theory* initially contemplated by Neumann and Morgenstern, assumed the Minimax Theorem demonstrated by von Neumann in von Neumann 1928; i.e., that all games possess a strategy for each player by means of which both obtain an optimum result depending on the case: maximising profits for one, minimising losses for the other.

the pattern on which games are designed in traditional Game Theory is based on the assumed motivational homogeneity that guides any form of human conduct in the field of economics: self-interest in the neoclassical sense.

According to its creators, the theory developed well for a few years after the book was published. They introduced new concepts and ideas that markedly enriched the initial proposal: for instance, mixed strategies[2] to respond to situations where there was more than one optimum response.[3] John F. Nash, Reinhard Selten and John Harsanyi —who won the 1994 Nobel Prize for Economics— then backed back the theory.[4]

Not far removed from the original idea, and based on the perfect rationality notion of *homo oeconomicus*, Nash stated that the Game Theory could be broadly extended, as it was valid for the types of games for *n*-persons and *n*-strategies, and for positive-sum games (1950a, b). This was backed by the *equilibrium* notion with a view to defining the general behaviour of economic agents when making decisions: choosing the best available option by bearing in mind all the other participants' strategies. Nash's equilibrium, as it is commonly known, implied that all games with a finite number of players and strategies contains at least an equilibrium in mixed strategies that allows all those involved to partially satisfy their own objectives. In this way, Nash took a great leap forward in developing the theory as he demonstrated that cooperation between potentially self-interested agents was not only possible, but beneficial for all the related parties.

In time, Nash's contributions ran up against at least two problems that were hard to solve. The first was to find games that included two or more equilibriums so it was necessary to set a valid criterion to discern, in each specific case, which of them they had to opt for: refinement.[5] The second problem included extensive games in which participants did not make a decision simultaneously, something that occurs in games in the normal way. Instead, participants made decisions at different times and when they knew their rivals' responses (Gintis 2000: 3–14). Finally, reciprocity emerged in extensive games, where it became a disruptive element that allowed cooperation between players which was not necessarily selfish.

These three problems in the *equilibrium* notion proposed by Nash were considerable, and Dresher and Flood ran a laboratory experiment with a strategy game, known as the *Prisioner's Dilemma*, to check whether Nash's thesis was true. Unexpectedly, however, after playing 100 games, the results of the experiment

---

[2] Mixed strategies refer to a state which leads to a finite number of pure strategies. This is the starting point for Nash's famous equilibrium.

[3] An optimum response is what Nash was later to call the dominant strategy, although this was better developed.

[4] As Vicent Salas-Fumas explains, "(…) non-cooperative game theory models situations where interdependences cannot be resolved through interacting binding agreements, so the solution is, *a priori*, undetermined. Nash, Selten and Harsanyi received the Nobel prize precisely for their contributions to overcoming indetermination through the concept of the equilibrium of the game" (Salas-Fumas 1995: 35).

[5] Refinement is a process to seek an equilibrum among different pure strategies, but not necessarily dominant ones (Gintis 2000: 27).

showed that both players had preferred cooperation to betrayal 60% of times, and non-equilibrium strategies 78% and 68% of times, depending on the case. This would introduce reasonable doubts about both Nash's equilibrium – expressed as mutual defection – and about *homo oeconomicus* (Flood 1952). As Nash pointed out when analysing the results of the experiment, the problem was that Dresher and Flood's intention to play 100 distinct games consecutively with the same two players had made the game iterated, with perfect information. This gave the players the chance to know their opponent's character and to act consequently in the next game either by punishing or correcting (Poundstone 2005: 193).

Despite not being aware of this, what Dresher and Flood had managed to observe for the first time in a laboratory with their experiment was a form of reciprocity that would later be termed *reciprocal altruism* (Trivers 1971) in biology and a *tit-for-tat strategy* (Axelrod 1984) in political sciences. It represented behaviour consisting of always cooperating in the first game and repeating the opponent's decision in subsequent games. One of the two players constantly used the *tit-for-tat strategy*, and forced the other player to cooperate, against his/her initial intentions. Selfishness did not therefore appear as the economic agent's only possible motivation, as reciprocity had not only imposed its logic, but had also strongly influenced both players' decisions. After learning the result of the experiment, as previously mentioned, the researchers began to think about whether it was necessary or possible to revise the theory to include new axioms or to change some of the existing ones to provide a plausible and consistent explanation of the rational economic agents' entire behavioural reality. This initiative led to a defensive reaction by some of the main theorists of the traditional proposal, and it was finally discarded (Flood 1952: 1).

Over the next three decades, the theoretical development of the notion of equilibrium, especially through the contributions of Selten and Harsanyi, provided relevant information for a better understanding of the strategic rationality underlying cooperative relationships between human beings in non-competitive contexts.

Firstly, Selten proposed the notion of *perfect equilibrium in subgames* in the mid-seventies to "(…) resolve games involving dynamic actions between players in which they cannot commit themselves in advance" (Salas-Fumas 1995: 37). This idea has turned out to be crucial to explain strategic rationality in interactive decision-making processes. This is particularly because it demonstrates that the unviability of commitment by the players implies that some of Nash's equilibriums can be ruled out as solutions, as they can be considered rather unreasonable (Salas-Fumas 1995: 37). Through the trembling hand concept, Selten introduced a degree of irrationality in the behaviour of the players through small mistakes in choosing the action to follow to achieve equilibrium,[6] making it possible to reduce the number of perfect equilibriums possible for a particular extensive game (Salas-Fumas 1995: 39).

In addition, Harsanyi achieved a notable development of cooperative Game Theory through an analysis model capable of formalising games with incomplete information (1967, 1968). His main idea consisted of transforming incomplete

---

[6] In 1982 Kerps and Wilson replaced *mistakes* with *beliefs* in one of their most interesting contributions: *sequential equilibrium*.

information into complete but imperfect information. To do this, he proposed to turn every participant into a specific player *type*, containing all the relevant information: characteristics, beliefs, values, and so on. At the beginning of the game, each participant is informed about the type of player they are, but not the player types their opponents are. In this way, Harsanyi made the uncertainty surrounding the game explicit and quantifiable for subsequent analysis.

By doing this, both Selten and Harsanyi managed to develop the notion of equilibrium based on bounded rationality like that proposed by Herbert A. Simon in 1955. He indicated that most people act conditioned by their emotional impulses, their cognitive capabilities and their possibilities of obtaining information. This offered a better comprehension of cooperation through the formalisation of some of the underlying factors and variables.

Besides the theoretical development of the notion of equilibrium, the emergence of *experimental economics* during the first half of 1960s[7] and *behavioural economics* at the end of the 1970s[8] presented empirical evidence that cooperation based on other forms of rationality, such as bounded rationality, was not only possible in economic contexts, it was recurring behaviour. By means of the *Prisoner's Dilemma* and, above all, new games like the *Ultimatum*, the *Chicken* or the *Dictator Games*, the postulate of human selfishness – the fundamental pillar of the theory – was rendered vague and, therefore, not as self-evident as had been believed. As with Dresher and Flood's experiment, cooperation based on reciprocal relational processes emerged suddenly and strongly when players were allowed the necessary freedom to decide (Zamagni 2006).

With the proliferation of studies about the possibility and potential of cooperation in the economic domain, in 1981 Friedrich von Hayek —winner of the Nobel Prize for Economics in 1974— warned about the dangers underlying cooperation for liberal societies. According to Hayek, cooperation, whose appearance and implementation were linked to feelings like altruism and solidarity, and to the existence of false appearances such as commonly shared objectives, was a survival mechanism used satisfactorily by primitive societies. The modern world, however, is large and highly complex, and has nothing to do with those small groups of hunter-gatherers, among whom coordination was relatively easy to achieve, nor with the logic of lib-

---

[7] Vernon Smith is considered to be the father of *experimental economics*, and his works *Experimental Auction Markets an the Walrasian Hypothesis* (1962) and *An Experimental Study of Competitive Market Behavior* (1964) are the starting point for it. However, the initial contributions of scholars like Edward H. Chamberlin in the 1940s, who sought a way of making an experimental study of markets and, above all, Heinz Sauermann Reinhard and Reinhard Selten in 1959, who made an experimental study of oligopolies using strategy games, should also be borne in mind. For further information on this, see Faccarello and Kurz (2016) and Kagel and Roth (1995).

[8] The studies by Ward Edwards, Amos Tversky, Daniel Kahneman and Richard H. Thaler —winner of the Nobel Prize for Economics in 2017—, carried out during the 1970s, in which they compared cognitive models for decision-making in situations of risk and uncertainty with economic models of rational behaviour, are the basis for the emergence of behavioural economics. In this respect, the study *Prospect theory: Decision Making Under Risk* (Tversky and Kahneman 1979) should be highlighted. However, Kahneman himself states that *Toward a positive Theory of Consumer Choice* published by Richard H. Thaler in 1980, is the "(…) founding text in behavioral economics" (2002: 438; 2007: 183).

eral economics, based on individual freedom, selfishness and perfect competition, which are the only conditions allowing it to survive and develop. Hayek also called for eradicating the anachronistic morality of those primitive societies and the feelings underlying it, such as altruism, solidarity and the joint search for shared goals. This morality, which was coherent at that time, and from which we still maintain instincts, was now seen as poorly adapted for today's society and an impediment for its proper development and survival (Hayek 1981). In today's context, where the extensibility and complexity of societies make any attempt to coordinate action unviable, only an individualistic and selfish morality can allow a differentiation element to be introduced for human beings from an evolutionary perspective.

> The evolution of a moral tradition that allowed us to construct a broad order of international collaboration demanded the gradual suppression of these two basic instincts, altruism and solidarity, especially in the pursuit of common goals with our fellow men; and it was made possible by the development of a new morality that primitive man rejected. (…) Indeed, it was essentially the evolution of property, contracts, freedom of feeling regarding what belongs to each, which became the basis of what I call civilisation (Hayek 1981: 72–73).[9]

Hayek's statements were yet another attempt to offer a plausible explanation for the paradox of human reciprocity and underlying cooperation without leaving behind the axiomatic framework of traditional economic theory. Yet a year after Hayek made his statements, Evolutionary Game Theory appeared, with studies beginning to show both the main benefits of unselfish cooperation for the economy (Bowles 2016) and the feelings underlying it and allowing it to emerge and be enhanced (Gintis et al. 2005). Some interesting ideas arose from this and were accepted by hopeful theorists. Introducing a dynamic component offered the possibility of being able to continue developing the theory by von Neumann and Morgenstern, consolidated principally by Nash, Selten and Harsanyi. Yet, far from initial expectations, the evolutionary element showed up something that had been unquestionable until that time: based on the complete rationality of *homo oeconomicus*, it was impossible to fully explain either the observable set of relationships in a given economic context, or economic progress itself.

3.2   Evolutionary Game Theory: Motivational Heterogeneity and Cooperation

The Evolutionary Game Theory was proposed in 1982 by biologist John Maynard Smith in his book *Evolution and the Theory of Game*. This theory came about from the idea of giving Game Theory a dynamic or evolutionary component to study animal behaviour (Gintis 2000, 2009; Schecter and Gintis 2016). But the progress he made in the refinement problem led him to extend his initial expectations, and the theory began to be used in a multidisciplinary way by biologists, economists, sociologists, psychologists and philosophers in their fields to study human behaviour.

---

[9] English translated by Guillermo Rodríguez-González (Hayek 2012).

The main difference between the so-called Evolutionary Game Theory and the conventional Game Theory lies in abandoning equilibriums and adopting strategic dynamics as a key point for studying human behaviour. This was a vital question that allowed more open positions to be adopted. Among other issues, the theory was reinterpreted from the basis of non-perfection and non-completeness, shedding some light on two very important questions offering hopeful results: firstly, it was possible to show how, and under which particular conditions, rational behaviour was, *a priori*, determined and was eventually spread by social learning processes. Secondly, according to economic theory, more rational behaviour was not always the most beneficial for those participating in the game in a competitive context (Zamagni 2006: 32–33). Both these issues opened up a major fissure in what had, until then, been the unavoidable conventional economic focal point because it did away with one of its fundamental axioms: the perfect and complete rationality of *homo oeconomicus*.

And so it was that, with the sudden appearance of this dynamic component, many experimental economists who had strongly criticised Neoclassical Theory for its naive representation of reality began to apply two of the most important contributions to Game Theory to their non-normative studies: a static notion of equilibrium –an evolutionarily stable strategy– and the specification of the dynamic selection process – replication dynamics.

The evolutionarily stable strategy represents the evolutionary equivalent of Nash's equilibrium within traditional Game Theory (Gintis 2000: 148). It is a behaviour strategy or pattern which, although used by most members of society, provides society with a maximum possible adaptive benefit, and remains robust against other individual strategies –which was the case with Nash's equilibrium– and against variations "(…) elected simultaneously by a small, but positive, fraction of players" (Zamagni 2006: 34). As Richard Dawkins argued, replication is the only possibility for any individual; that is, mimicking such performance if one does not wish to be penalised:

> An evolutionary stable strategy or ESS is defined as a strategy which, if most members of a population adopt it, cannot be bettered by an alternative strategy. It is a subtle and important idea. Another way of putting it is to say that the best strategy for an individual depends on what the majority of the population are doing. Since the rest of the population consists of individuals each one trying to maximize his *own* success, the only strategy that persists will be one which, once evolved, cannot be bettered by deviant individual. Following a major environmental change there may be a brief period of evolutionary instability, perhaps even oscillation in the population. But once an ESS is achieved it will stay: selection will penalize deviation from it (Dawkins 2016: 90–91).

Replication dynamics indicates that the value of a strategy in a game for a series of agents increases depending on how high profitability is in relation to the paid mean of the set of strategies (Gintis 2000: 191). This means the strategies above the mean, which have, therefore, been able to offer a better evolutionary advantage for a given society, have also increased presence at the expense of absorbing the strategies below it through a gradual domination process that ends up making them disappear[10] (Zamagni 2006: 34).

---

[10] Cf. to learn more about relication dynamics, see Gintis (2000: 188–219).

Assimilating both concepts allowed these economists to better understand the formation of social conventions, the impact and evolution of norms, cultural evolution processes, institutional change, the causes of collective action, the evolution of individual preferences and the role that all this plays in rational decision-making processes in highly competitive contexts, such as economic ones. In this way, they explained the main aspects of economic rationality through endogenous causes, such as consistency and durability at a given rationality level among its economic agents, or under the survival conditions of individual non-self-interested motivations (Zamagni 2006: 35). This meaning was given to the supposedly irrational decisions made which were, paradoxically, highly advantageous for all the agents involved.

In short, while conventional theory had been concerned about predicting behaviours through the observation, hypothesis, mathematisation and empirical verification of the preferences of those involved – revealed through their consumption habits – the emerging evolutionary economics had begun to show an interest in untangling the endogenous preferences involved in decision-making processes and, in this way, to attempt a plausible explanation for the numerous contradictions that the theory included ever since it emerged. For example, why did many participants in the Dictator Game tend to offer a fair share of the money when their opponent was merely a passive spectator of this attitude? If agents are exclusively guided by selfishness, it would not be worth considering any choices other than those that benefit them most. Similarly, why did the players in the Ultimatum Game, who have to accept offers, tend to reject offers below 30%? Any offer above 0 means optimising one's result – minimising losses. So, this conduct is nonsense if the Minimax Theorem is taken into account. Moreover, why do participants act more fairly in various games when they are allowed to have minimum communication with rivals? Or why do they prefer cooperation when they have the slightest chance of breaking the strictest game rules?

What evolutionary economics has contributed has not been ignored by many of today's theorists of the original Game Theory. Some, like political scientist Elinor Ostrom —the 2009 Nobel prize winner for economics— have absorbed their criticisms and contributions to enrich and develop the theory from within (Ostrom 2003). Among other things, Ostrom suggests that the mistake of the classical theory has been to maintain an acritical attitude to the adopted rationality model because this does not allow the possibility of agents being able to escape the problems and dilemmas underlying their activity. Agents' communication and emotional capacities and competences should be fairly evaluated to coordinate action for purposes that benefit them all.

For Ostrom, such matters are a challenge for both Game Theory – reviewing its own foundations to propose new models that help explain cooperation beyond self-interest – and Economic Theory – recognising that agents have the capacities and competences they need to be able to organise themselves and overcome conflicts of interest. This is especially true because, as laboratory experiments with strategy games and field studies are now demonstrating, cooperation is not only possible in economic contexts and it is desirable and much more efficient and beneficial for all those involved (Ostrom 2001: 19).

Clearly in line with Ostrom's ideas, other important economists have also criticised the simplicity of the predominant discourse in economics. For instance, Sen, in *On Ethics and Economy* (1987), who suggests that the contradictions underlying a rational choice based on particular objectives can no longer be ignored, above all when strategy game participants act against the objectives they acknowledge and which they ultimately wish to maximise. This tends to occur even when they do not consider complying with these behaviour rules to be intrinsically important. The 2001 Nobel laureate for economics Joseph E. Stiglitz, in *The Price of Inequality: How Today's Divided Society Endangers Our Future* (2012), indicates that the neoliberal proposal is not based on an in-depth understanding of modern economic theory, but on making a naive interpretation of economics, based on assumptions of perfect competition, perfect markets and perfect information. Herbert Gintis in *Game Theory Evolving: A Problem-Centered Introduction to Modeling Strategic Interaction* (2000), states that the problem of today's economic theory lies in its lack of interest in the motivational heterogeneity observed in laboratory experiments with strategy games. Thus, it is incapable of observing different types of *homo* –e.g. *oeconomicus, parachius, egualis* or *reciprocans*– and the role each of them plays in the economy. Meanwhile, Zamagni in *L'economia del bene commune* (2007), indicates that paralysing methodological reductionism prevents correct social and human economic development. In his own words,[11] "(…) It is not true that the driver of market competition lies only in economic agents' interest. Apart from being actually false, as confirmed by merely observing cases, this statement implies theoretical reductionism" (Zamagni 2007: 25–26).

More recently, Evolutionary Game Theory studies have been supported by the Neuronal Game Theory, a cross-sectional branch of neurosciences that contributes relevant data about the possibility and benefits of human cooperation, their intrinsic relationship with reciprocity, and the role played by *prosocial emotions* in different relational decision-making processes.

3.3   Neural Game Theory: Neuronal Correlates and Cooperation

Neuronal Game Theory came about in 2001 when Kevin McCabe, Vernon Smith —winner of the Nobel Prize for Economics in 2002—, Daniel Houser, Theodore Trouard and Lee Ryan began to use strategy games as a method for studying the cerebral basis of economic agents' behaviour. The difference between this theory and other Game Theory stances –e.g., the traditional or the evolutionary ones – lies in its attempt to predict agents' conduct by observing their brain activity during

---

[11] "(…) non è vero che il mercato è un'istituzione compatible solamente con la motivazione egocentrica dei suoi attori. Non è vero cioè che ciò che muove la competizione di mercato è *solo* il self-interest degli agenti economici. Questo è fattualmente falso, come la mera osservazione casual conferma, oltre che teoricamente riduttivo" (Zamagni 2007: 25–26).

decision-making processes in various activity areas, e.g., economics or politics. In this way, Neuronal Game Theory moves the centre of attention from a *posteriori* observation of economic agents' purchasing habits to an *a priori* discernment of the neuronal correlates underlying these behaviours.

Neuroeconomics, whose prime objective is to elucidate the cerebral basis involved in a rational economic agent's decision-making processes (Glimcher et al. 2009), came into being a few years earlier, in 1996, when Peter Shizgal and Kent Conover published "On the Neural Computation of Utility". However, this pioneering work and others focused on the discipline, and some others centred mainly on studying animal behaviour, did not deploy strategy games as a method to study brain activity. After publishing "A Functional Imaging Study of Cooperation in Two-Person Reciprocal Exchange" (McCabe et al. 2001), both this emerging discipline and Game Theory itself took a huge qualitative leap because, firstly, Game Theory offered new neuro-economic studies experiments and robustness and, therefore, confidence in the results. This was chiefly due to the fact that the theoretical basis of the games had been thought out over more than 50 years, which could not be said of other neuroscientific disciplines that had to create new methods or adopt methods from other study areas. In addition, the brain image techniques employed by neuroeconomics were an excellent complement for consolidating the Game Theory. It was therefore no longer necessary to fall back on the explanation offered *a posteriori* by subjects under study concerning a given response because their brains now *spoke* at the same time as the response was provided.

Since it came into being, complementing Game Theory and imaging techniques, it represented major advances in the field of economic rationality studies. Among other issues, it has verified: (a) the implication of feelings and emotions in different rational decision-making processes; (b) the possibility of striking optimum and highly beneficial equilibriums for related parties thanks to intangible resources like trust, reciprocity and reputation; (c) and the implementation of reciprocity as a condition for enabling collaborative interpersonal relationships.

(a) *The role of feelings and emotions in rational decision-making processes:* the agent's motivational heterogeneity and its role in rational decision-making processes have been a recurrent theme in most neuroscience disciplines. Antonio R. Damasio, a pioneer in the study of the cerebral basis of feelings and emotions, proposed in *Descartes' Error: Emotion, Reason, and the Human Brain* (1994) and *Looking for Spinoza: Joy, Sorrow and the Feeling Brain* (2003), an emotive and reflective structure of reason, inseparable from the rational decision-making process. According to Damasio, emotions have a cognitive and experiential basis reflected in the agent's decision through binding positive or negative feelings, generating a feeling of rejection or proximity when faced with our own responses or those of others.

In the same line of thought, neuro-economists Ernst Fehr and Bettina Rockenbach focused their works on the involvement of negative feelings in rejecting positive offers in strategy games, particularly when those considerably favouring a particular player are rejected as a punishment for what that player considers to have been inappropriate behaviour. Thus, in "Detrimental Effects of Sanctions on Human Altruism" (2003), Fehr and Rockenbach suggested that, considering homogenous rationality with ambitions for completeness, like that adopted by the traditional theory, major drawbacks are highlighted, making it inconsistent. This is mainly because it completely ignores players' capacity to make moral judgements. This refers to the negative effects deriving from applying sanctions to actions they consider unfair, because punishment incurs a high cost, not only for the guilty party, but also for the party who imposes the punishment. There are therefore underlying reasons for imposing punishment for the given action deriving from the player's commitment to these prosocial values, principles or rules.

Hence the fact that brain images taken in Ultimatum Game participants, for example, reveal that when the receiver of an offer perceives that a response is unfair, different areas of his/her brain are activated: the anterior insula, an area related to feelings; the dorsolateral prefrontal cortex, an area involved in cognition; and the anterior cingulate cortex, an area involved in pleasure and reward. Depending on the degree of activation of all these parts, the player makes one decision or another. The decision is therefore not only motivated by the player's self-interest, but also by a series of factors determining the player's final response. Among them, we find the possibility of maximising benefits, and also analysing the resulting prosocial feelings and emotions that lead players to be concerned about others' well-being, or about moral values, rules and moral principles, by means of which they are capable of feeling committed, regardless of whether they are offered an optimum.

Research is going on in neuropsychology in this sense. Recent studies like *Decreasing Unethical Decisions: The Role of Morality-Based Individual Differences* (Sturm 2017), have examined the process and variables involved in controlling the immoral decisions of economic agents. Among their conclusions, they highlight the double route of the process affecting decision-making through moral variables. Although the preliminary studies have been highlighting awareness and deliberation and fundamental characteristics of the process, this study stresses the role played by the subconscious part in limiting unethical behaviour at individual level.[12]

(b) *The possibility of cooperating to seek common objectives:* the cooperation theme has also been thoroughly studied by neurosciences. The pioneering study of using strategy games in neuroeconomics (McCabe et al. 2001), for instance, points out that the neural activation of those who participate in strategy games is shown by a much more active prefrontal cortex in players who maintain cooperative strategies than in those who decide not to. This means that non-self-interested cooperation is healthy in the economic domain because the bases of

---

[12] For more in-depth studies of moral decision-making processes based on neuropsychology, see Orlitzky (2016); Schwartz (2016); Dedeke (2013); Woiceshyn (2011); and Kahane and Shackel (2010).

selfishness (a) are far from the prefrontal cortex and (b) lack noteworthy activity when such cooperation is activated.

Other relevant neuroeconomics studies conducted in the field of relationality and in a given human activity context, like an economic one, have stressed the value of certain intangible resources in their appearance and reinforcement: trust, reciprocity and reputation. From all these studies, "Oxytocin increases trust in humans" (Kosfeld et al. 2005) should be highlighted. Through implementing a game of trust, this work empirically demonstrates that: (a) it is possible to alter an economic agent's behaviour with neuropharmacological manipulation; (b) there is a direct relationship between the levels of oxytocin in the brain and the appearance and reinforcement of the trust implied in non-self-interested cooperation processes; (c) such trust allows agents to take higher risks when attempting to maximise profits, but only if they are linked with interpersonal relationships. Among other issues, this study suggests that the predominant economic theory makes a serious mistake when it analyses all cooperative conduct from a single viewpoint, as the neurobiological bases involved in various types of relationships observable through strategy games respond to different brain areas and are poorly interrelated. Interpreting collective action by taking the self-interested player's position as a starting point therefore implies a bias that prevents the underlying reality being properly interpreted.

"What motivates repayment? Neural correlates of reciprocity in the trust game" (Van den Bos et al. 2009) is also significant in this sense. Its objective is to disentangle the neural correlates of reciprocity by brain images taken by implementing games of trust. This study reveals that, firstly, several brain regions associated with moral judgements (aMPFC, rTPJ), reward and excitement (VS, IC), and with inhibiting selfish impulses (ACC, rDLPFC), work together when individuals reciprocate. On the other hand, the greater the trust required of the player who has to make the first decision in a game, the more the others are prepared to cooperate with the him or her. What this indicates is that reciprocators act by bearing in mind the consequences for both themselves and others. Finally, individual decision-making processes are modulated by social values accumulated by various players. This study therefore suggests that an intangible resource like reciprocity is a key element for social interaction, and that reciprocal trust conditions the possibility of it being implemented and carried out.

The "Neural Basis of Conditional Cooperation" (Suzuki et al. 2011) is even more interesting. It is a study whose results, obtained by applying the iterated *Prisoner's Dilemma*, suggest that cooperation between people not related by family ties is a basic and essential trait of today's societies, is conditioned by expectations of responses from the related parties (reciprocity) and the negative feelings resulting from selfish conduct. Hence this study suggests that most agents (a) are willing to cooperate; (b) are concerned about discerning between co-operators and free-riders to be able to decide rationally with whom to relate reciprocally to meet their different interests, which may be personal, collective or made universal. The detection of a free rider activates their right dorsolateral prefrontal cortex (RDLPFC), which is the part of the brain associated with punishment for breaking rules in social interaction situations to inhibit the human tendency to relate with fellow citizens. Such RDLPFC activation has a cognitive, rather than a biological, basis resulting from direct experiences in the reciprocity capacity of the related parties.

Finally, it is worth highlighting "Indirect Reciprocity Provides Only a Narrow Margin of Efficiency for Costly Punishment" (Ohtsuki et al. 2009) which reveals, firstly, the role that *altruistic punishment* plays in implementing cooperation based on indirect reciprocity and, secondly, reputation as a two-way bridge between the reciprocal act and the trust needed to establish highly beneficial relationships for the related parties: "Consequently, there is only a small parameter region where costly punishment leads to an efficient equilibrium. In most cases, the population does better by not using costly punishment. The efficient strategy for indirect reciprocity is to withhold help for defectors rather than punish them" (Ohtsuki et al. 2009: 79).

(c) *From homo oeconomicus to homo reciprocans*: the different studies made of the role of feelings and emotions in different decision-making processes and the possibilities of striking optimum equilibriums suggest reciprocity to be a condition allowing not only strategic cooperation, capable of maximising the benefit for all those involved. Indeed, the majority of neuroeconomics studies have focused on specific aspects of reciprocity like the neural bases of altruistic punishment or the neural process that underlies human reciprocity during social interactions.

Studies like "Altruistic Punishment in Humans" (Fehr and Gächter 2002) and "The Efficient Interaction of Indirect Reciprocity and Costly Punishment" (Rockenbach and Milinski 2006), which is one of the most significant contributions made by the strong reciprocity theorists, have suggested serious interpretation deficiencies in the theoretical self-interest approach. This is particularly so because it is rendered dumb, as opposed to the empirically observable and verifiable fact that most agents pay costs to act in accordance with judgements about what is fair or unfair, mainly thanks to the prosocial emotions emanating from these judgements which motivate action.

Later studies, like "Neural correlate of human reciprocity in social interactions" (Sakaiya et al. 2013), among others,[13] reveal that some important questions lie behind reciprocity, forcing us to reflect on the margins of predominant economic rationality, and that a close relationship exists between this rationality and the possibility of specifying equilibriums to deal with common and highly beneficial objectives for all parties involved. Firstly, there is a link between a non-reciprocal attitude and the emergence of negative emotions in the agents who cooperate. Secondly, the perception that the punishment imposed

---

[13] For a more detailed look at these issues, see Nicklisch and Wolff (2012), Van den Bos et al. (2009), Ohtsuki et al. (2009), Strobel et al. (2011).

on those breaking the game rules is morally justified. Thirdly, a direct relationship exists between the identity of the other party and human reciprocity (person *vs.* machine). Fourthly, there are the positive feelings aroused in players by the people who carry out reciprocal actions (tit-for-tat *vs.* random).

Through these questions and others, Neural Game Theory offers data that corroborates the need to reconceptualise economic rationality to guide it towards a new emotional and relational paradigm. Other important findings include: agents' behaviour in highly competitive contexts is modulated by a behavioural and motivational heterogeneity ranging from the most basic selfishness to various forms of altruism or reciprocity; moral judgements play a key role in decision-making processes in economy; and behind the feelings and emotions that allow actions to be coordinated lies a strategic, but also a moral, dimension. These matters suggest the necessity of widening the margins of economic rationality emotionally, morally and, therefore, relationally, by introducing variables like feelings and prosocial emotions into the information base, as well as the values, rules or principles underlying the moral judgements involved in decision-making processes.

Neural Game Theory also contributes with arguments that explain and account for the various reciprocal behaviours observed and studied for decades by economists, psychologists, biologists, sociologists and philosophers in field studies and in laboratory experiments with strategy games. This is collaborative conduct, not necessarily of the self-interested kind, emerging, persisting and being reinforced by reciprocity, whose implementation paradoxically offers all those involved in the relationship the possibility of accessing what selfishness will never achieve: optimum economic profits.

Bibliography

Arrow, Kenneth J. 1951. *Social choice and individual values.* New York: Wiley.

Axelrod, Robert. 1984. *The evolution of cooperation.* New York: Basic Books.

Borel, Émile. 1921. La theorie du jeu et les equations integrales ä noyau symetrique. *Académie des Sciences (France)* 173: 1304–1308.

Bowles, Samuel. 2016. *Moral economy. Why good incentives are no substitute for good citizens.* New Haven: Yale University Press.

Damasio, Antonio R. 1994. *Descartes' error: Emotion, reason, and the human brain.* New York: Avon Books.

———. 2003. *Looking for Spinoza: Joy, sorrow and the feeling brain.* London: William Heinemann.

Dawkins, Richard. 2016 [1976]. *The selfish Gene.* Oxford: Oxford University Press.

Dedeke, Adenekan. 2013. A cognitive–intuitionist model of moral judgment. *Journal of Business Ethics* 126: 437–457. https://doi.org/10.1007/s10551-013-1965-y.

Faccarello, Gilbert, and Heinz D. Kurz, eds. 2016. *Handbook on the history of economic analysis volume III: Developments in major fields of economics.* Cheltenham: Edward Elgar Publishing.

Fehr, Ernst, and Simon Gächter. 2002. Altruistic punishment in humans. *Nature* 415 (6868): 137–140.

Fehr, Ernst, and Bettina Rockenbach. 2003. Detrimental effects of sanctions on human altruism. *Nature* 422 (6928): 137–140.

Flood, M. Merrill. 1952. *Some experimental games*, Research memorandum RM-789- 1. Santa Monica: RAND Corporation.

Gintis, Hebert. 2000. *Game theory evolving: A problem-centered introduction to modeling strategic interaction.* Princeton: Princeton University Press.

———. 2009. *The bounds of reason: Game theory and the unification of the behavioral sciences.* Princeton: Princeton University Press.

Gintis, Herbert, Samuel Bowles, Robert Boyd, and Ernst Fehr, eds. 2005. *Moral sentiments and material interests. The foundations of cooperation in economic life.* Cambridge: MIT Press.

Glimcher, Paul W., Colin F. Camarer, Ernst Fehr, and Russell A. Poldrack, eds. 2009. *Neuroeconomics. Decision making and the brain.* Amsterdam: Elsevier Academic Press.

Harsanyi, John C. 1967. Games with incomplete information played by "Bayesian" players, I-III. part I. The basic model. *Management Science. Special Issue: Theory Series* 14(3), 159–182. https://doi.org/10.1287/mnsc.14.3.159.

———. 1968. Games with incomplete information played by "Bayesian" players, I-III. part II. Bayesian Equilibrium Points. *Management Science. Special Issue: Theory Series* 14(5), 320–334.

Hayek, Friedrich A. 1981. Los fundamentos éticos de la sociedad libre. In *Ciclo de Conferencias sobre Fundamentos de un Sistema Social Libre.* Centro de Estudios Públicos, Santiago de Chile. http://www.eleutera.org/wp-content/uploads/2015/07/Hayek-Friedrich-Los-fundamentos-éticos-de-una-sociedad-libre.pdf.

———. 2012. *Free from envy: The legitimization of envy as a moral axiom of socialism.* Trans. Rodríguez-González, G. http://www.caminosdelalibertad.com/articulos/verArticulo/3317#.WRNZVhgrwcg. Accesed 25 September 2017.

Kagel, John H., and Alvin E. Roth, eds. 1995. *Handbook of experimental economics volume 2.* Princeton: Princeton University Press.

Kahane, Guy, and Nicholas Shackel. 2010. Methodological issues in the neuroscience of moral judgement. *Mind & Language* 25 (5): 561–582.

Kahneman, Daniel. 2002. Maps of bounded rationality: Psychology for behavioral economics. In *Les Prix Nobel*, ed. Tore Frängsmyr, 416–417. Stockholm: Nobel Foundation. https://www.nobelprize.org/nobel_prizes/economic-sciences/laureates/2002/kahnemann-lecture.pdf. Accessed 30 Sept 2017.

———. 2007. Maps of bounded rationality: Psychology for behavioral economics. In *A history of psychology in autobiography. volume IX*, ed. Gardner Lindzey and William M. Runyan, 155–190. Washington, DC: American Psychological Association.

Kosfeld, Michael, Markus Heinrichs, Paul J. Zak, Urs Fischbacher, and Ernst Fehr. 2005. Oxytocin increases trust in humans. *Nature* 435 (1): 637–677.

Kreps, David M., and Robert Wilson. 1982. Sequential equilibria. *Econometrica* 50 (4): 863–894.

McCabe, Kevin, Daniel Houser, Lee Ryan, Vernon Smith, and Theodore Trouard. 2001. A functional imaging study of cooperation in two-person reciprocal exchange. *Proceedings of the National Academy of Sciences of the United States of America* 98 (20): 11832–11835.

Morgenstern, Oskar. 1955. La teoría de los juegos y del comportamiento económico. *Económica* I (3–4), 345–375.

Nash, John F. 1950a. Equilibrium points in n-person games. *Proceedings of the National Academy of the United States of America* 36 (1): 48–49.

———. 1950b. The bargaining problem. *Econometrica* 18 (2): 155–162.

Nicklisch, Andreas, and Irenaeus Wolff. 2012. On the nature of reciprocity: Evidence from the ultimatum reciprocity measure. *Journal of Economic Behavior & Organization* 84 (3): 892–905.

Ohtsuki, Hisashi, Yoh Iwasa, and Martin A. Nowak. 2009. Indirect reciprocity provides only a narrow margin of efficiency for costly punishment. *Nature* 457: 79–82.

Orlitzky, Marc. 2016. How cognitive neuroscience informs a subjectivist-evolutionary explanation of business ethics. *Journal of Business Ethics*, Published online. https://doi.org/10.1007/s10551-016-3132-8, 144, 717.

Ostrom, Elinor. 2001. Reformulating the commons. In *Protecting the commons: A framework for resource management in the Americas*, ed. Joanna Burger, Elinor Ostrom, Richard B. Norgaard, David Policansky, and Bernard D. Goldstein, 17–41. Washington, DC: Island Press.

———. 2003. Toward a behavioral theory linking trust, reciprocity, and reputation. In *Trust & reciprocity. interdisciplinary lessons from experimental research*, ed. E. Ostrom and James Walker, 19–79. New York: Russell Sage Foundation.

Poundstone, William. 2005. *El dilema del prisionero. John von Neumann, la teoría de juegos y la bomba*. Madrid: Alianza. [English version: 1992. *Prisoner's Dilema: John von Neumann, Game theory and the puzzle of the bomb*. Doubleday: New York].

Rockenbach, Bettina, and Manfred Milinski. 2006. The efficient interaction of indirect reciprocity and costly punishment. *Nature* 444: 718–723.

Sakaiya, Shiro, Yuki Shiraito, Junko Kato, Hiroko Ide, Kensuke Okada, Kouji Takano, and Kenji Kansaku. 2013. Neural correlate of human reciprocity in social interactions. *Frontiers in Neuroscience* 7 (239): 1–12.

Salas-Fumás, Vicente. 1995. Los Premios Nobel de Economia, Harsanyi, Nash y Selten: El funcionamiento de los mercados desde la teoría de juegos. *Societat Catalana d'Economia* 12: 35–46.

Sauermann, Heinz, and Reinhard Selten. 1959. Ein Oligopolexperiment. *Zeitschrift für die gesamte Staatswissenschaft* 115: 427–471.

Schecter, Stephen, and Herbert Gintis. 2016. *Game theory in action: An introduction to classical and evolutionary models*. Princeton: Princeton University Press.

Schwartz, Mark S. 2016. Ethical decision-making theory: An integrated approach. *Journal of Business Ethics* 139: 755–776. https://doi.org/10.1007/s10551-015-2886-8.

Selten, Reinhard. 1978. The equity principle in economic behavior. In *Decisio theory and social ethics, issues in social choice*, ed. Hans W. Gottinger and Werne Leinfellner, 289–305. Dordrecht: Reidel.

Sen, Amartya. 1987. *On ethics and economy*. Oxford: Blackwell Publishing.

Shizgal, Peter, and Kent Conover. 1996. On the neural computation of utility. *Current Directions in Psychological Science* 5 (2): 37–43.

Smith, Vernon L. 1962. An experimental study of competitive market behavior. *Journal of Political Economy* 70: 111–137.

———. 1964. Experimental auction markets and the Walrasian hypothesis. *Journal of Political Economy* 73: 181–201.

Smith, John Maynard. 1982. *Evolution and the theory of game*. Cambridge: Cambridge University Press.

Stiglitz, Joseph E. 2012. *The price of inequality: How today's divided society endangers our future*. New York: W. W. Norton & Co.

Strobel, Alexander, Jan Zimmermann, Anja Schmitz, Martin Reuter, Stefanie Lis, Sabine Windmann, and Peter Kirsch. 2011. Beyond revenge: Neural and genetic bases of altruistic punishment. *NeuroImage* 54 (1): 671–680.

Sturm, Rachel E. 2017. Decreasing unethical decisions: The role of morality-based individual differences. *Journal of Business Ethics* 142: 37–57. https://doi.org/10.1007/s10551-015-2787-x.

Suzuki, Shinsuke, Kazuhisa Niki, Syoken Fujisaki, and Eizo Akiyama. 2011. Neural basis of conditional cooperation. *Social Cognitive & Affective Neuroscience* 6 (3): 338–347.

Thaler, Richard H. 1980. Toward a positive theory of consumer choice. *Journal of Economic Behavior and Organization* 1 (1): 36–90.

Tirole, Jean. 2017. *Economics for the common good*. Trans Rendall, S., Princeton: Princeton University Press.

Trivers, Robert L. 1971. The evolution of reciprocal altruism. *Quarterly Review of Biology* 46: 35–57.

Tversky, Amos, and Daniel Kahneman. 1979. Prospect theory: Decision making under risk. *Econometrica* 47 (2): 263–292.

Van den Bos, Wouter, Eric van Dijk, Michiel Westenberg, Serge A.R.B. Rombouts, and Eveline A. Crone. 2009. What motivates repayment? Neural correlates of reciprocity in the trust game. *Social Cognitive Affective Neuroscience* 4 (3): 294–304.

von Mises, Ludwig. 1998. *Human action: A treatise on economics.* Auburg: Ludwig von Mises Institute.

von Neumann, John. 1928. Zur Theorie der Gesellschaftsspiele. *Mathematische Annalen* 100 (1928): 295–320.

von Neumann, John, and Oskar Morgenstern. 1944. *Theory of games and economic behavior.* Princeton: Princeton University Press.

Woiceshyn, Jaana. 2011. A model for ethical decision making in business: Reasoning, intuition, and rational moral principles. *Journal of Business Ethics* 104: 311–323. https://doi.org/10.1007/s10551-011-0910-1.

Zamagni, Stefano. 2006. *Heterogeneidad motivacional y comportamiento económico. La perspectiva de la economía civil.* Madrid: Unión Editorial.

———. 2007. *L' economia del bene commune.* Rome: Città Nuova.

Chapter 4
Reciprocity Approaches: The Possibility of Human Cooperation

Abstract Finding an explanation for human cooperation in highly competitive contexts has become one of the main challenges for economics. Many field studies and laboratory experiments with strategy games have shown that human beings are predisposed to cooperate with their peers in a competitive context like the economic one, and that this is a conduct which most agents consider to be desirable. For many economists, behind this diversion of the theoretical model based on the self-interested rationality of *homo oeconomicus* lies the human capacity to reciprocate. This allows agents to establish interpersonal relationships to meet common objectives. The objective of this chapter will be to analyse the main reciprocity approaches proposed from sociobiology, evolutionary economics and humanistic economics from the ethical-critical viewpoint as a plausible explanation for cooperation in different areas of activity, particularly economics.

Traditionally, the predominant economic theory has not shown much interest in cooperation. Among other reasons, this is because it is structured on a determining proposal that limits its emergence and obstructs its development: human nature itself, hindered by selfish impulses (Mandeville 1705, 1724), renders useless all efforts to implement collective actions that allow highly beneficial common objectives for all participants to be fulfilled. In other words, the horizon of meaning for human beings is rooted in constantly satisfying their own well-being, which makes humans disembodied individualists who see fellow men and women as rivals to beat in competitive zero-sum games. Hence the theorists of the traditional economic hypothesis understand that only control and external coercion can generate the trust needed to be able to coordinate the action of an activity that requires interpersonal relationality.[1] Yet in recent decades, various disciplines, such as evolutionary economy and neuroeconomics, have provided relevant data and arguments about the reasons for human cooperation that have returned altruism and reciprocity to the forefront of studying the economic situation as a condition of the possibility of cooperation emerging and being reinforced.

---

[1] To learn the basic aspects of this argument, see Olson (1965).

© Springer International Publishing AG, part of Springer Nature 2018
P. Calvo, *The Cordial Economy - Ethics, Recognition and Reciprocity*,
Ethical Economy 55, https://doi.org/10.1007/978-3-319-90784-0_4

Along these lines, several works conducted over decades by different economists, sociologists, anthropologists, biologists, political scientists, psychologists and philosophers are worth highlighting, mainly in the conceptualisation of both terms. They have also described and developed distinct cooperative processes observed in various areas of human activity – the disparate behaviours and strategies undertaken by humans and animals which have, paradoxically, served to reassert universal selfishness and to demonstrate the poverty of an axiomatised economic model shaped by the economic agent's assumed perfect and complete rationality, ignoring critical reflection and prosocial feelings and emotions.

Altruism models underlie these cooperative behaviours and, above all, reciprocity. Their application and implementation in practice allows related agents to establish and develop joint projects that greatly benefit them all, such as reciprocal altruism of Robert Trivers, James Friedman and Robert Axelrod, indirect reciprocity of Richard Alexander and Sugden, reciprocal selfishness of Robert H. Frank, social reciprocity of Ostrom, strong reciprocity of Samuel Bowles, Gintis and Fehr, among others, the unconditional reciprocity of Luigino Bruni, and the transitive reciprocity of Zamagni.

The main objective of this chapter will be precisely to take a closer, critical look at the main explanations for human cooperation in the field of economics by offering guidelines for its development from a moral point of view. For this purpose, the study is divided into three sections. Firstly, proposals developed from sociobiology that offer an explanation for cooperation based on the agent's homogeneous motivation will be presented, in economic and other contexts. Secondly, this chapter will look closely at the different approaches developed from evolutionary economics in which application from the bounded rationality perspective offers a plausible explanation for the agent's feelings, emotions and underlying social/moral norms. Thirdly and finally, it will make an in-depth study of different considerations from humanistic economics which, beyond the results of cooperation, is particularly concerned with the intrinsic benefits of the relationship established, as this is the basis for the sustainability and potential not only of market economies, but also their institutions, organisations, companies and associated agents.

4.1 Sociobiological Approaches: Relationships, Tit-for-Tat and Reputation

For just over half a century, sociobiology has been concerned to find a convincing answer for human cooperation –the whys involved in relationality which, although widely observed in fieldwork and laboratory experiments with strategy games, find no rational explanation in the Darwinian perspective for natural selection.

In general terms, sociobiology "(…) is the study of the social structure of such species" (Gintis 2016: 126) and research on it has offered various cooperation explanations based on the agent's motivational homogeneity in economic and other contexts which are applied both to humans and other kinds of animal. These range from attempting to preserve genes –kin altruism– to establishing instrumental relations based on short-, medium- or long-term mutual benefit -reciprocal altruism – or constructing a good reputation to improve the expectations of possibly receiving future help – indirect reciprocity. These explanations have played a key role in maintaining the position taken by the predominant economic theory about human relationality in highly competitive contexts.

(i) *Kin altruism*

The first plausible explanation for cooperation was proposed in 1964 by biologist William D. Hamilton in "The Genetical Evolution of Social Behaviour". Hamilton, who was concerned about being able to explain the evolution of altruism,[2] observed cooperative behaviour in humans and animals that requires both close relationships and the acceptance of high costs before it can properly appear and develop. What Hamilton discovered was kin altruism, also known as kin selection.[3] It showed a type of cooperation intrinsically related to the possibility of generating evolutionary benefit for a group of genetically related individuals or animals.

Based on this observation, Hamilton pondered an evolutionary-type proposal of human cooperation, based on individuals' roles in the reproductive success of family members (Marechal 2009: 454). Yet, unlike the Darwinian viewpoint, which pays attention to the number of family members who manage to pair up and survive,[4] Hamilton was concerned about the quantity of alleles that managed to pass from one generation to the next (Curtis et al. 2008: 836; Bowles and Gintis 2011: 48). This point of view allowed the subject to be considered capable of influencing natural selection in two different ways: by means of *direct fitness*, which means that the subject makes his/her own copies via reproduction, or by *indirect fitness*, which means that the subject contributes to the reproductive success of his/her direct descendants or other family members with a high degree of kinship, such as siblings, nieces/nephews or cousins. In this way, Hamilton was able to provide a biologically plausible explanation of why altruistic behaviours exist in societies. Natural selection itself encourages and promotes the existence of such conduct at a cost for the subject when the production success of the family members of the individual in question and, thus of his/her genes, increases (Dawkins 1982, 2016). The altruistic act is, therefore, performed by thinking both about those who are carriers of the same genetic information, and the strategies allow a larger number of copies and increase the possibilities of transmitting this information to a new generation (Marechal 2009: 454).

The result of all this was the well-known inclusive fitness or Hamilton's rule[5]: $[r > c/b']$, which formulated the possibilities of altruistic behaviour being successful

---

[2] As Camilo J. Cela-Conde (1989) explained, sociobiology coined the inclusive fitness concept with the intention of attempting to offer a plausible explanation about the paradox aroused by altruism. Natural selection is assumed to have a tendency to favour individual fitnesses, so it seems paradoxical that so many people who display this non-individualistic fitness exist.

[3] The term kin selection was coined by John Maynard Smith in *Group Selection and Kin Selection* (1964) to refer to the idea expressed by Hamilton.

[4] As Dawkins argues, "(…) in the world of Darwinism, gains are not paid in money, but in descendants" (2016).

[5] The inclusive fitness or kinship rule would be related to both the direct fitness and the indirect fitness (Curtis et al. 2008: 836).

(Fletcher and Zwick 2006: 252). This implies that, for an altruistic act to benefit from the natural selection process, the cost [c] for the subject incurred by an altruistic act needs to be no higher than the benefit [b] obtained by it, set by the number of copies finally made of his/her genes. This is where the determining role of the relationship [r] that the altruist has with the beneficiary of the act comes into play. In this way, Hamilton's rule shows that natural selection favours altruists who mainly help their offspring or siblings because their action safeguards or increases the number of copies that allow more alleles to be passed on to the next generation. The more distant the kinship, the less effect the altruistic act has on the natural selection process.

This viewpoint suggests that the assumed altruistic attitude is merely a kind of covert selfishness (Marechal 2009: 454). That is, people help family members thinking of their own interests and of the sustainability of the transmitted genes, not of a collective or common interest. In this way, although the costs incurred could be high, and might even include the altruist's own life, the benefits from the genetic-evolutionary perspective are huge for those who act altruistically with their closest family members. However, the kin altruism problem observed by Hamilton in both human and animal behaviour lies in the fact that it offers a plausible explanation for only one specific type of cooperation, based on the survival of genes by accepting the costs and the family proximity of the people in the relationship. Yet human relationality is reflected in interactions that are not necessarily genetic or parental, which also have to be two-way in order to be sustainable and sustained in the medium term and the long term. For these and other reasons, biologists began to worry about the main concept that would prove to be fundamental for subsequent studies into how to establish mutually beneficial relationships in highly competitive contexts like economics: reciprocity.

(ii) *Reciprocal altruism*

While seeking a holistic explanation for human cooperation, in 1971 biologist Trivers proposed a concept known as reciprocal altruism or weak reciprocity.[6] This is a strategic behaviour observed in humans and animals where the cost of helping others is accepted provided there are reasonable expectations of a return in the future in case of need, which would at least cover the costs deriving from the action (Bowles and Gintis 2011: 59). This cooperation proposal went a step beyond kin altruism because it revealed a type of non-reducible cooperative action beyond subjects who maintained a genetic-parental relationship, extended to all those who were capable of generating expectations of a response for the help provided.

A decade later, political scientist Axelrod linked reciprocal altruism to the possibility of achieving cooperation in international political affairs in his work *The*

---

[6] Different studies indicate that reciprocal altruism has very little to do with uninterested disinterested attitude because the person performing the act does so expecting a future behavioural response from the other person in case of need. They therefore suggested that the most suitable name would be weak reciprocity (Bowles 2006, 444, 433) or direct reciprocity (Becchetti et al. 2010: 289).

Evolution of Cooperation (1984). Using *ad hoc* designed software, Axelrod decided to check the functional validity of different cooperative strategies (Axelrod 2003: 18). To this end, he suggested to a heterogeneous group of recognised specialists in the Game Theory –political scientists, psychologists, mathematicians, sociologists and economists– that they participate in an experiment, and he presented a strategy for playing the Prisoner's Dilemma, which was repeated against other rivals[7] (Axelrod 1986: 40, 2003: 30). The outcome was 15 different strategies with four distinct disciplines, which were translated into computer language and were input into a computer to compare them in different virtual games.[8] Each strategy competed against all the other available ones and against a copy of itself on at least one occasion.[9] It was striking that after 225 games, 120,000 game moves and 240,000 individual decisions, cooperation won the tournament. The tit-for-tat proposal of psychologist and mathematician Anatol Rapoport, consisting of cooperating in the first game and repeating the response offered by one's rival in the following rounds, managed to beat all the other strategies presented (Axelrod 1986: 40–41). It was the simplest strategy of all and yet still managed to obtain some apparently surprising results compared with the most elaborate strategy which, strangely enough, came last in the tournament (Dawkins 2016: 274).

Another striking fact for Axelrod was the comparison made between the strategies considered to be *nice*, as they were never the first to give up cooperating, and those classified as *nasty*, which took advantage of others' work the first chance they had. Eight nice and seven nasty strategies were presented, of which one was called Friedman, based on a resentful strategy.[10] A comparison of the two groups revealed an enlightening fact: all the nice strategies obtained better scores than the best of the unfair ones. That is, the option of playing unfairly did not appear to be the best option to maximise results (Dawkins 2016: 274).

Given these findings, Axelrod organised a second tournament and increased the number of participants. The list of possible competitors included all the participants from the first tournament[11] and all the players obtained information about the results and conclusions drawn from the first experiment (Axelrod 1986: 50). In the end, 63 different strategies were presented, some of which even reached the limits of *mercy*,[12] yet despite everyone knowing tit-for-tat was the strategy to beat, Rapoport once again won by sticking closely to it (Axelrod 2003: 30–31).

---

[7] Well-known theorists were among the participants, like Dawkins, Rapoport or Maynard Smith.

[8] It should be borne in mind that tournament players were not human beings, but computer programmes representing the strategies developed by each theorist in the group (Dawkins 2016: 271).

[9] As Axelrod explained, this particular characteristic defined the so-called round-robin-type tournament (2003: 30).

[10] Friedman's resentful strategy proposal did not work well at all (Dawkins 2016: 274).

[11] Although all the participants from the first tournament were asked to participate, they did not all agree to compete again; e.g. Dawkins presented a strategy in the first tournament but rejected Axelrod's offer to compete again (Dawkins 2016).

[12] Maynard Smith presented an extremely merciful version of tit-for-tat but did not manage to beat Rapoport's original strategy (Dawkins 2016: 275).

After analysing the experimental data, Axelrod concluded that the tit-for-tat strategy was (a) the best possible option when attempting to achieve cooperation in international politics; (b) it combined perfectly with the biological approach of reciprocal altruism developed by Trivers; (c) it was a collectively stable strategy (CSS)[13] that maintained certain basic features, by means of which it was possible to understand its tremendous success (Axelrod 1986: 61–67): niceness, punitiveness and mercy. Niceness because it began by cooperating and only stopped cooperating if the other did so first; punitiveness because if the other player stopped cooperating, he or she was immediately punished through the application of the tit-for-tat rule; and mercy because if the deserter showed a cooperative attitude again, punishment was lifted (Axelrod 1986: 60, 2003: 35–37; Bowles and Gintis 1998: 10–14; Dawkins 2016: 261–301).

Despite its success, reciprocal altruism was also unable to explain all the cooperative behaviours observed in humans. This demonstrates, firstly, how robust relationships can emerge based on mutual benefit and not on genetic motives, which the involved parties share, but it offers no plausible explanation for non-self-interested or non-dual behaviours (Bowles and Gintis 1998). When observed in fieldwork and laboratory experiments carried with the Ultimatum Game, these revealed the existence of many choices in which people prefer cooperation to desertion even though it is less advantageous. Reciprocal altruism, on the other hand, managed to illustrate how some people who do not know one another can build trust through maintaining iterated relationships, but was unable to explain the basis for the reasonable expectation that the other participant is a co-operator and will respond to help received. In one-shot games, where there is no possibility of preparing a short-mid or long-term future perspective, for instance, cooperation also surfaces in many cases. Thus, people who do not know each other trust one another, without having the chance to build enough trust by establishing a continuous relationship. This is an aspect for which reciprocal altruism has no initial response. This second question attracted the attention of biology to another key aspect of cooperation – reputation – which was found to fit into what is known as indirect reciprocity.

(iii) *Indirect reciprocity*

Indirect reciprocity was proposed by biologist Alexander in *The Biology of Moral Systems* (1987) as an attempt to bridge some of the gaps left by kin altruism and reciprocal altruism, as neither could offer a plausible explanation for the reciprocal attitudes observed among unknown agents in which neither kinship nor iterated relationships were feasible (Bowles and Gintis 2011: 68).

At first, indirect reciprocity described cooperative behaviour in humans and animals in which help was offered to those who had previously shown a similar attitude with other people. This made it a type of cooperation that emanated from observing reciprocal attitudes, while its results corresponded to a kind of inverted chain of

---

[13] An ESS cannot be invalidated by other mutant or rare strategies. The tit-for-tat strategy cannot be considered a ESS because it comes over as being unyielding with "nasty" strategies, but not with "nice" ones (Dawkins 2016: 280–281).

favours (Becchetti et al. 2010: 289–290). Later this proposal was improved thanks to Olof Leimar and Peter Hammerstein, who introduced into their simulations of indirect reciprocity game elements with a similar approach to that developed by Sugden in *The Economics of Rights, Cooperation and Welfare* (1986). These two authors realised that reputation strategy – standing strategy – and the good reputation concept – good standing – used by Sugden showed better theory performance (Leimar and Hammerstein 2001: 745–746). This hypothesis was corroborated later by Karthik Panchanathan and Robert Boyd (2001: 116), who showed in their works that this was a stable indirect reciprocity strategy in evolutionary terms, where those agents who followed a good standing strategy saw how their prestige faded when they refused help to someone with good standing. However, this was not the case when they rejected cooperation with agents who did not have good standing (Panchanathan and Boyd 2001: 119).

Indirect reciprocity, therefore, showed that reputation was a determining factor in cooperative actions between people who do not share the same genetic information, or that repeated interactions are not necessarily going to lead to a relationship. Earning a good reputation could help, on one hand, to maintain a minimum of trust needed for an agent to decide to collaborate with a stranger before establishing a repeated relationship and, on the other hand, to maximise profits while increasing the agents' possibilities of entering mutually beneficial cooperative processes for related parties (Bowles and Gintis 2011: 68–77). However, indirect reciprocity still does not tie up all the loose ends of the puzzle underlying human cooperation. One problem is that, as with reciprocal altruism, it does not achieve satisfactory behaviour beyond dual relationships. This means that, when it is applied to large groups, the proposal weakens and is difficult to maintain, as each member needs to know the other participants' actions to be able to cooperate in large-scale joint projects. As dual relationships are private in many cases, it is virtually impossible for all this information to be available. When a reputation is built on observed dual relationships, another problem arises because anyone left out of the relationship will find it very hard to recognise when a decision in the various interactions is of a deserter type and when it is of a cooperative type (Bowles and Gintis 2011: 70).

Kin altruism, reciprocal altruism and indirect reciprocity are common explanations of apparently generous acts performed among humans, and, underlying them, are capacities that are not exclusively human (Bowles 2006: 441). As stated by Bowles and Gintis (2003: 430), iterated interactions and interactions between family members are common in many species. They are behaviours selected through evolution for their adaptive capacity. In other words, traits designed by natural selection that guide behaviours towards purely self-interested mutual cooperation. As a result, the different explanations that sociobiology offers about relationality between humans begin from an acritical position and move towards the rationality assumed to govern individuals' behaviour, acting as a model for designing the traditional economic theory: universal selfishness, a prevalent and pre-reflective idea that has remained immovable for at least the last century and a half.

However, evidence provided by empirical studies, such as "In Search of *Homo Economicus*: Behavioral Experiments in 15 Small-Scale Societies" (Henrich et al.

2001) or other similar cases,[14] has suggested that human behaviour in economic contexts is much more complex than sociobiology has demonstrated. Other animal species also have the capacity to reciprocate (Cela-Conde 1989: 36; Dawkins 2016: 236–237), but underlying such complexity are careful ways of establishing relationships that are only within reach of the human species' cognitive, linguistic and physical capacities. These capacities are found behind the establishment and following of rules; the design of institutions that help to control and disseminate these rules; complex processes to internalise these rules; and the establishment of group relationships based on ethnicity and linguistic behaviour, rather than on similar genetic information (Bowles and Gintis 2003: 430).

4.2   Evolutionary Approaches: Moral Feelings, Social Capital and Altruistic Punishment

Evolutionary economics understands that relationality, on which reciprocal altruism is based, is an important element to bear in mind when explaining human and animal cooperation and cooperation among family members suggested by kin altruism and that the chain of favours of indirect reciprocity may be a good starting point from which to extrapolate cooperative behaviour beyond the family setting. From the perspective of evolutionary economics, it is also believed that none of these three approaches suffices to explain the relationality observable among individuals who have no family relationship whatsoever, who have no possibilities of establishing solid relationships through iteration, or who maintain no mutual relationship of convenience based on expectations of higher future benefits.

Firstly, none of these three explanations based only on the agent's self-interested motivation explains, for example, why in n-players games about public assets or in one-shot games, where relationships are impossible, there is no chance of punishing those who betray trust and take advantage of another player's cooperation. So, a large number of participants opt to collaborate (Bowles and Gintis 1998, 2006, 2011).

Secondly, there seems to be no argument plausible enough to support the idea that the first human beings developed iteration-punishment as a strategy to achieve and maintain cooperation in the group. This was because, firstly, the groups' peculiar situation at that time hardly encouraged such solutions. As they were groups of hunters-gatherers who constantly moved in search of food, it would have been relatively easy to avoid punishment by changing group (Bowles and Gintis 2003: 432). They also faced critical and extreme situations when the group's extinction was at risk from some kind of internal conflict, war, plague, famine or adverse environmental effects. Such critical periods have been very common throughout the human being's evolutionary history, and using iteration-punishment did not seem the most suitable mechanism to achieve survival-oriented cooperation (Bowles 2006: 442).

---

[14] See also Bowles (2006); Bowles and Gintis (1998, 2004, 2006, 2011); Fehr and Fischbacher (2005); Gintis (2000, 2010); Henrich et al. (2001, 2004).

Thirdly and finally, because applying the grim-trigger strategy, based on iteration-punishment, does not work properly when applied to large groups (Bowles and Gintis 2011: 85). In iterated games, the Folk Theorem tends to be used in order to show that in sufficiently iterated situations, with adequately low discount rates,[15] it is possible to obtain Nash's equilibriums with high cooperation levels between players using a grim-trigger strategy when these players maintain self-interested preferences over the results of their actions (Bowles and Gintis 2011: 80–83). Yet, as Axelrod acknowledged,[16] (2003: 60), its main problem lies in the fact that it does not appear to be sustainable beyond a dual relationship[17] (Bowles 2006: 441–442; Bowles and Gintis 2011: 83).

These three issues –iteration-punishment, anomalies in expected behaviour and the grim-trigger strategy – greatly simplify the limitations faced by the theory when only the universal selfishness axiom is applied to explain human cooperative behaviour in all its richness. It is here that many works on evolutionary economics have focused in order to reveal the endogenous motivations underlying the rational economic agent's behaviour; in other words, showing all the jigsaw pieces lying behind the explanation of cooperative behaviour in highly competitive contexts. This new concern has led to various explanations of cooperation based on reciprocity among agents; e.g. the reciprocal selfishness of Frank, Ostrom's social reciprocity and the strong reciprocity of Bowles and Gintis, among others.

(i) *Reciprocal selfishness*

In an attempt to explain how and why people relate to each other in highly competitive contexts like economic ones, in 1988 the evolutionary economist Frank proposed reciprocal selfishness, a pseudo-altruistic behaviour based on moral feelings, related to processes in which people gained a good reputation as reciprocators throughout their lifetimes to obtain, in extreme cases of need, the chance to be included in the relationality networks offering the greatest possibilities of subsistence.

In *Passions within Reason: The Strategic Role of the Emotions* (1988), Frank maintained that, while cooperation has been a key element for human evolution, the mark left by free-riders has been the fact that they exist. Even before there was any language, this has forced human beings to produce selection mechanisms capable of detecting who can be trusted and who is merely opportunistic, waiting for a good chance to maximise profit at everyone else's expense. According to Frank, between these mechanisms there would be a kind of reputation which, unlike the concept worked on by Sugden (1986), fell only within the scope of humans, as it involved moral feelings in its construction and reinforcement process.

---

[15] Zero or close to zero rates.

[16] Axelrod argued that "(...) the reciprocity that works well in the Bipersonal Prisoner's Dilemma simply does not work in the n-persons game version when there are more than just a few people involved" (2003: 60).

[17] One type of dual relationship could be the mutual exchange of assets.

For Frank, a resource like a good reputation allowed those involved to recognise and be recognised as cooperative beings, and to rule out and be ruled out as free-riders. This fact was crucial for human survival because, if relationality offers more possibilities of success, and co-operators tend to relate to one another and leave opportunistic people behind, then the better a good reputation is, the greater the chances of the person possessing it collaborating with others when circumstances allow it. Frank understands that this fact explains why altruistic people are quite successful in a competitive world like economics, even though the way they act incurs such high personal costs (Frank 1988). When relating to others, agents assess the chances of success by very positively evaluating the agents who, like altruists, clearly offer evidence for behaviour that is not merely selfish and is guided by good –in other words, moral– feelings. This is mainly because using such feelings to guide behaviour gives greater self-control to individuals when the short-term temptation for gain on an individual basis implies coming into conflict with the collective benefit (Frank 1988: 90).

This would therefore be a reciprocity proposal based on impure altruism or good selfishness because high costs are incurred when one acts guided by one's good feelings towards others, as with genuine altruism, but while seeking to shape a suitable reputation capable of generating profits in the medium and long term thanks to cooperation. Reciprocal selfishness, which combines the ideas of reciprocal altruism and indirect reciprocity, and which introduces moral feelings as a guide for action to improve the perception that others have of oneself, is, in this way, classified as eligible for possible collaboration. Thus, its structure is such that [A] helps [B] and [C] with a view to increasing his/her possibilities of being able to form part of those reliable cooperation networks whose relational activity allows the benefit of all those involved to be maximised.

This selfish reciprocity approach offers a feasible but insufficient solution for several reasons. Firstly because, as with indirect reciprocity, one of the questions that still has no definite answer is why people cooperate in one-shot games where there is no reference, such as a good reputation, for gaining the required trust. Secondly because reactive feelings, like moral ones, as defined by Strawson (1974: 6–9), show a link between human beings, which may have a clearly evolutionary feature for those people or groups that really take it seriously but which, above all, reflects a practical reason: humans' capacity to make moral judgements about what they consider to be fair or unfair; right or wrong. Humans can therefore be guided by them. Reciprocal selfishness looks at the potential of moral feelings, but does not go deeply into the reasons why they emerge with universal strength. These reasons might provide some clues as to why people cooperate when no good reputation reference exists. As Cortina argues, a reactive feeling like "(...) indignation does not owe its moral nature to having altered the interaction between two isolated people, but to the fact that a normative expectation has been attacked, which does not only serve for both these people, but for many more" (Cortina 2011: 145–146). It therefore seems necessary to also reflect on the moral judgements that enable and justify reactive feelings and can lie behind non-dual, non-family and non-iterated cooperation. Thirdly and finally, Frank's proposal still offers no solution to the problem that leads to non-dual interaction. In extreme situations where the solution involves the cooperation of large groups of n-persons, it is not possible to evaluate the good reputation of absolutely everyone involved in the process. This implies that, the bigger the group, the greater the possibility that free-riders go unnoticed and take advantage of the cooperation for their own benefit.

(ii) *Social reciprocity*

When attempting to find a solution to one of the human cooperation problems, such as how economic agents can relate to one another right from the start, and in situations demanding collaboration among n-persons, the political scientist Ostrom studied the Social Capital Theory. She understood this to be "(…) the value of trust built by social networks to facilitate individual and group cooperation in shared interests, and to organise social institutions on different scales" (Brondizio et al. 2009: 255). Based on this, Ostrom proposed a specific reciprocity approach as a plausible mechanism.[18]

The behavioural approach that Ostrom described and developed from 1998 began with a classical definition of the reciprocity concept as "(…) a continuing relationship of exchange that is at any given time unrequited or imbalanced, but that involves mutual expectations that a benefit granted now should be repaid in the future" (Putnam et al. 1993: 172). It therefore initially seemed to match the typical direct reciprocity structure; in other words, [A] does something for [B], and [B] responds likewise by giving or doing something for [A], regardless of quantity or quality, and in the short, medium or long term (Becchetti et al. 2010: 289). In time, Ostrom adjusted the proposal to motivational heterogeneity, apparently shown by the economic agent in different fieldwork and laboratory experiments with strategy games; to the typical features underlying it as a specific form of social capital; and to a certain influence of evolutionary economics, particularly based on strong reciprocity. All this gave her reciprocity proposal a certain degree of originality, which was defined as "(…) an internalised personal moral norm as well as pattern or social exchange" (Ostrom and Ahn 2003: xxi). This corresponds to both biological inheritance and the socialisation process humans follow to gradually shape their identity (Ostrom 1998: 10, 2003: 49).

From this perspective, which combines contributions of evolutionary economics and Social Capital Theory, Ostrom proposed reciprocity as an attribute of both people and relationships found in all societies. So it would be rather like a packet of strategies available to agents to be used in various collective action contexts or in some non-finite iteration social dilemmas, whose use is linked to some basic questions being fulfilled: (*a*) identifying who is involved in the cooperative process; (*b*) evaluating the possibilities of others being conditional co-operators; (*c*) cooperating initially if there is trust in the others being conditional co-operators; (*d*) not cooperating with those who do not display a collaborative attitude; and (*e*) punishing those who betray others' trust (Ostrom 1998: 10–11). So, for Ostrom, reciprocating meant "(…) reacting positively to others' equally positive conducts, but punishing their negative acts in some way" (Ostrom 2000: 12).

---

[18] Ostrom's first explorations into reciprocity are found in the article "A Behavioral Approach to the Rational Choice Theory of Collective Action", published in 1998.

In her fieldwork and laboratory experiments with strategy games, Ostrom also showed how using reciprocity in a context like that of economics becomes almost unavoidable for all agents capable of relating to others and is established as a condition of the possibility of this relationality moving towards an equilibrium status capable of maximising its benefit in an optimum, continuous and sustainable way (Cárdenas and Ostrom 2004: 311). However, the individualism of self-interested rationality is only able to accomplish suboptimum equilibriums, like those described by Nash, where a better strategy always exists than the one finally adopted by all the participants. For Ostrom, the continuous use of reciprocity allows agents to establish collaborative processes moving towards optimum benefit for all involved thanks to the reputation and mutual trust it generates.

Thus, in part, Ostrom's proposal takes a step beyond reciprocal selfishness. By revealing reciprocity to be a form of social capital, Ostrom managed to convincingly explain how two people or more can set up a mutually beneficial collaboration from the very beginning, without having to directly, dually and iteratively observe what the predisposition of the parties involved. Thanks to social capital, in that it builds citizen networks for transmitting information, potentially linked people can build the minimum trust needed to establish a relationship because of available circulating data about their mutual predisposition to reciprocate and to stick to any commitments made. Nevertheless, Ostrom seemed to suggest that the motivation underlying cooperation does not go beyond the search for maximum economic profit.[19] But if this were the case, it is incomprehensible why many people make decisions based on what they believe is fair or right, even when this means they have to pay a high cost for such action, as several evolutionary economics and neuroeconomics studies have shown.[20] So, it is not a matter merely of showing how cooperation considerably improves the profit of those involved, it is also important to specify the other motivations underlying the maintenance of robust, sustainable cooperation in competitive contexts like economic ones. However, reciprocal selfishness talks about the involvement of moral feelings in such cooperative processes as a motivation for an action, but does not explain why and how they arise. Strong reciprocity has contributed significantly to this, as it is behaviour observed only in humans rooted in the prosocial feelings emanating from collectively internalised rules offering a competitive advantage from the evolutionary viewpoint.

(iii) *Strong reciprocity*

At the end of the 1990s, evolutionary economists like Bowles and Gintis, anthropologists like Robert Boyd and neuro-economists like Fehr and Simon Gächter, among others, observed, in fieldwork and laboratory experiments with the Ultimatum

---

[19] Ostrom's relationality would be framed within a limited two-way rationality that considers both rational interest in personal well-being and interest in others' well-being (which, despite being self-interested, introduces feelings and pro-social emotions as something rational). Sen, however, argues that another level of rationality exists that is not self-interested, committed to that which we consider is right and fair. Ostrom does not consider this level.

[20] On this matter, see Henrich et al. (2001), and Fehr and Rockenbach (2003).

Game, a kind of reciprocal behaviour linked to typically human cognitive, psychological and linguistic capacities: strong reciprocity (Bowles and Gintis 1998; Bowles et al. 1997; Fehr and Gächter 1998; Fehr et al. 1997). This was a human tendency to collaborate with those who act similarly, and to punish behaviours that do not respect the social or moral rules involved, even when such conduct entails a high personal cost (Carpenter et al. 2009: 222; Fong et al. 2005: 282; Gintis 2000: 262).

Subsequent studies of strong reciprocity revealed that it was a social preference motivated by prosocial feelings and emotions stemming from rules. It has: (a) developed in the intersection between genetic transmission and human cultural learning; (b) evolved along with other human traits; (c) been internalised to end up becoming another specific and exclusive trait that identifies human beings, which confers humans a competitive advantage; and (d) moves between two different, but complementary, times: one conditioned and the other unconditioned. The analysis of the interest in particular well-being underlies all this, and is an important, but insufficient, source of knowledge about the causes altering the economic agent's behaviour (Bowles 2006: 11). As one-shot games show, perfect and complete rationality still has a long way to go before it can any of these attitudes, such as that of *homo oeconomicus*. Some people are able to act cooperatively with strangers right from the start, and can punish behaviours that take advantage of others' work despite the high cost it means for them (Bowles and Gintis 2011: 25).

Along these lines, analysing such behaviour modified by strong reciprocity reveals that individuals are adaptive agents and followers of rules. People economise with their limited cognitive resources by acting in accordance with evolutionarily developed behavioural rules, including the fact that "(...) there are ethical prescriptions that govern actions with regards to others; that is, there are social rules whose fulfilment is valued by the actor (e.g. the rule is internalised) and is supported by the social sanction" (Bowles 2006: 97). From this perspective, human cooperation exists, to a great extent, because people are motivated by prosocial preferences as they worry about others' well-being and follow values of justice values and rules of decent conduct (Bowles and Gintis 2011: 19).

The strong reciprocity approach is, therefore, a type of reciprocity rooted in human morality that combines the particular, collective and general interests of the agents who cooperate. This is a kind of social preference, which (a) is expressed in many people all over the world; (b) bears in mind both the result of the action and the process that determines it, plus interest in others' well-being; and (c) has a two-level structure: conditional and unconditional. On one hand, there is a level of cooperation with peers who show similar readiness: positive strong reciprocity (Fehr et al. 2002: 2); on the other hand, there is the level of imposing punishment on those who take advantage of others or break rules, even though this entails high personal cost: negative strong reciprocity. Both these levels are based, to a great extent, on the human capacity not only to generate social and moral rules, but to internalise them, and also on those moral feelings and prosocial emotions, such as shame or blame, which underlie cases when some of these rules are broken either by oneself or by others.

Strong reciprocity is a very good example of how and why collaboration is possible among large groups of people. The human capacity to create and internalise social and moral rules has given people the necessary resources to establish and maintain advantageous relationships for all those involved, even when there is neither the communication needed to gain a good reputation among participants nor a metarule that makes reciprocators punish free-riders. Regardless of the result of the action, a strong reciprocator can punish those who take advantage of others' efforts for endogenous reasons related to social and moral values, principles or rules; in other words, through negative feelings occurring when a reciprocal act creates disputes.

Yet despite strong reciprocity emphasising the role of social and moral rules, values, principles and feelings involved in the appearance and implementation of human cooperation, this continues to be purely conventional. Whereas moral issues always maintain an ambition to be universally valid, strong reciprocity does not attempt to find any plausible justification beyond its evolutionary feature or competitive advantage for a particular community or group. But there must be something else behind relationality, because otherwise there is no explanation for why societies are able to intersubjectively make rules that they then internalise, and which often go beyond the limits of what is evolutionarily valuable and economically beneficial for a group or society. Often these rules serve to coordinate action, and to resolve or avoid the dispute underlying all human relationality processes. The post-conventional reasons behind internalised rules are also important to see whether, apart from being beneficial, strong reciprocal behaviour is also morally justifiable.

Reciprocal selfishness, social reciprocity and strong reciprocity provide relevant information about how large-scale non-dual cooperation can be built and sustained. Firstly, by positive feelings about those who are ready to cooperate with others; secondly, by the human capacity to internalise rules that promote and favour cooperation; thirdly, by negative feelings that flow when social and moral rules are broken; and fourthly, by communication structures that allow the trustworthiness of potential partners in binding cooperation to be known without the need for previous experience of them. Yet many behaviours analysed by experimental economics have suggested that human cooperation does not boil down to the mere calculation of the other person's capacity to respond. In many cases, participants also recognise each other as worthwhile human beings who are worthy of respect and care, and for whom commitment to common projects is worthwhile, although they cannot always respond appropriately to help them.

Indeed, a considerable number of works have been created based on humanistic-type economics in north Italy in the last 20 years. We would highlight Bruni's proposal of unconditional reciprocity and Zamagni's transitive reciprocity. These reciprocal behaviours are involved in the appearance and reinforcement of the relational processes that provide intrinsic, rather than merely extrinsic, benefits for all the related agents by encouraging people's self-fulfilment and the cohesion of the economic sphere.

4.3   Humanistic Approaches: Solidarity and Empowerment

Given concern about unsustainable markets and the lack of suitable social, economic and human development, several economic and humanistic-type studies have paid attention to the relational processes that generate both intrinsic and extrinsic benefits for the system, for institutions, companies and organisations, and also for the economic agents involved.

From this perspective, two decades of work by Bruni on one hand, and Zamagni on the other, have observed and developed two reciprocity approaches involved in generating and reinforcing the relational assets required, among other things, for people's self-fulfilment and for the development and sustainability of the economy and society. On the one hand, there is solidarity or unconditional reciprocity, which allows relationships reaching out to care for people who are mutually recognised as being worthwhile and necessary. On the other hand, there is transitive reciprocity, which facilitates the establishment of relationships that move towards the empowerment and self-fulfilment of people who are mutually recognised as being unique and necessary.

Clearly, these are two very different, but complementary, perspectives whose main concern has been to recover relationality in the economy as a plausible solution for today's socio-economic problems: dehumanisation of markets, no social and human development, state welfare being unsustainable, inefficient appropriation of knowledge capital, an unhappy consumer society, inefficient use of scarce resources, environmental damage, and so on.

(i)   *Unconditional reciprocity*

Unconditional reciprocity was proposed and theorised by the economics Bruni in 2006 in *Reciprocità. Dinamiche di cooperazione, economia e società civile* and *Il prezzo della gratuità* after studying internal behaviour among the early Christian communities during the Classical period. It is a type of reciprocity based not only on care and solidarity, but also on the intrinsic reward obtained by the related parties, independently of the result of action.

In an attempt to ease the relational scarcity of today's economy, the cause of many of the problems that built up in society in the nineteenth century, Bruni maintained the idea of reintroducing fraternity into economic discourse. This concept was linked to achieving freedom and equality for marginalised agents whose main objective is to eradicate or minimise both absolute poverty – the number of people living below the poverty line – and relative poverty – social and economic inequalities between people (Bruni 2008: 141–143). Bruni therefore proposes implementing and reinforcing reciprocity in practice. In particular, he meant a specific type of reciprocal behaviour displayed by the first Christian communities who lived between the first and fourth centuries AD and whose main characteristics were caring and unconditionality.

Unconditional reciprocity, as proposed and developed by Bruni, is a behavioural approach that comes very close to altruism. Because of the intrinsic rewards obtained by the related agents, it is not linked to any possible strategic use of cooperation. Thus, Bruni bases his work on different psychological studies, especially those by Sugden, and reveals an approach that is highly influenced by indirect reciprocity: [A] reciprocates with [B] in the hope that his/her attitude generates a reciprocal process between [B] and [C]. The substantial difference lies in the action of [A] not being conditioned by the extrinsic results that [A] manages to obtain, or by the response [B] may give. Anyone who acts in this way does so by thinking of opening and contributing to the development of a mutual help process between peers in which care is provided to those who need it to improve their capabilities and not merely to help them. In turn, this person will help other people with different needs in the future. All this is done without making care conditional on the possible response from the person who receives help because the intrinsic assets generated in whoever cares for his/her peers – including self-fulfilled people – are sufficient for the purpose (Bruni 2008: 124).

This is reciprocity based on the Christian banquet and linked to living in communion: gifts and gratitude. It is behaviour whose action is not motivated by the other person's response – altruism – but whose intrinsic results depend to a great extent on the response the other person gives – reciprocity (Bruni 2008: 128–129). This intrinsic reward the agent obtains when acting in this way which, according to Bruni, permits unconditionality, "(…) must be high enough to compensate for the costs assumed in material payment terms" (Bruni 2008: 130).

Yet the idiosyncrasy of such an unconditional reciprocity proposal makes it difficult to uphold and implement in a broad, open and plural economic context. This is firstly, because it encounters the problem of how to combine various models of good living with the generation of intrinsic results, which clearly refer to a follow-up from a given moral viewpoint not shared by all economic agents. Secondly, justifying the tendency to relationality from a merely psychological viewpoint linked to a specific moral perspective is a complicated matter. Finally, leaving the continuity of a reciprocal process to depend only on intrinsic results in a domain like economics, regardless of the external results it produces or the other person's attitude and readiness, demands a degree of emotional euphoria and behavioural senselessness to be able to completely ignore free-riders over and over again.

Although it is true that this type of unconditional reciprocity with solidarity is observed in various areas of human activity, even in the economic area, Bruni's explanation for its appearance and implementation makes sense only when applied to specific communities whose foundations are linked to shared values and beliefs, especially if they are the religious kind. Yet if we do away with religion, the unconditional reciprocity proposed by Bruni hints at a very important matter for human cooperation that has not been dealt with by sociobiology, or evolutionary economics: the mutual acknowledgement by the potentially bindable parties involved when they come up against worthwhile people who therefore deserve care and protection. Such acknowledgement by the related parties goes deeply into the same bases as the foundations of human cooperation and provides a motivational explanation that is not merely economistic or evolutionist of its appearance and development. Zamagni's transitive reciprocity proposal works in the same way. It is a type of reciprocity that creates relationships that tend towards providing self-fulfilment for the related parties' thanks to the acknowledgement of mutual dependence.

(ii) *Transitive reciprocity*

Transitive reciprocity was proposed in 1997 by the economics Zamagni in his work *Paradossi Sociali della crescita ed economia civile* as a reaction to the lack of relationality amassed by the dominant economic theory. According to the author, this negatively affects both economic development at all levels and social and human development.

Zamagni understands that, for society to really prosper, it is necessary to shape excellent character among its inhabitants by promoting the acquisition of civic virtues in accordance with the community's common good. In this, the promotion of transitive reciprocal behaviours plays a crucial role, like that observed in different civil society organisations. This is particularly because they allow collaborative relationships to be built in which the most important results are not economic profits they generate. Instead, the essential products are the intrinsic results – friendship, sympathy, gratitude, alterity, respect, identity, self-fulfilment, etcetera– leading to the assets involved in proper economic development, such as cohesion, trust, reputation, commitment or participation.

Transitive reciprocity is therefore related to acts of empowerment that lead the other person to give a suitable behavioural response, either in terms of quality or quantity, as a result of the positive feelings that flourish thanks to the help received. In order to avoid its instrumentalisation, transitive reciprocity takes on a triple structure: [A] helps [B] and expects that this help allows [B] to adequately reciprocate with either [A] or [C], and that the inclusion of one or more other people does not damage the relationship that has begun. So, the most important point of the cooperation generated by transitive reciprocity is not the economic outcome produced, but the relationships shifting towards the empowerment underlying it which are necessary for the possibility of self-fulfilment for the related parties for proper the proper development of economic activity.[21]

For Zamagni this transitive structure of the reciprocal action is based on three basic points: (a) the gift or reciprocal help is not the purpose, but the means through which a relationship begins, moving towards the self-fulfilment of the binding or bindable parties; this means a chain of reciprocal acts which creates a strong chain among those involved; (b) unlike an exchange of equivalents or pure altruism, reciprocity does not intend to give to receive or merely to attend to another person,

---

[21] As previously mentioned, Adam Smith seemed to suggest one kind of transitive reciprocal behaviour – inclusive reciprocity – which was strikingly similar to that developed by Zamagni. Smith warned about was how unfruitful it was for society to both give without expecting and to receive without acting. So, benevolence is positive, as long as it is used in the context of relationships controlled by the logic of reciprocity.

but to empower the other person and improve his or her capacities; (c) the purpose of transitive reciprocity is to create strong, long-lasting links between the related parties, and also economic ones. From these, it is possible to generate and reinforce those relational assets which, implied in people's self-fulfilment, and in terms of happiness in the eudaimonic sense, allow the economy and society to develop properly (Bruni and Zamagni 2007).

Yet far from simply describing the reciprocal act and its intentional and/or unintentional consequences, Zamagni goes further by showing concerned about reconstructing the conditions of the possibility of transitive reciprocity – of the *ligatio* that *ob-liges* – the people who are bound, or potentially bindable to strive to be, or remain, in the relationship through reciprocity. Along these lines, Zamagni proposed mutual acknowledgement as the starting point for cooperation: a reciprocal act that precedes a gift or help and which is the source of the motivation needed to establish stable and enriched relationships for all related parties and feelings and emotions, like gratitude, which appear when people mutually acknowledge their dependence on others as a condition of possibly fulfilling their good living plans.

Basically, the various reciprocity approaches described by sociobiology, evolutionary economy and humanistic economy[22] reveal that the behaviour model on which the preponderant economic theory is based has been cast in a mould whose correspondence with reality is extremely fragile and tenuous, and can be attributed only to a small group of people: *free-riders* (Bowles and Gintis 2011). Beyond being a mere exchange of equivalents governed by external coercion, human beings appear to possess emotional and motivational heterogeneity, and the capacity to be committed to that which has good reasons to be valued and defended. For some 500,000 years now (Mediavilla, 03 November 2015), this has allowed the human race to develop and promote different reciprocal behaviours that are to varying degrees selfish or altruistic, or more or less conditioned or unconditioned. These are capable of making cooperation among humans arise in different contexts and circumstances.

Observing these behaviours reveals, firstly, that reciprocity is an intangible, relational and communicative asset that needs to be complemented with other similar assets, such as reputation and trust, to be properly implemented and developed in practice. Secondly, the feelings and emotions that enable such assets appear to flow from following (positive feelings) or rejecting (negative feelings) those values and rules that societies are involved in and defend. In other words, positive emotions and feelings allow agents to want to relate to one another and to trust in other people's goodwill to meet the implicit and explicit commitments made, while negative feelings activate punitive processes against those who contravene the reciprocal

---

[22] There are studies in economic and business ethics about other reciprocal behaviours in humans. For example, work is being done about the possibility of institutional-type reciprocity; in other words, an indirect form of relationality which, based on the act of offering help to others in exchange for this help benefitting the development and enrichment of a given institution, requires that the reciprocator should pay the high costs.

expectations of behaviour, where punishers act motivated by the interests of the community which they belong to and feel part of.

However, the main problem underlying many of the proposals described, especially the evolutionary kind, lies in the normative framework. It is our genetic code or our brain which, from generation to generation, stores and transmits this emotive memory built from specific requirements and given experiences from past groups or societies. This perspective implies that the available information can merely be what is left over, or the impression of what was once a reciprocal expectation of social or morally valid behaviour and the feelings and emotions involved in the rules being followed or breached in a given era. So, reciprocal cooperation is not anchored only in an evolutionary process. The requirements, expectations and problems of the prehistoric groups of hunter-gatherers or of societies shut off from the Classical and medieval worlds have very little to do with what is expressed and debated in today's complex and plural societies, where hundreds of cultures and points of view on good living coexist side by side. Thus, these feelings and emotions require critical reflection to provide reasons for their existence and, in this way, to convert them into stimuli that truly motivate action.

A suitable normative framework can be developed from reciprocity itself; that is, by mutually acknowledging the value and capacity of the related parties, as Bruni and Zamagni's works demonstrate so well. As Zamagni (2009) argued, the *ligatio* that *obliges* people to relate to one another comes before the act of giving and receiving, and is related to the mutual acknowledgement of the parties' vulnerability. Only through relationships with others can their good living plans and their maximum happiness fully develop and be fulfilled. This acknowledgement generates mutual gratitude and other feelings and emotions related to the possibility of carrying out collective actions that mutually benefit the parties. However, this mutual acknowledgement perspective is greatly concerned with the emotions of the related parties and not so much with the capacities that underlie the construction, justification and cleansing of those values – rules and principles which, as suggested by strong reciprocity, are the source of associated feelings and emotions when they are followed or breached. Perhaps it is here where another different, but complementary and necessary, element of reciprocal acknowledgement should come into play: that acknowledging the communicative capacities of the parties involved or affected so they can argue and reach agreements about what affects them or is their responsibility.

Cordial ethics could play a key role in all this, as proposed and developed by Cortina in her latest works (2007a, b, 2010, 2013, 2017). This is a proposal of minimums reconstructing the conditions of the possibility of public works through reciprocal acknowledgement. Here justice and emotion go hand-in-hand in the continuous process of constructing and reviewing this guiding framework, which must guide all mutual cooperation in any area of human activity. Basically, the emotive and affective part of reciprocity is stressed in it, without ignoring the necessary critical-reflexive element concerning the moral validity of behaviours.

Thus it is a kind of acknowledgement anchored in the human capacity to feel emotions about oneself and others, and to also dialogue and make judgements about what is fair and unfair in order to construct all collective actions from respectful reciprocal behaviours with the minimums that a plural post-conventional and morally developed society expects and desires. This would be a society whose individuals are able to dialogue about the correctness or validity of rules and to estimate, as Cortina would say, the value of fairness (2010: 17).

Bibliography

Alexander, Richard. 1987. *The Biology of Moral Systems*. New York: Aldine.
Axelrod, Robert. 1984. *The evolution of cooperation*. New York: Basic Books.
———. 1986. *La evolución de la cooperación*. Madrid: Alianza.
———. 2003. *La complejidad de la cooperación. Modelos de cooperación basados en los agentes*. Buenos Aires: Fondo de Cultura Económica de Argentina.
Becchetti, Leonardo, Luigino Bruni, and Stefano Zamagni. 2010. *Microeconomia. Scelte, Relazione, Economia Civile*. Bologna: Il Mulino.
Bowles, Samuel. 2006 [2004]. *Microeconomics: Behavior, Institutions, and Evolution*. Princeton: Princeton University Press.
Bowles, Samuel, and Herbert Gintis. 1998. Is equality Passé? Homo reciprocans and the future of egalitarian politics. *Boston Review* 23 (6): 1–27.
———. 2003. The origins of human cooperation. In *The Genetic and Cultural Origins Of Cooperation*, ed. P. Hammerstein, 429–444. Cambridge, MA: MIT Press.
———. 2004. *Homo Economicus and Zoon Politikon: Behavioral Game Theory and Political Behavior*, 1–16.. http://www.umass.edu/preferen/gintis/Homo%20Economicus%20and%20 Zoon%20Politikon.pdf. Accessed 25 Sept 2017.
———. 2006. Social preferences, homo economicus and zoon politikon. In *Work of Contextual Political Analysis*, ed. Robert E. Goodin and Charles Tilly, 172–186. New York: Oxford University Press.
———. 2011. *A Cooperative Species. Human Reciprocity and Its Evolution*. Princeton: Princeton University Press.
Bowles, Samuel, Robert Boyd, Ernst Fehr, and Herbert Gintis. 1997. Homo reciprocans: A research initiative on the origins, dimensions, and policy implications of reciprocal fairness. *Advances in Complex Systems* 4 (2–3): 1–30.
Brondizio, Eduardo S., Elinor Ostrom, and Oran R. Young. 2009. Connectivity and the governance of multilevel social-ecological systems: The role of social capital. *The Annual Review of Environment and Resources* 34 (1–3): 253–278.
Bruni, Luigino. 2006. *Reciprocità. Dinamiche di cooperazione, economia e società civile*. Milan: Bruno Mondadori.
———. 2008 [2006]. *El precio de la gratuidad*. Madrid: Ciudad Nueva.
Bruni, Luigino, and Stefano Zamagni. 2007 [2004]. *Civil Economy: Efficiency, Equity, Public Happiness*. New York: Peter Lang.
Cárdenas, Juan-Camilo, and Elinor Ostrom. 2004. What do people bring into the game? Experiments in the field about cooperation in the commons. *Agricultural Systems* 82: 307–326.
Carpenter, Jeffrey, Samuel Bowles, Herbert Gintis, and Sung-Ha Hwang. 2009. Strong reciprocity and team production: Theory and evidence. *Journal of Economic Behavior & Organization* 71 (2): 221–232.
Cela-Conde, Camilo-José. 1989. Altruismo moral y altruismo biológico. *Taula* 12: 34–47.
Cortina, Adela. 2007a. Ethica cordis. *Isegoría. Revista de Filosofía Moral y Política* 37: 113–126.

————. 2007b. *Ética de la razón cordial. Educar en la ciudadanía en el siglo XXI.* Oviedo: Nobel.

————. 2010. *Justicia Cordial.* Madrid: Trotta.

————. 2011. *Neuroética y Neuropolítica. Sugerencias para la Educación Moral.* Madrid: Tecnos.

————. 2013. *¿Para qué sirve realmente... la ética?* Barcelona: Paidos Iberica.

————. 2017. *Aporofobia, el rechazo al pobre. Un desafío para la democracia.* Barcelona: Paidós Ibérica.

Curtis, Helena, N. Barnes Sue, and Adriana Schnek. 2008. *Biología.* Buenos Aires: Editorial Médica Panamericana.

Dawkins, Richard. 1982. *The Extended Phenotype: The Gene as the Unit of Selection.* Oxford: Oxford University Press.

————. 2016 [1976]. *The Selfish Gene.* Oxford: Oxford University Press.

Fehr, Ernst, and Urs Fischbacher. 2005. The economics of strong reciprocity. In *Moral Sentiments and Material Interests. The Foundations of Cooperation in Economic Life*, ed. Herbert Gintis, Samuel Bowles, Robert Boyd, and Ernst Fehr, 151–191. Cambridge, MA: MIT Press.

Fehr, Ernst, and Simon Gächter. 1998. Reciprocity and economics: The economic implications of homo reciprocans. *European Economic Review* 42 (3): 845–859.

Fehr, Ernst, and Bettina Rockenbach. 2003. Detrimental effects of sanctions on human altruism. *Nature* 422 (6928): 137–140.

Fehr, Ernst, Simon Gächter, and Georg Kirchsteiger. 1997. Reciprocity as a contract enforcement device: Experimental evidence. *Econometrica: Journal of the Econometric Society* 65 (4): 833–860.

Fehr, Ernst, Urs Fischbacher, and Simon Gächter. 2002. Strong reciprocity, human cooperation and the enforcement of social norms. *Human Nature* 13 (1): 1–25.

Fletcher, Jeffrey A., and Martin Zwick. 2006. Unifying the theories of inclusive fitness and reciprocal altruism. *The American Naturalist* 168 (2): 252–262.

Fong, Christina M., Samuel Bowles, and Herbert Gintis. 2005. Reciprocity and the welfare state. In *Moral Sentiments and Material Interests. On the Foundations of Cooperation in Economic Life*, ed. Herbert Gintis, Samuel Bowles, Robert Boyd, and Ernst Fehr, 277–302. Cambridge, MA: MIT Press.

Frank, Robert H. 1988. *Passions Within Reason: The Strategic Role of the Emotions.* New York: W. W. Norton & Company.

Gintis, Herbert. 2000. *Game Theory Evolving: A Problem-Centered Introduction to Modeling Strategic Interaction.* Princeton: Princeton University Press.

————. 2010. Behavioral ethics. In *Creating consilience: Integrating the Sciences and the Humanities (New Directions in Cognitive Science)*, ed. Edward Slingerlan and Mark Collard, 318–333. New York: Oxford University Press.

————. 2016. *Individuality and Entanglement: The Moral and Material Bases of Social Life.* Princeton: Princeton University Press.

Hamilton, William D. 1964. The genetical evolution of social behaviour, I&II. *Journal of Theoretical Biology* 7 (1): 1–52.

Henrich, Josep, Robert Boyd, Samuel Bowles, Colin Camerer, Ernst Fehr, Herbert Gintis, and Richard McElreath. 2001. In search of Homo Economicus: Behavioral experiments in 15 small-scale societies. *American Economic Review* 91 (2): 73–78.

Henrich, Josep, Robert Boyd, Samuel Bowles, Colin Camerer, Ernst Fehr, and Herbert Gintis. 2004. *Foundation of Human Sociality: Ethnography and Experiments in Fifteen Small-Scale Societies.* Oxford: Oxford University Press.

Leimar, Olof, and Peter Hammerstein. 2001. Evolution of cooperation through indirect reciprocity. *The Royal Society* 268: 745–753.

Mandeville, Bernard. 1705. *The Grumbling Hive, or Knaves Turn'd Honest.* London: Sam Ballard.

————. 1724 [1714]. *The Fable of the Bees: Or, Private Vices, Public Benefits.* 3rd ed. London: J. Tonson.

Marechal, Patricia. 2009. Selección de Grupo y Altruismo: El Origen del Debate. *Scientia Studia* 7 (3): 447–459.

Maynard Smith, John. 1964. Group selection and kin selection. *Nature* 201: 1145–1147.
Mediavilla, Daniel. 2015, November 3. Michael Tomasello: "Para mejorar la sociedad no podemos obviar lo negativo de nuestra biología". *El País*. https://elpais.com/elpais/2015/10/20/ciencia/1445363532_639418.html
Olson, Mancur. 1965. *The Logic of Collective Action: Public Goods and the Theory of Groups.* Harvard: Harvard University Press.
Ostrom, Elinor. 1998. A behavioral approach to the rational choice theory of collective action. *American Political Science Review* 92 (1): 1–22.
———. 2000 [1990]. *El Gobierno de los Comunes. La Evolución de las Instituciones de Acción Colectiva.* Mexico: Fondo Cultural de Economía.
———. 2003. Toward a behavioral theory linking trust, reciprocity, and reputation. In *Trust & Reciprocity. Interdisciplinary Lessons from Experimental Research*, ed. E. Ostrom y James Walker, 19–79. New York: Russell Sage Foundation.
Ostrom, Elinor y T.K. Ahn 2003. Una Perspectiva del Capital Social desde las Ciencias Sociales: Capital Social y Acción Colectiva. *Revista Mexicana de Sociología* 65 (1): 155–233.
Panchanathan, Karthik, and Robert Boyd. 2001. A tale of two defectors: The importance of standing for evolution of indirect reciprocity. *Journal of Theoretical Biology* 224 (1): 115–126.
Putnam, Robert D., Roberto Leonardi, and Raffaella Nanetti. 1993. *Making Democracy Work: Civic Traditions in Modern Italy.* Princeton: Princeton University Press.
Strawson, Peter F. 1974. *Freedom and Resentment and Other Essays.* London: Methuen.
Sugden, Robert. 1986. *The Economics of Rights, Co-operation and Welfare.* Oxford: Basil Blackwell.
Trivers, Robert L. 1971. The evolution of reciprocal altruism. *Quarterly Review of Biology* 46: 35–57.
Zamagni, Stefano. 2009. Fraternity, gifts and reciprocity in Cáritas in Veritate. *Revista Cultural Económica* 27 (75–76): 11–29.

Chapter 5
Cordial Recognition: The Communicative and Affective Link in Human Relationships

Abstract Evolutionary and Neuronal Game Theory depicts an emotional and moral anchorage for human cooperation. The *ligatio* that *ob-liges* the parties requires critical reflection that validates both the stimuli that engenders and promotes it and their sense of being. This appropriate normative frame can be developed from reciprocity itself; that is, through mutually recognising the value of the bound or bindable parties for their affective competence, for their ability to feel emotion for themselves and others and for their communication capacity for dialogue and for reaching agreements with others on different matters concerning the world. The aim of this chapter is to look in-depth at the ethical and affective basis reciprocity through reciprocal recognition theory, particularly in the works by Jürgen Habermas, Axel Honneth and Adela Cortina.

Recognition Theory and its relationship with reciprocity are nothing new. In the seventeenth century, Hobbes tentatively approached it in the *Leviathan* (1651) in his 19 theses on the law of human nature. Firstly, and as previously mentioned, in his fourth law –Gratitude– Hobbes considered that lack of reciprocity was one of the main causes of the state of war among men. In other words, as people are selfish by nature, any action to help someone else had to be understood as seeking a particular objective rather than as an act of benevolence, compassion or charity. Otherwise, the behavioural non-response to any help received was considered ingratitude, which produced negative feelings that led to warlike processes as revenge for the insult and for the restitution of the contribution made. Secondly, in his tenth law –Against Arrogance– Hobbes maintained that, once the desired state of peace had been achieved, its durability depended on no-one demanding from anyone else anything they would not demand for themselves, which required the prior and mutual recognition of a natural equality (Hobbes 1651: 77) because, as his ninth law of nature – Against Pride- stated, "If Nature therefore have made men equall, that equalitie is to be acknowledged. (…) That every man acknowledge other for his Equall by Nature. The breach of this Precept is Pride" (Hobbes 1651: 77).

However, as Robert R. Williams showed in *Hegel's Ethics of Recognition* (1998), the mutual recognition perspective as a foundation of morality dates back to the eighteenth and nineteenth centuries thanks to the works of two main references of

German idealism: Johann G. Fichte and Georg Wilhelm Friedrich Hegel. Fichte introduced the reciprocal recognition concept into his work *Grundlage des Naturrechts nach Prinzipien der Wissenschaftslehre* (*Foundations of Natural Right*) (1796), and later Hegel developed it from the moral and political philosophy point of view in works from the Jena period, and in his work *Grundlinien der Philosophie des Rechts* (*Elements of the Philosophy of Right*) (1821), by transforming it into a "(…) fundamental intersubjective structure of ethical life" (Williams 1998: 26). Thus, based on a moral reflection, Hegel offered a plausible alternative to Hobbes by showing that the motivation underlying the construction of the State is not fear of violent death, but an ethical motive related with the struggle to recognise: "(…) indignation felt by people when others do not recognise them, when they have to experience *non*-recognition – invisibility – and consequently have the desire to be recognised" (Cortina 2007: 164).

Since then, different currents of thought have shown an interest in reciprocal recognition in the twentieth and twenty-first centuries, particularly in the fields of philosophy and sociology, and theorists like Georges Herbert Mead, Paul Ricoeur, Alex Honneth, Jürgen Habermas and Adela Cortina, among others, have worked on it. Moreover, some economists, like Zamagni, have seen the possible emotional anchorage of human cooperation in this reciprocal behaviour. In other words, it is an element that comes before giving, and the origin of the sense of gratuitousness, producing the *ligatio* that *ob-liges* agents to seek the relationship and to be in it.

Yet the *ligatio* that *ob-liges* corresponds not only to merely emotional aspects. As Evolutionary and Neuronal Game Theory shows, human cooperation requires a suitable motivational, heterogeneous and extendible framework, but also an ethical anchorage that validates both the stimuli that engenders and promotes it and their sense of being. This moral and emotional framework of human cooperation can be observed and developed from reciprocity itself; that is, through the mutual recognition of both the value of the bound or bindable parties and their capacity for dialogue and reaching agreements about different matters concerning the world and for feeling emotion about themselves and others.

The aim of this chapter is therefore to show the emotional and moral element underlying reciprocal recognition through the works of three highly distinguished authors: Habermas, Honneth and Cortina. For this purpose, the Habermasian Theory of Reciprocal Recognition will firstly be analysed, paying attention to its role in specifying discursive processes allowing people to understand different things in the world. Secondly, we look closely at the Honnethian Theory of Reciprocal Recognition, which is concerned with its role in processes that guarantee a given society's members can satisfy their good living aspirations: their maximum happiness. Thirdly and finally, the Cortinian Theory of Reciprocal Recognition is shown which, starting from a Kantian perspective, combines aspects of justice and affectivity.

5.1 Reciprocal Recognition in Habermas: The Communicative Link of Relationality

In the 1970s and 1980s, Habermas (1991, 1999, 2001) included the reciprocal recognition concept to develop his Communicative Action Theory and, along with Karl-Otto Apel (1985, 1998, 2008), he put forward an ethical discourse proposal for moral foundations. Unlike other contemporary reciprocal recognition theories, the Habermasian reflection was not based on Hegelian thought, but on Kantian thought, which made his proposal original.

Discourse ethics, in terms of the proposed moral foundations with ambitions for universality, sought a rationality criterion for discerning and criticising the validity or justice of a norm. Moral norms, which concern all human beings without distinction, imply having to find some justification for them being made universal. To this end, discourse ethics proposed discursively transforming the formal Kantian principle of free will, moving from *I think* to *We argue* (Cortina 1993: 170) by establishing a dialogue process based on a concept of a person as a valid interlocutor capable of talking and acting, and on equality, which demands including all those affected by the criticised norm in the process (Cortina 2007: 43–47). In this way, discourse ethics managed to show the communicative rationality underlying argumentative processes that are inclined towards an understanding that exists among people who wish to reach an agreement about various worldly matters, such as the norms and principles that guide, control and coordinate interpersonal interactions, in which reciprocal recognition plays a key role. From this perspective, the main point for Habermas is to understand the process from the demand to recognising the other person as a subject capable of maintaining a dialogue about that matters affecting him/her or for which he/she is responsible.

> Whereas the communitarians appropriate the Hegelian legacy in the form of an Aristotelian ethics of the good and abandon the universalism of rational natural law, discourse ethics takes its orientation for an intersubjective interpretation of the categorical imperative from Hegel's theory of recognition but without incurring the cost of a historical d solution of morality in ethical life. (Habermas 2001: 109)

Thus, the formal Kantian principle becomes a procedural principle (D) of discourse ethics in that "(…) only those norms which in practice discourses could motivate the approval of all interested parties can hope to be valid" (Habermas 1999: 73, 1991: 101). As Honneth acknowledged (1998: 20), this matter is intrinsically linked to the Kantian notions of human, universal and egalitarian dignity, which has the human self-legislation capacity to provide itself with its own laws, and to be committed to respect and follow them. This is its own fundamental principle (Kant 2005: 92). As Kant argued in *Grundlegung zur Metaphysik der Sitten* (*Groundwork of the Metaphysic of Morals*) (1785), "(…) morality is the condition under which only a rational being can be a legislating member in the kingdom of ends. Thus morality, and humanity, insofar as it is capable of morality, is that which alone has dignity" (2005: 93). In this way, the Kantian notion of human dignity underlies the idea that, as far as being rational and, therefore autonomous, the human being is a purpose in itself; a being who not only possesses a relative worth, a price, but also an inner worth: dignity. So, autonomy for Kant is constituted as "(...) basis of the dignity of human nature and of every rational nature" (2005: 94).

Habermas started with such an unconditional and unconditioned moment, represented in the Kantian idea of human dignity, to structure his proposal. Yet he went even further and linked its sense and inviolability to the living world of interpersonal mutual recognition relations, not merely to the abstraction of a *noumenal* world, which lies far from the ways of specific lives or any particular *ethos*[1]:

> The community of moral beings creating their own laws refers, in the language of rights and duties, to all matters in need of normative regulation; but only the members of this can place *one another* under moral obligations and expect *one another* to conform to norms in their behavior. (...) "Human dignity" as I would like to show, is in a strict moral and legal sense connected with this relational symmetry. It is not a property like intelligence or blue eyes, that one might "possess" by nature; it rather indicates the kind of "inviolability" which comes to have a significance only in interpersonal relations of mutual respect, in the egalitarian dealings among persons. (Habermas 2003: 33)

This approach to *the world of life* via the Kantian concept of human dignity allowed Habermas to develop his proposal for reciprocal recognition of an affective nature. In other words, it is not only concerned about equality, but also about the alterity of potentially or virtually related subjects, particularly when Habermas was criticised by Feminist Theory about communicative reason.[2] These criticisms demonstrated the lack of a *generalised other being*, in that a depersonalised, decentralised and disembodied being was shown, which also came into conflict with the requirements for a *specific other person* which required recognition for the differences constituting his/her own collective identity. At this point, Habermas accepted the criticism and recognised alterity as a constitutive part of his proposal.[3]

> In its detranscendentalized version, Kant's "free will" no longer descends from the sky as a property of intelligible beings. Autonomy, rather, is a precarious achievement of finite beings who may attain something like "strength," if at all, only if they are mindful of their physical vulnerability and social dependence. If this is the "purpose" of morality, it also explains its "limits." It is the universe of possible interpersonal relations and interactions that is in need as well as capable of moral regulation. Only within this network of legiti-

---

[1] As Habermas stated on this matter, "(...) we should not let ourselves be inveigled, by this step of abstraction leading to 'human dignity' and to Kant's single 'human right' into forgetting that the moral community of free and equal subjects of human rights does not form a 'kingdom of ends' in the noumenal beyond, but remains embedded in concrete forms of life and their ethos" (2003: 37).

[2] Cf., for further information about criticism of communicative reason from Feminist Theory, Gilligan (1982) and Benhabib (1992a, b).

[3] At this point, Habermas works on the internal connection between the principle of justice –expecting equal respect and equal rights for all individuals– and the solidarity principle – concern for others' well-being (2001: 67–70).

mately regulated relations of mutual recognition can human beings develop and – together with their physical integrity – maintain a personal identity. (Habermas 2003: 34)

For Habermas, the problem with the Kantian notion of human dignity lies in the fact that it focuses basically on the equality viewpoint, and ignores the differences, which are considered matters relating to mankind's universal inclinations and dispositions with a market price (Kant 2005: 93). However, for Habermas, human dignity is not linked only to the equality principle. From the ethical-discursive transformation of the formal Kantian principle of free will, human dignity also refers to the reciprocal recognition of alterity and to mutual respect for the existing differences constituting the particular identity of each intersubjectively related subject. So, the procedure of the discursive formation of free will necessarily pays attention to the close internal relationship between two aspects: the autonomy of some individuals who cannot delegate their representation to anyone, and their primary inclusion in intersubjectively shared ways of life (Habermas 2001).

In this way, for Habermas, reciprocal recognition, like valid interlocutors and beings who possess communication competences, is equivalent to recognition as members of an *ideal communication community* who insist on maintaining their specific identity, which distinguishes them from others and is intersubjectively built through reciprocal recognition relationships in a linguistic community, whether collective or individual (Habermas 1991: 111–113). Habermas therefore demonstrates autonomy established based on the human capacity not only to govern their own lives, but to also build their identities in intersubjective relationships to others.

> Discourse does not break the social tie of community belonging, not even when the agreement that everyone is expected to reach aims beyond each specific community's limits. (…) The discursive formation process of collective free explains that there is an internal connection of both aspects: autonomy of non-exchangeable individuals and their inclusion in intersubjectively shared ways of life. Individual's equal rights and equal respect for their personal dignity are sustained by a network of interpersonal reciprocal recognition relations. (1991: 112–113)

Basically, the Habermasian recognition theory pays attention to the relationship between reciprocal recognition and questions about justice. In other words, their involvement in the constitution and proper implementation of those dialogue processes moving towards an understanding among people of different worldly matters; for example, which reciprocal expectations of behaviour are, or could be, morally justifiable.

In this sense, the Habermasian recognition is based on the empiricist proposal by Peter Strawson in *Freedom and Resentment and other Essays* (1974) to show the cognitive basis for feelings and the moral dimension underlying them. Based on the example of resentment used by Strawson, in *Moral Consciousness and Communicative Action* (1990) Habermas stresses three of Strawson's fundamental considerations allowing an emotivist phenomenology in a context of communicative action (Habermas 1990: 45–50).

Firstly, that the person responsible for acts in which another person is injured can apologise and, if this is accepted, there is no possibility of feelings of humiliation or resentment occurring to the same degree. According to Habermas, this led Strawson to consider that personal relationships involving grievance, such as resentment, "(…) are possible only in the performative attitude of a person taking part in interaction. The objectivating attitudes of the nonparticipant observer annuals the communicative roles of I and thou, the first and second persons, and neutralises the realm of moral phenomena as such. The third-person attitude causes this realm of phenomena to vanish" (Habermas 1990: 46–47).

Secondly, diverse moral feelings are intrinsically connected in the case of internal relationships. As Habermas explains, grievance generates indignation; indignation is compensated with apology; apology is the result of remorse, guilt and scruples; the acceptance of apology generates gratitude, and so on.

Thirdly, the moral nature of indignation is related to the breach of expected behaviour valid not only for grievance and the person causing the grievance but also for all participants in a specific society. For Habermas, the idea is crucial because only in this way is it possible to explain why the feeling of remorse or guilt arises in the person who has committed the offence.

Fourthly and finally, there is an intrinsic relationship between the validity of the applicable norm and the obligation to comply with it. Also, the validity of the current norms implies that they are reasons to uphold those legitimately in force. The result is that moral emotivism would proceed from a breach of the intersubjective understanding and the moral validity of a relationship between the legitimacy of the norms and the internal obligation to comply with them (Alútiz 2002). As Habermas states, "To say that *I ought* to do something means that I *have good reason* for doing it" (1990: 49).

In this way, the phenomenology of Strawson's ethical awareness generates a maieutic force that can "(…) open the eyes of empiricist in his role as moral skeptic to his own everyday moral intuitions" (Habermas 1990: 45). This is particularly because of the moral feeling it is based on: indignation. This constitutes the basis for human reactions to grievances suffered by oneself or others, thereby revealing the underlying moral dimension. It is a moral dimension whose manifestation in the world comes from the attitude of the participants in the interaction, as the reaction through indignation does not occur immediately, as it does with other non-moral feelings such as fear or anger, but rather due to the "(…) disgraceful wrong done to one by another (Habermas 1990: 46–47). From all this, therefore, it can be deduced that resentment and other affective reactions represent the expression of a moral judgement referring to suprapersonal patterns of judgement of norms and mandates and that "(…) the moral-practical justification of a form of action aims at an aspect *different* form the feeling-neutral assessment is made from the point of view of the general welfare" (Habermas 1990: 50).

5.2 Reciprocal Recognition in Honneth: The Affective Link of Relationality

In the 1990s, Honneth, a disciple of Habermas and an outstanding member of the third generation from the Frankfurt School, was also concerned about developing the reciprocal recognition theory. However, Honneth did so by starting with Hegelian writings from the Jena period, and not with Kantian thought as his mentor did. As a result, Honneth published *Kampf um Anerkennung. Zur moralischen Grammatik sozialer Konflikte (The Struggle for Recognition. The Moral Grammar of Social Conflicts)* (1992a), a work that presented reciprocal recognition as a driver of social change and of the processes involved in fulfilling people's different life projects.

In *Multiculturalism and the Politics of Recognition: An Essay* (1992), Charles Taylor introduced two liberalism-related political forms of recognition: policies of equality – based on recognising the universal rights that all humans possess – and policies of difference – based on constructing each subject's individual identity.[4] For Taylor, both political-liberal postures come into conflict and are irreconcilable, so a State must discern which of them is more suitable for its purposes and act accordingly. In other words, it must support and defend the relationship between both forms of recognition that creates clashes between the people or groups who feel ill-treated, as they are unrecognised in their alterity. Taylor therefore believes it is impossible to avoid this struggle for an identity based on a liberal proposal and he backs a third, very different, alternative route to this political system (Habermas 1999: 192–194).

To overcome this Taylorian conflict, Honneth used Hegel's work written he was a teacher at the University of Jena, when he was mainly concerned about reconstructing the history of developing ethical life (*Sittlichkeit*) and used the reciprocal recognition concept proposed by Fichte in his writings *Grundlage des Naturrechts nach Principien der Wissenschaftslehre (Foundations of Natural Right)* (1796) to support him. While he searched for a basis in natural rights, Fichte was convinced that "(…) subjects can only achieve awareness from their freedom when the mutual use of autonomy is demanded and, consequently, they are recognised as free beings" (Honneth 1998: 23). As Fichte argued, "(…) we would then have the *complete object* of the concept of right; namely, *a community among free beings as such*. It is necessary that every free being assume the existence of others of its kind outside itself" (2000: 10). This idea, along with some other of Fichte's earlier statements, might lie in the same, a similar, or even a different, direction, and Hegel was convinced that humans' experience of social recognition is the basis of self-awareness.[5] After making this necessary connection between self-awareness and intersubjective

---

[4] Habermas, according to Taylor, has worked to refute the assumed antagonism between these two types of recognition (1999: 189–227).

[5] Some of these ideas come from thinkers like Machiavelli, Hobbes or Rousseau (Honneth 1998: 23).

recognition relations, Hegel understood that (a) recognition experience is intrinsically committed to making "(...) progress in ethnicity relations" (Honneth 1998: 23), and (b) "(...) the dynamic exchange relation that must exist between the intersubjective acquisition of self-awareness and the moral development of entire societies" responds to a struggle for recognition occurring in three different spheres: the sphere of law, the affective sphere and the sphere of ethical life (*Sittlichkeit*) (Honneth 1996: 8).

Accordingly, for Hegel, the shift from one sphere to another takes place during a struggle between subjects seeking mutual recognition: maintaining their differences, their own self-conceptions, and basically their freedom. Through this constant struggle for recognition, new dimensions emerge that produce new recognition demands from subjects, and then it is back to the struggle (Honneth 1998: 24). As Honneth argues, "(...) to a certain extent, demanding that the person him/herself is recognised always in new dimensions causes an intersubjective conflict, whose dissolution can only consist in an ever-widening sphere of recognition" (1996: 24). With this idea, Honneth presented the Hegelian notion of struggle for recognition as a conceptual tool that is "(...) suitable for untangling social experiences of injustice, and for understanding the motivational source of social struggles" (Pereira 2010: 323). With this notion, Honneth revealed that it was possible to discern which orientation had gone hand-in-hand with the historical progress of humanity and, from this point, drew the normative horizon to guide progress towards "(...) what is the ideal of good living that converges with a certain formal ethnicity", formed by various "(...) structural elements that make successful self-fulfilment possible" (Pereira 2010: 323).

From this perspective, and still in line with Hegel's works, Honneth argued that the recognition process occurs dialectically through three dimensions – individual, social and moral – with a *telos* or normative horizon. So, from a moral perspective, Honneth demonstrates three forms of recognition which, despite being independent of each other, favour three different levels of positive self-fulfilment in humans and society (1992b, 1995, 1996, 1997, 1998):

- First form of recognition: love or care. This form is built on a private/family setting governed by affective relationships, where subjects are recognised as individuals and set a level or practical self-fulfilment related to self-confidence. This form of recognition is linked to emotions and is shaped a primitive relationship between mother and child when, during the first years of life, subjects gain the confidence to do things alone with their mother's care and love. However, a form of scorn exists that denies recognition at this same stage and therefore destroys the possibility of achieving self-esteem. This amounts to ill-treatment or violation in both psychological and physical senses.
- Second form of recognition: moral right or respect. This form occurs in a public/social setting governed by relationships between members of a moral community, where subjects are recognised as possessing rights and responsibilities and

accessing a level of practical self-fulfilment related to self-respect. Here, subjects are recognised as individuals going on to be accepted as community members and becoming the holders of moral rights and responsibilities, giving them equal universal treatment. This level is the equivalent to Kantian tradition universalism, as moral respect for human dignity. In comparison, subjects can see themselves being denied recognition at this stage by, for instance, being excluded from certain rights inside a society. That means they are deprived of their autonomy, which, consequently, means denying their recognition, either deliberately and directly or through scorn directed towards their image. This undermines the possibility of subjects reaching an optimum level of practical self-fulfilment which, at this level, is linked to the formation of self-respect.

– Third form of recognition: solidarity or loyalty. This form is expressed in a community setting governed by the achievement principle, where subjects are recognised as certain people who possess capacities of constitutive value for the community, and where a level with self-fulfilment related to self-esteem is set. This is the recognition of certain faculties or capacities that subjects possess, depending on how they positively affect a society's common objectives. As in the above stages, a form of scorn also exists that limits or denies recognition at this stage. This represents the disgrace that these subjects or groups experience when, for instance, they are excluded or socially cut off for belonging to a minority culture or ethnic group.

From these three forms of recognition, Honneth drew two main conclusions to develop the theory. Firstly, the struggle for recognition cannot solely be attributed to a struggle to meet material requirements or to achieve the individual or group's mere survival. Social struggle also corresponds to a question of moral feelings caused by perceiving injustice in the face of scorn or moral insult suffered by an individual when being denied recognition. Through it, it is possible to build one's own identity and, consequently, practical self-fulfilment. Secondly, the moral viewpoint does not correspond to a specific form of reciprocal recognition, nor to a hierarchy of the various reciprocal recognition forms. The moral point of view underlies the fulfilment of the three forms of reciprocal recognition presented:

> With this analysis, we show a recognition morale which, along with the Kantian concept, the tradition of the ethics of caring for oneself and communitarian considerations can claim a legitimate place. In all three traditions, one of the criteria that correspond to the three forms of recognition will come into play with which, as a set, we will protect our personal integrity as human beings. (Honneth 1996: 16)

Consequently, in his reciprocal recognition theory, Honneth ignored the issues of justice with which Habermas had been so concerned in the two previous decades to focus on the processes guaranteeing members of society the possibility of fulfilling their good living objectives; their maximum happiness.

5.3   Reciprocal Recognition in Cortina: The Cordial Link of Relationality

In the first two decades of the twenty-first century, Cortina has worked on developing the reciprocal recognition theory by, like Habermas, taking the Kantian view as a starting point rather than a Hegelian one as Honneth did. Nevertheless, Cortina's proposal substantially differs from the Habermasian perspective, and focuses mainly on matters of justice. It commences with cordial reason ethics combining concern about seeking what is fair –that unconditional and unconditioned element present in recognising dignity as a purpose in itself which all humans deserve – and concern about discovering the possibility of knowledge involved in the human capacity to feel emotions for, love or be fond of another person to the proper degree. One of the main pillars of this point of view is reciprocal recognition:

> (…) Cordial reason ethics is found in the reciprocal recognition tradition, which acquires a philosophical status in the Hegelian texts from the Jena period and in the *Elements of the Philosophy of Right*, in the work by Georges Herbert Mead, in the discourse ethics of Karl-Otto Apel and Jürgen Habermas, and continues until our day in the works of Paul Ricoeur and Axel Honneth, but moves along other tracks. (2010: 15)

This is an ethical approach which, linked to an ethical-discursive current with moral foundations that does not disparage reasons of the heart, shows reciprocal recognition as a basic category of social life, drawing on both religious tradition and philosophical thought (Cortina 2001: 152). This is firstly based on the mutual recognition of the ties that link people with each other. Such alliances, not pacts, are created by people after they mutually recognise one another as vulnerable and incomplete beings who need to relate to other people to be able to enjoy a fully human life. This acknowledged as far back as the book of *Genesis*, which stresses human beings' inviolability or absolute value, and the need that people have to enter relational processes with their fellow beings to be able to build and develop. Based on this, it can be stated "(…) the relational character of human beings, which show the inadequacies of any selfish individualism. This was because in the beginning there was no individual alone, nor was there a community, but one person in relation with another person" (Cortina 2001: 16). On the other hand, based on mutual recognition we can state "(…) those who know and feel like gifted beings" in terms of communicative capacity (Cortina 2010: 15) are competent as cordial interlocutors to be able to, and want to, reach agreements about what is fair and proper. This is a way of creating a – cordial – link between people based on the Socratic tradition, which has continued through transcendental pragmatics. By means of dialogue, people create a link when they mutually recognise one another as being capable of speaking and acting as competent autonomous beings, and are able to participate in those processes of dialogue in which things they are interested in or that affect them are at stake. Hence, their autonomy is the result of their communicative capacity and justification is therefore seen as having a value, not a market price.

In this way, Cortina puts forward a notion of mutual recognition rooted in foundations – in what is fair and true – and in experience: compassion. In other words, it begins from an unconditioned element which, in turn, needs to be enriched from experience before it can properly and robustly be deployed (2001: 153). This is a cordial perspective that reveals two different, but necessary and complementary, moments of reciprocal recognition: an *a priori unconditional moment*, anchored in the mutual recognition of equal dignity among all those beings allowed to speak and act; and an *a posteriori experiential moment*, which gives the *unconditioned moment* the motivating strength it requires to come into being and develop properly. This motivating strength emanates from human capacity to feel emotion based on what one does and what others do, and to shape an excellent character by acquiring virtues.

As Cortina argues, both these moments of reciprocal recognition are indissoluble because fairness could hardly occur without the mutual emotive capacities of bound or bindable people. Among other things, this is because without "(…) the capacity to appreciate the value of justice, even if a norm is fair, would not be important without the capacity to appreciate that other interlocutors are worthy. The fairness of the norms that should be at your service is irrelevant. (…) Anyone who lacks the capacity to appreciate values that allow the life of others and one's own life to be conditioned is incompetent for moral life" (Cortina 2010: 17). So, whereas discursive ethics only consider the "(…) formal logical dimension of reason: the human capacity to set valid ambitions of talking and solving them", cordial or compassionate ethics also recognise the cordial dimension of reason: the human capacity to appreciate, feel and acquire virtues to form an excellent character (Cortina 2001: 15–16). This is "(…) not only reason capable of arguing, but reason embodied in a body, human reason" (Cortina 2001: 16). From this perspective, Cortina attempts to:

> (…) develop the cordial dimension of a minimum ethics which, with one foot still in discourse ethics, reveals the competences of the communicative link, and goes further and exceeds it by giving it flesh and bone. It will therefore be named cordial ethics, *ethica cordis*, and its task is to show how the communicative link relies not only on the argumentative dimension and not only reveals a capacity to argue about what is true and fair, but also depends on a cordial compassionate dimension, without which there cannot be communication. (2007: 171)

In short, it is a cordial recognition concept based on cordial reason concerned with the morality of norms and without disparaging moral values and feelings. In other words, impure reason linked to history and to the human traditions from which it is built, developed and sustained by criteria which it both draws up and criticises "(…) norms with an ambition to be universal" (Cortina 2010: 113–114).

In these three authors and their different reciprocal recognition proposals, it is possible to discern the normative and affective foundation that makes possible relationality in various areas of human activity which, as well as being self-interested, also concerns economics. Firstly, and based on the Kantian concept of dignity as a rational capacity for self-legislation, Habermas shows that reciprocal recognition conditions the possibility of relationality allowing rational processes based on what is true and fair. Through mutual recognition of one other as valid interlocutors capable of speaking and acting, people are included in an ideal community where there is talk and dialogue about the moral validity of norms.

On the other hand, Honneth leaves aside the issues of fairness and truth worked on by Habermas to concern himself with what is good, with how the reciprocal recognition of alterity is established as a *sine qua non*-condition for meeting people's self-fulfilment horizon. When a human being is denied recognition, negative feelings flow through him/her and others, becoming obstacles to practical self-fulfilment. In this way, Honneth shows that reciprocity forms a constitutive part of good living. Also, underlying all this is a reciprocal recognition moral aspect taking into account both the Kantian concept of human dignity and the moral feelings implied in people's self-fulfilment processes.

Finally, Cortina reveals the twofold implication of reciprocal recognition: firstly, people are mutually recognised as beings able and competent to feel emotions about what they and others do. Secondly, they are beings able and competent to dialogue and reach agreements about what affects them and what they are responsible for. This is a reciprocal recognition proposal in the cordial sense and is basically concerned about what is fair, and about good occurring and developing. In this way, Cortina's Cordial Recognition Theory manages to show how it is possible to establish reciprocal relationships that are highly beneficial for all the participants in a context of human activity like economics. This has its unconditioned moment from which feelings and emotions flow, motivating the desire to relate to others, a factor also been appreciated by Bruni and Zamagni in their respective reciprocity theories. This is a necessary initial moment in which to establish a mutually beneficial cooperative relationship when no type of direct or indirect information on the potentially bindable parties exists. It is also an unconditioned moment based on which it is possible to understand how all these principles and norms that allow coordinated action among *n*-people to emerge, and be validated and enriched. It is also the source of feelings and emotions associated with the person feeling respected or violated, as the strong reciprocity of Bowles, Fehr and Gintis, among others, so rightly points out.

Consequently, this special kind of mutual recognition developed by Cortina is shown as a condition of the possibility of human cooperation in the practical sense, and also in an economics sense because it allows the recreation, based on the underlying reciprocity, of the minimum conditions of trust needed to establish and implement the reciprocal behaviours observed by sociobiology and evolutionary and humanistic economics: the cordial recognition that emerges and develops thanks to unconditional and unconditioned reciprocal behaviour – cordial reciprocity.

Bibliography

Alútiz, Juan Carlos. 2002. *Las Fuentes Normativas de la Moralidad Pública Moderna. Las Contribuciones de Durkheim, Habermas y Rawls.*. Doctoral thesis, University of Navarra. http://www.unavarra.es/puresoc/pdfs/tesis/alustiz/indice.pdf. Accesed 12 Dec 2017.
Apel, Karl-Otto. 1985. *La transformación de la filosofía. Tomo II. El a priori de la comunidad de comunicación.* Madrid: Taurus.
———. 1998. *Teoría de la verdad y ética del discurso.* Barcelona: Paidós.

————. 2008. Globalisation and the need for universal ethics. In *Public Reason and Applied Ethics: The Ways of Practical Reason in a Pluralist Society*, ed. Adela Cortina, Domingo García-Marzá, and Jesús Conill, 135–154. Aldershot: Ashgate.

Benhabib, Seyla. 1992a. *Situating the Self: Gender, Community, and Postmodernism in Contemporary Ethics*. New York: Routledge.

————. 1992b. Una revisión del debate sobre las mujeres y la Teoría Moral. *Isegoría* 0 (6): 37–63.

Cortina, Adela. 1993. *Ética aplicada y democracia radical*. Madrid: Tecnos.

————. 2001. *Alianza y contrato. Política, ética y religión*. Madrid: Trotta.

————. 2007. *Ética de la razón cordial. Educar en la ciudadanía en el siglo XXI*. Oviedo: Nobel.

————. 2010. *Justicia cordial*. Madrid: Trotta.

Fichte, Johann G. 1796. *Grundlage des Naturrechts nach Prinzipien der Wissenschaftslehre*. Jena/Leipzig: Felix Meiner Verlag.

————. 2000. *Foundations of Natural Right. According to the Principles of the Wissenschaftslehre*, ed. Frederick Neohouser. Cambridge: Cambridge University Press.

Gilligan, Carol. 1982. *In a different voice: Psychological theory and women's development*. Cambridge, MA: Harvard University Press.

Habermas, Jürgen. 1990 [1983]. *Moral Consciousness and Communicative Action*. Cambridge: Polity Press.

————. 1991 [1984]. *Escritos Sobre Moralidad y Eticidad*. Barcelona: Paidós.

————. 1999 [1996]. *La inclusión del otro*. Barcelona: Paidós.

————. 2001 [1991]. *Justification and Application. Remarks on discourse ethics*. Trans. Ciaran Cronin. Cambridge, MA: MIT Press.

————. 2003 [2001]. *The Future of Human Nature*. Cambridge: Policy Press.

Hegel, Georg Wilhelm Friedrich. 1821. *Grundlinien der Philosophie des Rechts*. Berlin: Felix Meiner Verlag. [English vertion: 1991. *Elements of the philosophy of right*, ed. Allen W. Wood. Cambridge: Cambridge University Press].

Hobbes, Thomas. 1651. *Leviathan*, ed. C.B. Macpherson. Harmondsworth: Penguin.

Honneth, Axel. 1992a. *Kampf Um Anerkennung. Zur Moralischen Grammatik Sozialer Konflikte*. Frankfurt am Main: Suhrkamp.

————. 1992b. Integridad y desprecio. Motivos básicos de una concepción de la moral desde la teoría del reconocimiento. *Isegoría. Revista de Filosofía Moral y Política* 5: 78–92.

————. 1995. *The Struggle for Recognition. The Moral Grammar of Social Conflicts*. Cambridge, MA: MIT Press.

————. 1996. Reconocimiento y obligaciones morales. *RIFP. Revista Internacional de Filosofía Política* 8: 5–17.

————. 1997. *La lucha por el reconocimiento. Por una gramática moral de los conflictos sociales*. Barcelona: Crítica.

————. 1998. Entre Aristóteles y Kant. Esbozo de una moral del reconocimiento. *Logos. Anales del Seminario de Metafísica* 32: 17–38.

Kant, Immanuel. 1785. *Grundlegung zur Metaphysik der Sitten*. Riga: Johann Friedrich Harknoch.

————. 2005. *Groundwork of the Metaphysics of Morals*. Toronto: Broadview.

Pereira, Gustavo. 2010. Reconocimiento y criterios normativos. Entrevista a Axel Honneth. *Andamios* 7 (13): 323–334.

Strawson, Peter F. 1974. *Freedom and Resentment and other Essays*. London: Methuen.

Taylor, Charles. 1992. *Multiculturalism and the Politics of Recognition: An Essay*. Princeton: Princeton University Press.

Williams, Robert R. 1998. *Hegel's Ethics of Recognition*. Los Angeles: University of California Press.

Chapter 6
Cordial Reciprocity: The Ethical Basis of Human Cooperation

Abstract Reciprocity is one of the main challenges for twenty-first-century economic science because of its leading role in specifying and developing human cooperation. Beyond the exchange of equivalents controlled by contracts and guaranteed by Law, reciprocity, in the many forms it takes, allows us to think about the possibility of establishing different types of cooperation among agents to meet the shared objectives that are highly beneficial for them all. However, the various reciprocity approaches do not explain why agents tend to relate to one another when they have no information about the bindable parties' response capacity. This is mutual recognition of the value that they deserve as people, and of effective and communication capacities so they can feel emotions for themselves and for others, and can use dialogue and reach agreements about the different things in the world to allow the minimum conditions of trust needed to establish and implement those reciprocal behaviours observed by sociobiology and by evolutionary and humanistic economics. This chapter aims to look in-depth at the unconditional and unconditioned reciprocity that underlies this type of mutual recognition, which is cordially constituted, to show the role it plays in the appearance and promotion of behaviours that enable human cooperation in highly competitive contexts like those in economics.

The role played by reciprocity in economics is a recurrent theme for social anthropology. In *Stone Age Economy* (1972), Marshall Sahlins compiled and systematised the majority of knowledge that the discipline achieved using the works of Marcel Mauss, Bronislaw Malinowski, Karl Polanyi, Raymond Firth, Edward Evan Evans-Pritchard, Elman R. Service, Marvin Harris and Richard B. Lee, among others. With these authors, Sahlins showed that many forms of reciprocity exist, and that they have played a determining role in the survival and development of primitive societies throughout history.

> The actual kinds of reciprocity are many in any primitive society, let alone in the primitive world taken as a whole. "Vice-versa movements" may include sharing and counter-sharing of unprocessed food, informal hospitality, ceremonious affinal exchanges, loaning and repaying, compensation of specialised or ceremonial services, the transfer that seals a peace agreement, impersonal haggle, and so on and on. (Sahlins 1972)

© Springer International Publishing AG, part of Springer Nature 2018 91
P. Calvo, *The Cordial Economy - Ethics, Recognition and Reciprocity*,
Ethical Economy 55, https://doi.org/10.1007/978-3-319-90784-0_6

Sahlins also arranged the different forms of reciprocity observed in ancient societies into three main types: generalised, balanced and negative. *Generalised reciprocity* has to do with transactions between agents with similar economic and social interests and can be considered altruistic, provided the response time and expected reward have not been previously defined (Sahlins 1972: 212). *Balanced reciprocity* groups the direct, immediate and equivalent exchanges that take place among agents with different economic and social interests that can be considered of the self-interest type, and which "(...) consist of the usual delivery of the equivalent of the received item with no delays; "(...) that is, the simultaneous exchange of the same classes of goods in the same quantities" (Sahlins 1972: 213). Finally, *Negative reciprocity* focuses on those direct and immediate exchanges between agents with contrasting interests, and can be considered selfish, seeking to maximise profits at the expense of another agent by obtaining more profits from a transaction by acting with impunity (Sahlins 1972: 213–14).

For Sahlins, the reciprocal behaviours making up the different typologies have accompanied societies for thousands of years. They appeared and have developed as a way of enabling relationships relating to internal and external social and economic exchanges. Through these exchanges between the n-individuals of the same community, and also among the n-communities and n-individuals of different societies, it is possible to meet requirements, such as peace or food, which improve their survival expectations. So, based on these ideas and others, Sahlins presents the origin and foundation of economics, moving away from conventional economic discourse, in which instrumental and homogeneous rationality is one of the several options available for economic agents:

> (...) but there is a curiosity worth remarking: Here has been given a discourse on economics in which "economising" appears mainly as an exogenous factor! The organising principles of economy have been sought elsewhere to the extent that they have found outside man's presumed hedonist propensity, a strategy for the study of primitive economics is suggested that is something the reverse of economic orthodoxy. It may be worthwhile seeing how far this heresy will get us. (Sahlins 1972: 252)

Among other things, Sahlins stresses the way in which reciprocity formed part of economic relationships in ancient societies and how it underlies ethical aspects. This is true to the extent that the inhabitants of the Trobriand Islands used a specific term to refer to economic ethics – *pokala* (Sahlins 1972: 225) – relating to the gifts and reciprocity expected and demanded by members of a highly hierarchised group. Economics therefore emerges as if intrinsically linked to ethical reciprocity and an ethics of reciprocity. In other words, it is linked not only to reciprocal behaviour underpinned by aspects of justice, but also to a consideration about the moral validity of reciprocal behaviours.

The objective of the present chapter is to look closely at the ethical foundations of cooperation in different areas of human activity, particularly in economics, through a proposal of cordial reciprocity. To this end, this chapter first shows when, how and why reciprocity appears and develops in humans, with some outstanding contributions made in social and evolutionary anthropology, evolutionary economics and neurosciences. Secondly, the place and leading role of reciprocity in the human cooperation structure in different areas of activity are shown. Thirdly and finally, a proposal is made for the ethical foundations of reciprocity through the theoretical cordial reason proposal put forward by Cortina, a model taking into account both the effects and the necessary ethical-critical moment that any behaviour needs if it is to live up to what is observable, desirable and expected by a *cordial society*.

6.1 Emergence of Reciprocity: From Group Subsistence to Satisfying Common Interests

Like cooperation, reciprocity also failed to arouse the interest of the preponderant economic theory. Although it is a type of behaviour necessary for completing business transactions and obtaining profit, as noted by Sahlins, or Adam Smith in *An Inquiry into the Nature and Causes of the Wealth of Nations* (1776), the apparent fragility characterising such relationships generates a field of uncertainty whose effects distort the proper development of the economy and, therefore, profit-making. To overcome this hurdle, neoclassical-type economics was concerned with clarifying and applying external coercion mechanisms and instruments to the relationship itself to guarantee previously concluded agreements. It is here, rather than in the mere exchange of equivalents controlled by contracts and guaranteed by the State through law, that economic relationships based on other forms of reciprocity have attracted no interest from conventional theory. Strangely enough, anthropologist Richard Goul indicated in "To have and not to have: the ecology of sharing among hunter-gatherers" (1982) that reciprocity appeared thousands of years ago as an adaptive measure to ameliorate the uncertainty created by constant fluctuations in available food supply, and that, in societies, the higher the risk index, the more sharing takes place.

Hence, in evolutionary anthropology, Michael Tomasello has pointed out that human cooperation appeared some 500,000 years ago at a critical time for group survival (Mediavilla, 03 November 2015). Hominids –heidelbergensis, rhodesiensis, antecessor, and other species– understood that achieving and promoting cooperation meant a competitive advantage from the evolutionary perspective of food being scarce. This was accessible thanks to two basic aspects: the capacity of participants showing empathy to those who maintained reciprocal behaviours, which was much greater towards the people in the group, and fairly sharing any benefits achieved. The appearance of this form of cooperation was a primary version of the selfish reciprocity described by Frank in *Passions within Reason: The Strategic Role of the Emotions* (1988). Here, people earned a reputation as reciprocators throughout their lives. In extreme cases of need, this offered them the chance to be included in the relationality networks providing better chances of survival.

In time, reciprocal selfishness developed, while other forms of cooperation appeared based on reciprocity approaches. These were much more complex and allowed interests not necessarily linked to the chances of survival to be met in cases of extreme evolutionary pressure. Accordingly, reciprocal altruism or weak reciprocity has been stressed. This is strategic behaviour in which the costs deriving from helping others are paid, provided the expectations of them being returned in the future in a case of need are reasonable. Indirect reciprocity is an inverted chain of strategic behaviours where help is offered to those who have shown a similar attitude to other people to shape a good reputation as a reciprocator. In this way they are considered a person worthy of being helped. Strong reciprocity is a tendency to collaborate with those who act in a similar fashion and, for the good of the group or society, to punish behaviours that do not respect the social or moral rules involved, even if this entails a very high personal cost. Institutional reciprocity is an indirect form of relationality which, based on offering help to others on the basis that the help will beneficially develop and enrich a given institution, requires that the person who offers help pays the costs. Underlying these and other approaches observed is the idea that human cooperation emerges thanks to an intangible, relational and communicative virtue such as reciprocity. Yet this virtue also needs to be complemented with other similar virtues, such as reputation and trust so it can be deployed and suitably developed in a practical domain.

The possibility of cooperation has been backed in recent years by contributions made by emerging areas of knowledge such as neurosciences, mainly through one of its disciplines, neuroeconomics, whose main objective focuses on elucidating the cerebral bases involved in the behaviour and decision-making processes shown by the rational economic agent (Glimcher et al. 2009). Among other relevant points, neuroeconomics has shown that: (*a*) the cerebral bases of cooperation have nothing to do with self-interest (McCabe et al. 2001); (*b*) agents' behaviours in highly competitive contexts are shaped by a behavioural and motivational heterogeneity ranging from the most basic selfishness to different forms of altruism and reciprocity (Damasio 1994, 2003); (*c*) it is feasible to strike optimum balances that are extremely beneficial for all the related parties, thanks to intangible virtues like trust, reputation and reciprocity (Kosfeld et al. 2005; Ohtsuki et al. 2009; Sakaiya et al. 2013); (*d*) moral judgements play a key role in relational decision-making processes (Fehr and Gächter 2002; Rockenbach and Milinski 2006). Moreover, practical neurophilosophy has indicated that the moral judgements implied in these feelings and emotions appearing emanate from moral values and principles built by the people involved through dialogue, and, therefore, from the virtues involved in coordinating action — trust, reputation and reciprocity. There is an underlying strategic and emotional dimension, which is also a moral one (Cortina 2012).

What all this suggests is that the individual search for maximum profit is not a choice based on a human being's natural tendency towards self-interest, but is a possibility that lies further along the series of strategies available for related agents. The problem is that this option offers only the chance to strike the balances that are unable to go beyond suboptimum profit, just as Ostrom shows in her fieldwork and laboratory experiments using strategy games (1990, 2003). This apparently suggests that the most sensible option would be to specify and seek objectives that are commonly beneficial for all related parties, and this requires cooperation. How to make these appear and develop it is a question involving having to look very closely at the elements making up their internal structure.

6.2 Role of Reciprocity: The Axiological Structure of Human Cooperation

Evolutionary Game Theory in economics, anthropology and neurosciences, in the form of neuroeconomics and practical neurophilosophy, have markedly enriched debate about the possibility of cooperation in different contexts of human activity, even in such a competitive area as economics. However, there are still gaps in understanding the internal structure of cooperation, particularly concerning the relationship established by other virtues – reciprocity, reputation and trust – and the role it plays in their establishment and development or regarding the possibility of generating and promoting them in practice.

In line with this, in "Toward a Behavioral Theory Linking Trust, Reciprocity and Reputation" (2003), Ostrom proposed a structure of cooperation based on the idea that the reciprocal behaviours of people, groups and organisations build a good reputation, which is the foundation of the necessary trust for them to guide others directly (in observed experience) or indirectly (social capital). This should be borne in mind when proposing, specifying and meeting objectives that are commonly beneficial to all parties involved.

By introducing social capital, Ostrom extends the margins of the possibility of human cooperation. While reciprocal altruism, indirect reciprocity or strong reciprocity do not go any further than merely two-way relationships, as the trust needed to cooperate with someone else entails previously having observed their behaviour, Ostrom shows that it is possible to cooperate by means of the indirect information circulating through citizen participation networks. In other words, establishing participative relationships moving towards meeting common objectives, people, groups or organisations can either provide individual experience, directly observe the other person's behaviour, or use shared experience and collect information about the other person's reputation in different citizen participation networks.

Underlying this is a one-way pyramid structure of human cooperation where reciprocity is the base, trust is the peak and reputation is the body and mechanism operating between them. Along these lines, Ostrom (2003) starts with the idea that it is possible to achieve optimum profit by participating in relational and cooperative processes. Based on this idea she implicitly draws up a list of sentences:

(A) To participate in relational processes, you have to be considered worthy of trust
(B) To be considered worthy of trust, you have to have a good reputation
(C) To have a good reputation, you have to generate direct or indirect information about your tendency towards reciprocity
(D) To generate direct or indirect information about your tendency towards reciprocity, you have to practically perform binding and observable actions

The problem with Ostrom's proposal is that it is a paradox or contradiction, and one that is not easy to solve because the possibility of putting into practice these binding – reciprocal – behaviours (D) expects people, groups or organisations to be introduced into relational processes, which leads them to the starting point because it demands trust (A). As a result, we obtain the following sentences (B, C, D, and A):

(A) Only if *(B)*
(B) Only if *(C)*
(C) Only if *(D)*
(D) Only if *(A)*

Moreover, Ostrom starts from an individualistic perspective, where the existence of an observer and an observed person is necessary, and when the starting point of relationality is collective and, consequently, demands reciprocity, reputation and mutual trust. Thus, all the binding or bindable parties are, at the same time, observers and observed. In other words, Ostrom's proposal is applicable only in the assumed case that there is a pre-existing relational process, and that someone/something – a person, a group or an organisation – knows the reputation of the process, and also knows that the related agents wish to join it. It is, therefore, a reciprocal relationship that has been previously built, in which external (observed) agents present their candidacy by showing they are willing to cooperate by adopting reciprocal attitudes that can be observed by internal agents (observers). Yet it is impossible to determine the role of the process when attempts are being made to construct a new relational process in which the agents are unaware of the reputation and trust of at least one of their number: who is to be the observer and who the observed. In this case, it is not possible to build trust individually through observable experiences.

The solution involves going through the relational processes that are perceptible in practice and are not strictly limited to obtaining direct or indirect information about the conduct of potential agents. They also include our reasonable expectations of one other related to technical qualities and capacities as well as moral and emotional ones. These expectations are the basis of all possible routes to relationality and allow a break with the individualistic perspective and the contradiction underlying the one-way pyramid structure proposed by Ostrom.

So, when a participative process is established, two different interrelated, complementary and indissoluble levels are activated. On one hand, there are reasonable expectations based on mutually recognising the technical, communicative and affective capacities and skills that the parties amass and through which they seek to relate in order to specify, commit to and meet shared objectives. Although this level is extremely fragile, it allows a minimum of trust to be built so that the parties take the first step and establish the relationship. Moreover, the experiences of the parties' tendencies towards reciprocal participation are observed. Once again, this level is fragile, but not as fragile, and it makes the relationship robust through the direct and indirect information about the values guiding agents' behaviour in the relationship as well as information about the soundness and social and moral validity of these values. Both levels form a whole: they are two parts of a single entity, as observable experiences enrich and consolidate reasonable expectations, and reasonable expectations cleanse and justify observable experiences.

Thus, it is not a one-way pyramid structure with reciprocity as the base, trust as the peak and reputation the mechanism between them, as proposed by Ostrom.

Instead, it is rather two-way and circular, with multiple possible combinations thanks to expectations about our behaviours, our reputation or our trust, which we might reasonably expect. These reasonable expectations allow the minimum trust required to begin the relationship, without the need for previous direct or indirect information about the reputation and trust of the parties involved.

This level of expectation also stems from reciprocity, the mutual recognition of technical (strategic know-how) communicative (moral know-how) and affective (emotional know-how) qualities, competences and skills of human beings that allow the building of the minimum trust needed to begin a relationship without requiring prior direct or indirect information about the reputation and trust of the parties involved. People mutually recognise each other as beings with the ability to speak and act; with communication capacities to enter practical discourses whose objective is to be intersubjectively understood concerning the worldly matters that affect them or for which they are responsible (Habermas 2001). However, they also mutually recognise one another as beings gifted with feelings and the capacity to feel emotions for themselves and for others, competences without which it is impossible to implement such procedures, to be committed to undertake them, or to appreciate their own accomplishments (Cortina 2010). Therefore, as Cortina proposes, this reciprocity arises from the ethics of cordial reason (2007a, b, 2010, 2013, 2017).

Reciprocity has a previous aspect based on cordiality –the expectations arising from cordial recognition and enabling a minimum, but sufficient, reputation to be gained from the willingness and commitment of the parties who wish to be related: cordial reciprocity. Yet there is also a later moment built from experience through behaviour demonstrating through practice that expectations deservedly depend on the parties' trust: reciprocal altruism, reciprocal selfishness, strong reciprocity, institutional reciprocity, indirect reciprocity, transitive reciprocity, unconditional reciprocity, social reciprocity, inclusive reciprocity, and so on.

In this sense, the contributions made by Developed and Evolutionary Game Theory, social and evolutionary anthropology and neurosciences, through neuro-economics and practical neurophilosophy (Cortina 2012), reveal that: cooperation is possible thanks to a virtue like reciprocity. This is a heterogeneous set of behavioural responses with a strategic, moral and emotional dimension that has to be addressed so that relationality emerges and develops appropriately. Relationality requires feelings and emotions and these feelings and emotions arise from values, rules and principles, shared collectively or universally. Social or moral values, rules and principles are specified, justified and enriched in dialogue terms by the affected people. These discourse dialogues are possible thanks to there being cordial recognition among people who are aware they can talk and act, and can experience emotions for themselves and for others.

Consequently, relationality among economic agents is feasible and implements and empowers reciprocity, particularly cordial reciprocity, in the practical sphere. In other words, it is an unconditional and unconditioned interpersonal relationship where beings who can speak and act mutually recognise their emotional, feeling- and dialogue-based capacities so that they can be understood and commit themselves to the framework in which to act and undertake personal, collective or universal objectives in any area of human activity, and the close relationships linking them. All reciprocal behaviours that may appear and develop, as appropriate, regardless of whether they are self-interested, should start from this minimum level of dignity that represents mutual recognition when faced with beings capable of dialogue, assessment, emotions, acting and making commitments in any area of activity, even economics. These factors are cordially related to make sense of different things, experiences, projects and decisions in the living world.

6.3   Ethics of Reciprocity: Reconstructing the Conditions Allowing Human Cooperation

The reciprocity models observed or proposed in various disciplines show how, beyond a mere exchange of equivalents governed by external coercion, human beings are capable of establishing beneficial relationships with fellow citizens in a context of highly competitive action that is assumed to be as individualistic as the economic context is. Yet the vast majority of these approaches lack a frame of reference capable of guiding such reciprocal conduct toward the horizon that gives the actions meaning and legitimacy. The disciplines that have attempted this, such as the strong reciprocity of Bowles and Gintis, among others, and Zamagni's transitive reciprocity,[1] have not managed to do this in enough depth. Firstly, strong reciprocity founders in functional ethics (Gintis 2000, 2010), and is mainly interested in clarifying the role of the moral and social rules in the emergence and proper development of collaborative conduct in a given society. Secondly, transitive reciprocity goes no further than the relevant, but insufficient, ethics of the virtue or ethics of improvement (Zamagni 2007, 2008, 2009, 2010, 2017), which is concerned about sensibly elucidating the virtues and emotions that form a constitutive part of an excellent character according to the interests of a given society in order to, among other things, allow those involved to develop their good living plans in relation to everyone else.

Indeed, putting into practice one type of reciprocity like that underlying cordial recognition, as developed by Cortina through her *ethica cordis* proposal (2007a, b, 2010, 2011, 2013, 2017), would allow the necessary post-conventional moral viewpoint to be introduced into the various reciprocity approaches that have been observed and developed based on sociobiology, evolutionary economics, humanistic economics or moral philosophy. This could then guide implicit behaviours towards their required moral legitimacy and social sense. There are several issues in line with this:

Firstly, in etymological terms, the word reciprocity comes from the Latin *reciprocitas, −atis,* whose root *reciproc* is related to the verb *reciprocare,* which means *a to-and-fro relationship* (*re*-iteration and *procurare*-to obtain).[2] Thus, in etymo-

---

[1] To examine this special reciprocity type more deeply, see Calvo (2012, 2013).

[2] To examine the verb *procurare,* see Moussy (2008).

logical terms, this term reveals that the factual realisation of reciprocity demands two complementary and indissoluble moments: that of offering (something) and that of responding (from something); both are reciprocal as they maintain expectations of a behavioural response from the other party.[3]

Secondly, in order to set up an act of offering something to establish a reciprocal relation, some reasonable expectations should have been previously generated about the other person's suitable response capacity. These expectations are generated by the direct or indirect information available about the parties' tendency to behave reciprocally (Ostrom 2003) or, if this were not the case, through the mutual recognition of the dignity and bindability emanating from the communicative and emotional capacity of the related, or potentially related, parties.

Thirdly, the reciprocity that lies behind the reasonable expectations that arise from direct or indirect information about the reputation of the binding or bindable parties is related to the different behaviours observed by economics, sociology, anthropology, biology or philosophy, such as reciprocal altruism, indirect reciprocity, social reciprocity, strong reciprocity, unconditional reciprocity, transitive reciprocity, inclusive reciprocity and institutional reciprocity. Meanwhile, the reciprocity involved in the possibility of creating reasonable expectations when the potentially bindable parties have no previous, direct or indirect information available on the other person's tendency towards reciprocity, is related to knowledge of the dignity and bindability that underlies the communicative and emotional capacity of the potentially bindable parties.

Fourthly, for reciprocity to appear in practice – that is, the actions of giving with reasons (the proposal level) and suitably responding (response level) actually occurring – another action needs to be occur: acceptance of the proposal. This intermediate level allows the conditions for the possibility of reciprocity to be rebuilt. This is the source of the justification resulting from both accepting and rejecting the collaboration proposal:

(i) *Clarity*: The person receiving the collaboration proposal through a resource has to know the exact reasons underlying it. In other words, understanding that it is a reciprocal action, and not a merely altruistic one. A suitable response is expected if it is accepted.

(ii) *Reality*: The person receiving the collaboration proposal through a resource has to weigh up whether it is in line with his/her good living projects. If the project is not related to his/her reality, then accepting help and starting with the relational process may be trivial or counterproductive for the person's own well-being

(iii) *Emotivity*: The person receiving the collaboration proposal via a resource has to assess it as being interesting and desirable to be able to participate in, and to be committed to the relational process. Help is very often rejected because of

---

[3] The *Diccionario de la Lengua Española* (2014) defines reciprocity as "Mutual correspondence between someone/thing and someone/thing else", and the *Oxford English Dictionary* (2017) defines reciprocity as "The practice of exchanging things with others for mutual benefit, especially privileges granted by one country or organization to another".

the resulting consequences, the resulting degree of commitment, or the negative feelings it produces

(iv) *Justice*: The person receiving the collaboration proposal via a resource makes moral judgements about the person who proposes it, the proposal itself, the resource, the project and the consequences of the relational process. If the proposal or resource originates from, for example, drug trafficking or organised crime, the receiver might reject the collaboration proposal as he/she understands that it violates legitimate expectation's behaviour, even though the consequences that result from the relationship may be highly beneficial for him/her. At this level, cordial recognition comes into play, where disdain generates negative feelings that impoverish, restrict or destroy the possible or existing relationship, such as tediousness, hate or shame felt by the receiver, as Richard Sennett argued (2003), or resentment and indignation, as pointed out by Strawson (1974).

Fifthly and finally, if any of the possibility conditions is broken – *clarity*, *reality*, *motivation* or *justice* – there is a risk that the receiver does not accept help and the relationship does not actually take place.[4] Nevertheless, the reciprocity underlying the mutual recognition of the parties' dignity and bindability behaves differently from the other reciprocity approaches observed in the practical domain, because not recognising either the other person as an absolute value or the close link between them implies inhumanity. It therefore becomes a contemptible and reprehensible act that cannot possibly be justified. Consequently, it becomes a type of reciprocity that may not only occur, but is also morally expected, as Cortina would say (2007a, 2010), to take root in the sphere of intersubjectivity.

These five issues reveal the potential of cordial reciprocity as a cooperation horizon in a moral sense. This reciprocal act lies behind the possibility of cordial recognition addressed by this work, and also at the moment prior to the relationship, where the potentially bound or bindable parties recognise their dignity and the close link that binds them, as well as the mutual communicative and emotional capacities they have to understand each other and to make commitments to the framework for action and to undertaking specific, collective and universal objectives in any area of human activity. This compassionate approach will constitute the unsurpassable framework for all reciprocity proposals that humanely take pride in setting the minimums for recognition and respect between the parties involved or affected, without whom it is not possible to build an interpersonal relationship which tending towards personal, collective or general benefit that makes social and moral sense.[5]

---

[4]When one of the conditions is in doubt or breached, there is the possibility of enriching and reestablishing collaboration through a dialogue process that clarifies, adapts, motivates or argues in accordance with the expectation in question.

[5]As previously mentioned, strong reciprocity, through social and moral rules, and transitive reciprocity, through virtues and affective reciprocity, also attempt to rebuild the normative frame of cooperation. What cordial reciprocity contributes is another relevant and complementary moment of mutual recognition: the dignity of people capable of dialogue and reaching agreements about the moral legitimacy of the social rules applied or applicable. Without this communicative recognition,

Accordingly, it is worth stressing eight basic traits that define and characterise this cordial reciprocity:

(i)   Two-way: it is an interpersonal two-way relationship based not only on mutual respect for emotional, feeling- and dialogue-based capacities any party may have, but also on the parties' active participation.

(ii)   Compassionate: a reciprocity type whose roots lie in developing compassionate reasons where the rational combines the emotional, feeling- and dialogue-based arguments of those involved in the processes of fulfilling an own or mutual objective.

(iii)   Unconditional: a reciprocity type based on freedom relationships, where the external coercion that obliges the parties to fulfil the recognition compromises reached is impossible. This approach is based on mutual behavioural expectations whose sense and legitimacy give it the strength of links and commitment, but it is moral rather than legal.

(iv)   Unconditioned: a relationship whose specification has not been restricted to the proportional response made by others. In other words, although some do not recognise the dignity of others, the other parties recognise in them their value as people because the relationship is intrinsically linked with the mutual recognition of whoever faces these others, which is absolute, and also a purpose in itself that offers good reasons to wish that it is decently preserved.

(v)   Vital: a reciprocity type that takes root in the world of life, and whose sense and inviolability is linked to the mutual recognition experiences about those specific life forms and particular *ethos*.

(vi)   Communicative: this reciprocity type is nourished and enriched based on the commitment and active and dialogue-based participation of all those involved or affected.

(vii)   Inclusive: a reciprocity type that pays attention to all human beings, without distinctions, irrespectively of the differences and peculiarities of each person, and of whatever their maximum happiness may be.

(viii)   Universal: a reciprocity type that maintains an intersubjective and universal perspective. In other words, their expectations that come into play do not correspond to the particular and strategic interest of given individuals and societies, but rather to general and legitimate interest, which all beings who deserve to be considered in dignity may have, and whose performance has positive effects on all human societies and their citizens.

By means of these basic traits, cordial reciprocity is postulated as a condition of the possibility of cooperation that is not merely strategic emerging, developing and operating, capable of making optimum profits in economic contexts. Recognition and active respect for what is recognised creates solid links among the parties, which allow a relationality that moves towards making a maximum economic profit

---

we will not be able to find out which rules are morally valid, and without affective recognition, we will not wish to know what is fair. As Cortina rightly points out, both moments are necessary and complementary (2007a, b, 2010, 2013, 2017).

for themselves or the other party. All reciprocal behaviour emerging and appropriately developing, whether or not it is self-interested, should start from this minimum dignity constituting the mutual recognition of facing beings who are able to dialogue, assess, become emotional, act and be committed in any area of activity, even economics. This is cordially related in order to make sense of different things, experiences, projects and decisions from the vital world.

Basically, reciprocity is a condition of the possibility of those optimum balances capable of making excellent profits among those involved or affected. However, the different reciprocity relationships that related agents are capable of successfully establishing and dealing with in each case is one thing, while the framework allowing the guidance of the development of these highly beneficial behaviours for those involved, without losing sight of the horizon point of action that gives them not only a sense of existence but also, and consequently, the moral and social legitimacy to act, is something else entirely. Any reciprocal behaviour that wishes to rise to the challenge of cordial society – mature, emotional, felt, dialogic-based and committed – should begin with this minimum constituted by mutual recognition when faced with beings capable of dialogue, assessment, feeling emotions, acting and being committed in any area of activity, even the economic one – in other words, cordially relating to making sense of different things, experiences, projects and decisions from the vital world.

So, regardless of their interest, the different reciprocity approaches that individuals adopt to feel worthy of relating to others, such as reciprocal altruism, indirect reciprocity, reciprocal selfishness, social reciprocity, strong reciprocity, institutional reciprocity, unconditional reciprocity and transitive reciprocity, should begin with this same unsurpassable minimum that represents the related agents' dignity and bindability. In other words, cordial reciprocity that allows them to rise to the challenge of a cordial society that actively recognises and respects its citizen's communicative and affective capacities.

Based on all these issues, the need to extend the margins of economic rationality in an emotive and communicative – and thus a relational and moral – sense, is evidenced by introducing variables into the information, such as feelings and prosocial emotions, as well as the values, rules or principles underlying the moral judgements involved in various decision-making processes (Van den Bos et al. 2009; Ohtsuki et al. 2009; Strobel et al. 2011). On them depends the efficient management of intangible goods, like reciprocity, reputation and trust, which condition the possibility of relational processes that move towards private, collective and generalisable interests in economic contexts emerging, developing and being sustained.

Bibliography

Calvo, Patrici. 2012. *Racionalidad económica: aspectos éticos de la reciprocidad.* Castellón de la Plana: Serveis de Publicacions de la Universitat Jaume I.
————. 2013. Economía civil desde una ética de la razón cordial. *CIRIEC. Revista de Economía Pública, Social y Cooperativa* 79: 115–143.

Cortina, Adela. 2007a. Ethica cordis. *Isegoría. Revista de Filosofía Moral y Política* 37: 113–126.
———. 2007b. *Ética de la razón cordial. Educar en la ciudadanía en el siglo XXI.* Oviedo: Nobel.
———. 2010. *Justicia cordial.* Madrid: Trotta.
———. 2011. *Neuroética y Neuropolítica. Sugerencias para la Educación Moral.* Madrid: Tecnos.
———. 2012. Neuroética, presente y futuro. In *Neurofilosofía práctica*, ed. Adela Cortina, 9–38. Granada: Comares.
———. 2013. *¿Para qué sirve realmente… la ética?* Barcelona: Paidós Ibérica.
———. 2017. *Aporofobia, el rechazo al pobre. Un desafío para la democracia.* Barcelona: Paidós Ibérica.
Damasio, Antonio R. 1994. *Descartes' Error: Emotion, Reason, and the Human Brain.* New York: Avon Books.
———. 2003. *Looking for Spinoza: Joy, Sorrow and the Feeling Brain.* London: William Heinemann.
Diccionario de la Lengua Española. 2017. *Reciprocity.* http://dle.rae.es/srv/fetch?id=VRiTmmB. Accessed 25 Sept 2017.
Fehr, Ernst, and Simon Gächter. 2002. Altruistic punishment in humans. *Nature* 415 (6868): 137–140.
Frank, Robert H. 1988. *Passions within Reason: The Strategic Role of the Emotions.* New York: W. W. Norton & Company.
Gintis, Hebert. 2000. *Game Theory Evolving: A Problem-Centered Introduction to Modeling Strategic Interaction.* Princeton: Princeton University Press.
———. 2010. Behavioral ethics. In *Creating Consilience: Integrating the Sciences and the Humanities (New Directions in Cognitive Science)*, ed. Edward Slingerlan and Mark Collard, 318–333. New York: Oxford University Press.
Glimcher, Paul W., Colin F. Camarer, Ernst Fehr, and Russell A. Poldrack, eds. 2009. *Neuroeconomics. Decision Making and the Brain.* Amsterdam: Elsevier Academic Press.
Gould, Richard. 1982. To have and not to have: The ecology of sharing among hunter-gatherers. In *Resource managers: North American and Australian Hunter-Gatherers*, ed. Nancy M. Williams and Eugene S. Hunn, 69–91. Boulder: Westview Press.
Habermas, Jürgen. 2001. Justification and application. In *Remarks on Discourse Ethics.* Cambridge, MA: MIT Press.
Kosfeld, Michael, Markus Heinrichs, Paul J. Zak, Urs Fischbacher, and Ernst Fehr. 2005. Oxytocin increases trust in humans. *Nature* 435 (1): 637–677.
McCabe, Kevin, Daniel Houser, Lee Ryan, Vernon Smith, and Theodore Trouard. 2001. A functional imaging study of cooperation in two-person reciprocal exchange. *Proceedings of the National Academy of Sciences of the United States of America* 98 (20): 11832–11835.
Mediavilla, Daniel. 2015, November 03. Michael Tomasello: "Para mejorar la sociedad no podemos obviar lo negativo de nuestra biología". *El País.* https://elpais.com/elpais/2015/10/20/ciencia/1445363532_639418.html
Moussy, Claude. 2008. L'histoire du latin procurare: une "préhistoire" du français procurer? *Revista de Estudios Latinos* 8: 17–29.
Ohtsuki, Hisashi, Yoh Iwasa, and Martin A. Nowak. 2009. Indirect reciprocity provides only a narrow margin of efficiency for costly punishment. *Nature* 457: 79–82.
Ostrom, Elinor. 1990. *Governing the Commons. The Evolution of Institutions for Collective Action.* Cambridge: Cambridge University Press.
———. 2003. Toward a behavioral theory linking trust, reciprocity, and reputation. In *Trust & Reciprocity. Interdisciplinary Lessons from Experimental Research*, ed. Elinor Ostrom and James Walker, 19–79. New York: Russell Sage Foundation.
Oxford English Dictionary. 2017. *Reciprocity.* https://en.oxforddictionaries.com/definition/reciprocity. Accessed 25 Sept 2017.
Rockenbach, Bettina, and Manfred Milinski. 2006. The efficient interaction of indirect reciprocity and costly punishment. *Nature* 444: 718–723.
Sahlins, Marshall. 1972. *Stone Age Economy.* Chicago: Aldine. Atherton.

Sakaiya, Shiro, Yuki Shiraito, Junko Kato, Hiroko Ide, Kensuke Okada, Kouji Takano, and Kenji Kansaku. 2013. Neural correlate of human reciprocity in social interactions. *Frontiers in Neuroscience* 7 (239): 1–12.

Sennett, Richard. 2003. *Respect in a world of inequality*. New York: Penguin.

Smith, Adam. 1793 [1776]. *An Inquiry into the Nature and Causes of the Wealth of Nations*. London: A. Strahan and T. Cadell.

Strawson, Peter F. 1974. *Freedom and Resentment and Other Essays*. London: Methuen.

Strobel, Alexander, Jan Zimmermann, Anja Schmitz, Martin Reuter, Stefanie Lis, Sabine Windmann, and Peter Kirsch. 2011. Beyond revenge: Neural and genetic bases of altruistic punishment. *NeuroImage* 54 (1): 671–680.

Van den Bos, Wouter, Eric van Dijk, Michiel Westenberg, Serge A.R.B. Rombouts, and Eveline A. Crone. 2009. What motivates repayment? Neural correlates of reciprocity in the trust game. *Social Cognitive Affective Neuroscience* 4 (3): 294–304.

Zamagni, Stefano. 2007. *L'economia del bene comune*. Rome: Città Nuova.

———. 2008. Reciprocity, civil economy, common good. In *Pursuing the Common Good: How Solidarity and Subsidiarity Can Work Together*, ed. Margaret Archer and Pierpaolo Donati, 467–502. Vatican City: The Pontifician Academy of Social Sciences.

———. 2009. Fraternity, gifts and reciprocity in Cáritas in Veritate. *Revista Cultural Económica* 27 (75–76): 11–29.

———. 2010. Reciprocidad y Fraternidad. El Papel de los Sentimientos en la Economía. In *XXI Seminario Étnor de Ética y Economía. ¿Lecciones Aprendidas? Nuevos Caminos para el Crecimiento y Nuevas Formas de Vida Ética en las Estrategias Empresariales del Siglo XXI*, ed. Jesús Conill, 55–66. Valencia: Fundación Étnor.

———. 2017. Economics as if ethics mattered. In *Economics as a Moral Science. Virtues and Economics*, ed. Peter Rona and Zsolnai Laszlo, vol. 1, 21–41. Cham: Springer.

Chapter 7
Cordial Rationality: The Language of Human Cooperation

Abstract The role played by reciprocity and other intangible assets for the economy, as well as the confirmation of the motivational heterogeneity and moral commitment that underlie them, demonstrate the need to extend the margins of economic rationality in an affective and communicative sense in order to introduce into the information base variables like *prosocial emotions,* and the values, norms or principles forming part of economic agents' conduct and decision-making processes. From the ethical and emotional anchorage proposed through cordial reciprocity, and without ignoring the necessary strategic-technical dimension of economic rationality, the aim of this chapter is to elucidate a suitable proposal for economic rationality to guide and provide information about economic agents' conduct and decisions in the area of economics.

With *Les Misérables* (1862), Victor Hugo offered a deep, close reflection about the conflicting forces, good and bad, that govern society: faith and reason, order and chaos, law and ethics, indolence and compassion and so on, together with the negative consequences stemming from states that dominate and repress each other.

Using the historical events that took place in Paris in June 1832, Hugo described the processes of struggle between opponents of all these conflicting forces through the stereotyped figures of the two main characters in his work: the relentless and disciplined Javert, a police officer who has made law his religion, and honesty and order his good living project; and the benevolent and unwary Jean Valjean, a former prisoner who desires freedom, and who never thinks twice about helping his fellow men, even though such action costs him his own well-being. Above all with Javert and Valjean, Victor Hugo recreates the crossing of two currents of thought which, emerging during the French Revolution, were coming to an end in the last decades of the nineteenth century: Neoclassicism and Romanticism. They presented two apparently conflicting ways of understanding freedom: as reason that leaves social and moral feelings and emotions on one side, and as experience linked to satisfaction with one's own good living projects and with those of others. In *Les Misérables,* Hugo showed his inclination towards the freedom of the Romantics, a yearning for the time of his youth, but he opts to break down the walls of conflict and reconcile the two postures, avoiding both paralysing conventionalism and dangerous relativ-

© Springer International Publishing AG, part of Springer Nature 2018 105
P. Calvo, *The Cordial Economy - Ethics, Recognition and Reciprocity,*
Ethical Economy 55, https://doi.org/10.1007/978-3-319-90784-0_7

ism. Society needs to know what is fair to be able to create good rules that promote stability, peace, balance, and so on, but to also to be able feel and become emotional for oneself and for others to be able to appreciate justice and its consequences.

This is precisely the path Hugo describes, from the historical context depicted in *Les Misérables* between 1815 and 1832 to the publication of his novel in 1882, very similar to that of economic Neoclassicism until it became well-established. However, this form of Neoclassicism was concerned with instrumental reason – elucidating the most efficient means to achieve a given objective: seeking maximum profit. Freedom, therefore, was considered as the capacity to individually strive for one's own well-being by acquiring goods and services on the market, not to establish fair laws and be committed to follow them or to undertake one's good life plans in relation to others. So, Neoclassicism was not only stripped of all prosocial feeling and emotion in rational decision-making processes, it also disapproved of any critical reflection that wished to go beyond individualism, efficiency and maximising personal interest.

Yet, as in a passage taken from *Les Misérables,* which describes the organisation and tasks of Valjean's prosperous factory in Montreuil-sur-Mer, the current advances made in various disciplines suggest the need to extend the margins of economic rationality to reconcile these three important and complementary moments, so that efficiency, justice and compassion can go hand-in-hand in the process of developing the economy, society and human beings in general. Any solution needs to be able to live up not only to the observations from the fieldwork and laboratory experiments with strategy games, but also to the desires and expectations of a *cordial society* with a post-conventional level of moral development depending on it.

The objective of this chapter is to elucidate a theoretical model of rationality giving information about the emotional heterogeneity and moral commitment behind a series of agents' conduct in highly competitive contexts like economic ones. For this purpose, it firstly looks closely at the *ultra-social reason* proposed by Tomasello based on evolutionary anthropology. This emerges in the first years of humans' lives, and allows purposes to be considered and performed with *shared intentionality* through cooperation. Secondly, we examine in-depth the *compromised reason* proposal, which underlies Amartya Sen's capacities approach. This proposal considers the need to bear in mind the feelings and emotions emanating from agents' concern for their own well-being and that of others, and from the commitments they acquire concerning matters with good reasons to be valued. Finally, guidelines are offered to extend the margins of economic rationality in the effective and ethical-critical sense through the *cordial reason* proposed and developed by Cortina.

7.1 Ultra-Social Reason: From the Self-Interested *I* to the Shared *mutuum*

Given the recent advances in experimental economics, neurosciences, social anthropology or practical philosophy, it is increasingly difficult to find arguments that defend methodological absolutism, studying social reality as if human beings were fundamental particles of the subatomic world – quarks, neutrinos, electrons – and rational reality based on homogeneous motivation of human beings, which boils down to any behaviour that will possibly satisfy their own interests, in line with neoclassical economics. The various questions raised to date suggest the need to deal with redesigning economic rationality to adapt it so it can live up to what is expected at a given time in history.

The predominant economic theory, however, stems from the assumption that the logic of collective action itself determines human beings' incapacity to establish interpersonal relationships that can satisfy common objectives that are advantageous for all parties involved with no suitable control or external coercion and offering the necessary trust.[1] For decades, this discourse, although it lacks justification, has notably influenced the way economic institutions and organisations are designed (Stiglitz 2012), and the way public policies are drawn up and applied (Krugman, 18 April 2013). This limits the horizon of possibilities for societies and different areas of human activity.

Paradoxically, from a coevolutionary perspective, anthropologist Tomasello has shown that cooperation appears very early in human life, just after the age of one. He has demonstrated that cooperation is related to capacity for reciprocity and with being committed to and with dealing with a common objective by abandoning the *I* perspective, and adopting the *We* outlook. He adds that all these issues arise among the most intelligent primates (Tomasello 2010: 50–70) and suggests that such mutualist interpersonal rationality has been taken the form of following three basic processes throughout human biological-cultural evolution: (1) developing cognitive-social skills and motivation for communication and coordinating action towards a common purpose; (2) developing a type of trust capable of enabling and maintaining non-instrumental cooperative action, which is not necessarily two-way; (3) developing certain group institutional practices for drawing up a set of rules to control and guide mutual action and considering their deontic character, as well as managing and ensuring shared collaborative action (Tomasello 2010: 74–75).

When comparing experiments with strategy games used with children, monkeys and chimpanzees – when using a social game or an adapted Ultimatum Game – Tomasello observed that babies aged 14–18 months cooperate and help others altruistically. In other words, they do so without expecting any equitable response from the other person and even without making help conditional on the goodwill of the person asking for it, or there being any kind of kinship between the parties. In other experiments with social games, one was used in which a stranger threw a personal object to the floor and asked the child to help him/her to pick it up. Most of the children picked it up, even though they were aware that it could have been thrown intentionally and there would be no reward involved for offering assistance. So, the experiment apparently indicates that altruism in children is not the result of some form of socialising, cultural exchange or parental intervention (Tomasello 2010: 50), but corresponds to a "(…) natural inclination to understand others' situation when they face difficulties" (Tomasello 2010: 34).

---

[1] To learn about the basic aspects of this argument, see Olson (1965).

When children are 2–3 years old, which is when their linguistic capacities begin to develop, socialising and direct experience begin to play a determining role in their relations with others. During this period, they will become aware of the cost of consequences deriving from indiscriminate altruistic cooperation and developing the faculty to reciprocate, and will direct their actions only at those they consider can be trusted – that is, those the children have good reasons to believe will not take advantage of them and who could offer an equitable response to the help received (Tomasello 2010: 51, 67).

When a child matures in this sense, specific forms of cooperation emerge from their interpersonal relationships linked to kinship altruism, reciprocal altruism and indirect reciprocity at a very early stage. Here, the rules and values of a given group, a sense of justice, the making of value judgements and reputation of the self and others begin to play a key role in help or cooperation actions. Children realise their behaviour is being observed and judged by other people according to the community's social rules. So they act by mimicking this attitude and attempting to influence or control the judgements others make of them. This is precisely what the sociologist Erving Goffman, the father of microsociology, defined as *controlling and handling impressions*: a dramaturgical process by which someone builds his or her own public profile, which is presented to others in an attempt to guide, control or redirect the opinions others have of them, and the kind of things they can and cannot do (Goffman 1956: 1–9).

It is at this childhood stage when one of the determining factors of human cooperation emerges: the plural subject. This is the time when children develop their capacity to recognise and undertake a mutually shared purpose whose performance makes sense only if everyone collaborates. Fieldwork and experiments with primates have demonstrated that animals do not have such capacities. They can identify a common objective, such as hunting or defending the group, and collaborate in satisfying it, but they are incapable of dealing with the project without putting the *I* viewpoint to side (Tuomela 2007). If someone stops collaborating, they continue without trying to communicate with that person to get him/her involved again or to reproach his/her conduct. What all this seems to suggest is that their behaviour is linked to "(…) a kind of instrumental relationality destined to the individual's personal gains" (Tomasello 2014b: 193). No shared intentionality therefore exists in the performance process.

Children aged 14–24 months, however, act quite differently because, as plural subjects, they are able to identify a (*our*) common objective and implement it based on an intentionality shared by everyone. So, when someone related to this *our* stops participating, the others immediately communicate with this person to ask him/her to continue collaborating (Tomasello 2014a: 80–123, 2014b: 189). For them, it is a necessarily interdependent act, a purpose whose fulfilment only makes sense and is possible if all the members that share it actually collaborate. When this our is breached by someone involved not being committed, the rest try to re-establish cooperation by implementing communication processes (Warneken and Tomasello 2006: 1301–1303). Consequently, for children, the project makes no sense from the

I viewpoint, which seems to show that their behaviour has been mediated by a kind of ultra-social rationality concerned with the group's gains (Tomasello 2014b: 188).

From this point of view, and as their communication, cognitive and ontogenetic competences develop in order to assimilate and internalise mutual expectations of behaviour, preschool children not only comply with socially grasped rules, they also become guarantors that these will be followed without the mediation of any competent authority; e.g., parents or teachers (Tomasello 2010: 59–60). This takes place between 3–5 years of age, when they genuinely become aware that a group identity, social rationality and mutual interdependence exist allowing social rules to be perceived "(…) as supraindividual bodies that involve a social strength irrespectively of (…) instrumental considerations" (Tomasello 2010: 61). This allows them to start relating with others by means of more complex forms of reciprocity, such as reciprocal selfishness, indirect reciprocity in its more developed form, social reciprocity and strong reciprocity,[2] which, when deployed, demand prosocial rules and feelings capable of motivating the cooperation process and altruistic punishment from any punishable acts that do not correspond to mutually generated behavioural expectations (Bowles and Gintis, 2011: 19; Vaish et al. 2010: 1661–1668).

As a result, from the evolutionary anthropology perspective, it appears to be suggested that children go from altruistically helping others to cooperating with those who seem trustworthy by applying and implementing reciprocity in different ways. Yet as soon as they acquire more autonomy and group awareness, they begin to leave aside their initial solipsistic perspective and make a commitment to the idea of *our*, which allows them to consider "(…) common challenges with others who are normatively committed to both parties" (Tomasello 2010: 123). So the first signs of independence appear, children begin showing an interest in their reputations and those of others, and in the social rules involved, and they start worrying about following them and them being followed, and about shaping a public ethos by becoming linked with these rules. Such an ethos guides, controls or redefines the impressions the children may have of themselves or others. These matters allow much more complex relationships to be established, which is beyond the scope of other animals.

The rules that boost cooperation thus do not correspond only to respect for authority or the group to which people belong, nor to a reciprocal expectation of making profits in the mid or long term (Tomasello 2010: 63–65), especially when what is at risk is non-two-way and indirect cooperation with large groups of people involved. Instead, the response is to the positive and negative emotions linked to fulfilling or breaching commitments. Children feel ashamed and guilty when they do not stick to rules, with punishment for not doing what they should, and they feel angry when others breach a reciprocal expectation of behaviour, so they are capable of reproaching them for their attitude and demanding accountability from them. Cooperative rules therefore "(…) stem from the mutual recognition of our independence and from the natural relations we have when faced with our frustrations and those of others" (Tomasello 2010: 110).

---

[2] To go further into these reciprocity approaches, see Calvo (2012: 133–166).

All this underlies the idea of an ultra-social or cooperative reason allowing people to establish and maintain interpersonal relational processes in various areas of human activity (Tomasello 2014b: 192–193). One reason that appears and develops in the first years of human life allows humans to be actively committed to following-up and fulfilling rules they have apprehended, even when no implicit reward is expected, when an authority figure might disapprove of a breach of the rules, or when there is no cost involved in punishing the acts of those who do not stick to them. So, a normative horizon underlies cooperation that goes beyond kinship, nepotism or the instrumental potential inherent in such behaviour and linked to recognising another person's dignity, one's own vulnerability, or esteem for anything which there are good reasons to value. In other words, a type of reciprocity that escapes the mere instrumentalisation of related subjects coincides with and penetrates the area of recognition, cordiality, intersubjectivity. This is based on any type of interpersonal cooperation and collaboration that wishes to, in the words of Ortega y Gasset, "(...) live *at the height of our time*, with an exaggerated consciousness of the historical circumstances" (1960: 95).

7.2 Compromised Reason: Self-Interest, Sympathy and Moral Compromise

The fact that reciprocity is recurrent in various laboratory experiments with strategic games, even in those arbitrarily designed to control its appearance and to avoid the theory showing any inconsistency, drew the interest of most experimental economists. Since the 1980s, experimental economics has been concerned with clarifying the implementation and possibility of reciprocity in a context of activity such as economics.

Experimental economics studies have therefore managed to show the inconsistency of the entire rationality of *homo oeconomicus*, an axiomatised proposal intended to continue to provide information about all economic reality in its own language. This is a tendency towards relationality, a contemptible concept for a predominant theory based on methodological individualism and on the natural tendency of agents to constantly maximise their own benefit. This is mainly because its truth denies the theory itself, proving that reciprocity means the rational agent is self-interested, but compassionate; individualistic, but cooperative; rational, but emotional.

Studies have also revealed that their inclusion in the information base requires a search for rationality capable of absorbing the motivational heterogeneity observed in the behaviour of economic agents. As a basic element to create and maintain interpersonal relationships, reciprocity opens the door to achieving balances that greatly benefit all those involved. This enables agents to plan and specify common objectives from an *Our* perspective where the related parties can normatively commit themselves to their tasks. Yet such achievements require a rationality that evaluates the related people's capacity to feel, which, perfect, complete rationality does not do in conventional theory.

Accordingly, it is worth stressing the various economic rationality proposals which, like Simon's bounded rationality, Ostrom's emotional rationality and Sen's compromised rationality provide information about the possibility of specifying non-instrumental cooperation in practice capable of achieving the maximum benefit for all the related parties.

Firstly, the bounded rationality that Simon proposed in the "Behavioral Model of Rational Choice" (1955) admits the mark that human feelings and emotions leave on an economic agent's actions and decisions. This leads us to think about the possibility of human cooperation, although only in part. By recognising feelings and emotions as elements outside reason, bounded rationality inhibits the possibility of both materialising a *mutuum* from which common purposes highly beneficial for the participants to be considered and making the necessary commitments to undertake them.

Secondly, the emotional rationality that underlies the theoretical proposal by Ostrom[3] (1990, 1998, 2000, 2003, 2012) is fuelled by Simon's bounded rationality, but goes further by considering the motivational heterogeneity to be rational. This characterises economic agents' behaviour, making it possible, among other things, to contemplate and specify common objectives from the *Our* perspective. Ostrom therefore considers an interest in one's own well-being and that of others as being rational, as an optimum balance between agents is possible only through both moments.[4]

Thirdly, the compromised rationality developed by Sen (1977, 1987, 2000, 2002, 2009) from his capacities approach considers the need to bear in mind the feelings and emotions emanating from agents' concern about one's own well-being and that of others throughout the rational decision-making process, and also from related commitments with good reasons to deserve value and respect, irrespectively of their market price, the profits they make, or the personal cost involved in defending them.

From this perspective, Sen proposes a rationality structured around three complementary levels: self-interest, sympathy and commitment. On the one hand, Sen classifies personal interest as being extraordinarily fruitful because the motivational strength it possesses (Sen 2000). However, Sen also considers that this fact does not suffice to explain any behaviour observed in an economic context (Sen 2000) or justify that it should remain only as a utility (Sen 1984) or be limited to one's own well-being (Sen 2000). If so, economic theory would raise the figure of the rational fool to new heights with a simple mental portrait from the social point of view (Sen 1977, 2002). So, Sen believes it is necessary to reconstruct a more realistic structure of human rationality:

> The purely economic man is indeed close to being a social moron. Economic theory has been much preoccupied with this rational fool decked in the glory of his one all-purpose preference ordering. To make room for the different concepts related to his behavior we need a more elaborate structure. (Sen 1977: 336)

---

[3] See Calvo (2012a) for this economic rationality approach study by Ostrom.

[4] Accordingly, Ostrom argues that if rationality is interpreted based on the criterion of the largest possible profit, it would be senseless for the economic discourse to marginalize those emotions allowing optimum balances whose performance is far superior to that observed for merely selfishic behaviour (1990, 2000, 2003, 2012).

Based on this idea, Sen proposes the possibility that interest in one's own well-being allows interest in others' well-being as a determining factor for its accomplishment (1977: 327–328). This is a level where moral feelings, and not just cost-benefit calculations, play a decisive role in rational behaviour and decision making. This possibility does away with the assumed self-sufficiency of individualism, and, for economic agents, it restores the social reality underlying the feeling and legitimacy of their behaviours, based on which they develop their good life plans in relation to others.

Yet, for Sen, this sympathetic dimension does not provide information about some behaviours observed in the economic sphere. These would include, those in which high costs are paid for the decisions made by agents, negatively affecting their well-being. This shows that a committed dimension of the economic reason exists going beyond personal interest –whether through selfishness or sympathy– making sense of the sacrifices individuals make to achieve social justice or community well-being (1977: 328–329).

As a result, Sen understands that economic rationality can be entirely accepted in an ethical approach to conduct as an alternative behaviour model. This is firstly because moral values, commitments, rules and feelings play a determining role in contemporary economics despite the obvious ostracism they have suffered in recent centuries (Sen 2000). Secondly, it allows behavioural models that are not interpreted exclusively based on self-interest, and better correspond to the economic agent's social reality while implying a richer, more fruitful approach to economics in every sense (Sen 1987). As the economist Sen recognises, not all achievements in modern economy can be attributed to a system that depends on selfish beings moved only by maximising personal well-being. There is much more behind their behaviour, attitudes or decisions, and ethics form an integral part of their preferences (Sen 2000, 2002, 2009).

The rationality proposals put forward by Simon, Ostrom and Sen underlie the behavioural, emotional and communication aspects providing information about human cooperation in areas of activity that are presumably as unfavourable as economics. Among other aspects, these show how feelings and emotions play a critical role in the whole rational decision-making process; how interpersonal relationality emerges and develops thanks to agents' being committed to that which has good reasons to be valued; and also how people are capable of punishing behaviours that breach the values, rules and principles involved in an established relationship, even if this attitude comes with a high personal cost. The level of commitment stresses human altruism, which is not biological, and takes economic rationality closer to the necessary moral viewpoint that allows relationality: reciprocal recognition. So, as we have seen from experimental economics, we have seen the role altruism plays in the practical domain through some of the more developed reciprocal behaviours, such as strong reciprocity (Bowles and Gintis 1998, 2003, 2004, 2006, 2011) or social reciprocity (Ostrom 2003) in particular. This behaviour may punish – either to dissuade, chastise or correct – acts that go against mutual expectations of behaviour in, for instance, cooperative action moving towards achieving any common goal set by the participants.

From this point of view, the altruism involved in human cooperation is partly seen as being different from the biological altruism observed in the first year of children's lives. This is particularly the case because it does not stem exclusively from behavioural preferences that are evolutionarily selected and genetically inherited, but from the mutual recognition of those who, as Cortina would say (2007a, b, 2010, 2013, 2017), are seen as and felt to be cordial interlocutors, capable of feeling emotions on their own and others behalf; of appreciating anything with good reasons to be considered valuable, and of holding dialogue and reaching agreements about the meaning of things in the living world where they develop their maximum happiness in relation to others. From this cordial recognition (Cortina 2010), which also occurs thanks to reciprocity, and from cordial reciprocity, stem the mutual expectations about the dignity and capacity of the related parties that allow the establishment of dialogue processes providing information about the agreements reached as to how to altruistically punish those who take advantage of others for their own benefit. The altruism involved in cooperation therefore arises from the reasonable expectations of the people involved about human capacity to deal with relational reality based on freedom, the *mutuum*, commitment, dialogue and reciprocity, and allows the implementation of interpersonal cooperation capable of striking balances that are optimally beneficial for all related agents.

This relationality perspective reveals that the suprasocial rationality linked to human's cooperative processes possesses a shared mutuum that is one of its dominant aspects, as Antonio Genovesi pointed out back in the eighteenth century (1786: 199–200) and as Tomasello currently indicates (2010, 2014b). However, Genovesi also stresses that this *we*-ness is not sufficient to explain human cooperation. Consideration and undertaking of purposes with shared intentionality necessarily then implies affective relationality in which the value of the other related people and the consideration of what is mutual takes precedence over the person's *own* considerations. It is dialogue-based relationality based on which we can understand each other from the shared goals and commitments involved in the undertaking – a relationality involving feelings that is able to encourage an interest in implementing and respect and responsibility for the commitments made.

It is therefore cordial relationality like that underlying the Cortina's reasoned approach, where participation is fuelled by both the motivation of possibly making maximum profits, and also from the sense that mutual recognition confers dignity and human bindability, as well as the capacity of parties that reach agreements and are responsible for commitments made. In other words, a human cooperation approach that depends on a specific type of reciprocity – *cordial* – and also the Kantian commitment of mutual respect for another person's dignity (Kant 2005) as "(…) they are beings capable of reciprocally recognising the right to pact and the duty to fulfil pacts" (Cortina 2010: 118–119).

7.3   Cordial Reason: The Arguments of the Head and the Heart

From Latin *cor, cord, cordis,* from medieval Latin cordialis, which means heart, effort, encouragement or strongly felt (Oxford English Dictionary 2017; Diccionario de la Lengua Española 2017), but also affection, talent and spirit (Cortina 2007b: 214), cordiality has been historically constructed with reasons stemming from the head and the heart, from justice and care, from honesty and compassion. For Cortina, a rationality that lives up to what history expects at any given time is built from cordiality, based on reasons from the head and the heart. So it has to be developed within the framework of public civic ethics, from the commonly evaluated minimums of justice based on enriched, dignified dialogue and allowing peaceful coexistence and the interpersonal relationality involved in fulfilling maximum happiness for people in different good life projects that are not worthy of the name if they are not related to other people. For this reason, discourse ethics "(…) is an optimum basis for civic ethics of a morally, pluralistic society, provided it does not content itself merely with its procedural dimension, but also presents its cordial dimension" (Cortina 2007a: 113).

With the Kantian transcendental method, the discourse ethics proposed by Apel and Habermas in the 1970s and 1980s, and developed later by the Valencia School[5] reconstruct the rational basis of speech in order to offer a criterion of rationality intended to be universally valid. From this, it can be ascertained which rules can be classified as being morally valid. In other words, an attempt is made to identify and show which conditions enable an understanding among beings with communication competences, because it is precisely these unsurpassable elements that make it possible to guide and criticise both knowledge and action (Cortina 2007b: 176–177).

To this end, the original proposal starts by understanding people as beings with the gift to talk and act, with communication capacities to relate to their peers and to intersubjectively understand the best ways to coordinate a given social praxis (Cortina 2007b: 176–177). Kant's idea of human dignity – that human beings are endowed with value rather than having a price (Kant 2005) – understands that in places where people participate either actively or passively they must be considered to have purposes rather than as mere instruments to serve individual interests. From this point, the subject can express him/herself as a valid interlocutor who is able to argue about that which affects him/her as part of a practical discourse with certain logical rules (Cortina 1992).

This idea is based on the Habermasian communicative action proposal, which reveals that the true purpose and primary use of language – the *telos* – is to reach an understanding among participating subjects (Habermas 1987: 145). Based on Austin and Searle's speech acts theory, Habermas understands all acts of speech to reflect a propositional level, a pragmatic level and a performative level. In other words, the participants propose descriptions – the propositional level – and put forward these

---

[5] To learn what the Valencia School contributed to discourse ethics, see Cortina (2008: 10–27).

proposals – the performative level. However, for the speech act to take place, the listener needs to understand and accept what the message states and requests, which leads to a third level – the pragmatic level – which underlies the logical-formal conditions of an understanding between the related parties (Habermas 2001).

As Habermas explains (1987: 393–394), it is only possible to reach intersubjective understanding if: (a) the receiver understands the message from the sender; (b) the receiver understands that this message is true; (c) the receiver considers that the propositional content of the message is true; (d) the receiver believes that the message is backed by correct rules. When these four formal validity intentions – intelligibility, truth, veracity and honesty – are fulfilled in dialogue, it is feasible to reflect on communication action that leads to understanding among the participants. This is known as *linguistic understanding* and it acts as a "(…) mechanism to coordinate action that adapts the action plans made and the teleological activities undertaken by the participants so they can create an interaction" (Habermas 1987: 138).

The key idea lies in the discursive process which, according to Habermas, comes into play when any of the formal validity intentions is debatable and does not, therefore, lead to an understanding. A situation may arise when, in a communication, a valid interlocutor questions any of the basic assumptions because either he/she does not understand the message or is in doubt about its sincerity, the truth of the proposals or honesty of the rules followed (Habermas 1987: 394). In such cases, according to discourse ethics, there is the possibility of re-establishing dialogue to be able to meet the objective: intersubjective understanding. If what is at stake is the intention of intelligibility or veracity, the valid interlocutor may ask for explanations or reasons which, if given, will re-establish communication. However, if what is being doubted is the intention of truth or honesty, then it is necessary to establish a theoretical or practical discourse depending on each case in which the participants attempt to show the truth of the proposals or the correctness of the rules on which they base themselves to re-establish communication through language and by sticking to the rules of the argument used.

In this way, discourse ethics reveals the pragmatic and transcendental proposals whose normative content is synthetically specified through the universalisation principle [U]: "(…) if rules are valid, the lateral results and consequences that foreseeably follow the general fulfilment of the rule, in order to fulfil the interests of each one, must be accepted without being under coercion by anyone" (Habermas 1991: 101–102).

This universalisation principle [U] places the moral viewpoint in the reciprocal recognition of all those affected by the rule as valid interlocutors who are qualified with communication competences and are able to enter discussions in processes where the moral validity of a rule or action affects them. It also shows the need to reach a rational consensus among everyone, by establishing a counterfactual, inclusive, symmetrical, egalitarian, non-coactive dialogue where the only acceptable strength is "(…) the coercion of the best argument". In this way, the universalisation principle [U] gives dialogue a moral nature or value as it transforms into an essential mechanism to agree which rules are fair or correct (García-Marzá 2004: 103).

So this is a form of ethics that is seen as procedural, universalist, critical and deontological: universalist because it addresses all the rules, no matter where they come from, and refers to everyone affected by them; critical because, far from remaining immovable to validity, it offers orientations that can untangle the validity of the rules; procedural because it is not concerned about content, rules and values, but about the formal process that allows those affected to decide the rules that must govern common activity; and, finally, deontological because it aims to discern and limit this unsurpassable frame that should be considered by any activity in order to not to do something inhumane (García-Marzá 2004: 105). In other words, it should meet the minimums of justice present in any society with a post-conventional level of moral development largely taking the form of human rights and active respect.

This approach allows an understanding of the importance of dialogue for economic organisations and companies. By establishing relationships with those involved in or affected by their activity based on a dialogue leading to understanding and intersubjective agreement, the organisation or business can think about generating the credibility and legitimacy required to generate and reinforce the necessary intangible resources and to manage their activity beneficially, sustainably and feasibly.

As Cortina argues (1990: 183–215, 1996: 119–134), despite its potential, discourse ethics has its limits, especially in the field of applying ethics. Here it is necessary to introduce an ethical-discursive proposal that offers a way of applying moral rules that is not necessarily linked to the State's coercion mechanisms or to any strategic processes in given contexts, which is also in harmony with these civic morals and is the basis of plural societies with post-conventional moral development.[6] This ethical-discursive proposal developed will continue to be framed within three main aspects.

The first question deals with overcoming/surpassing Kantian ethnocentrism. Discourse ethics believes it has achieved this by moving from *I think* to *We argue*. Yet, based on a developed proposal, it is understood that it is necessary to recognise that reason is historical and the transcendental method is hermeneutic-critical, so "(…) a maturity process is necessary in a reflection when it depends on the level of moral, political and legal conscience reached" by society (Cortina 1990: 188–189).

The second question is about excess proceduralism in the original theory. While it seeks to maintain its basic characteristics –formalism, universalism, deontologism and cognitivism– a modest ethical system is proposed that runs the risk of being diluted in other philosophical disciplines. To avoid this, a developed proposal suggests that its field of action is not limited to rules, but also includes the moral good, the reason for the action, and its moral purposes, values and virtues in the reflection setting (Cortina 1990: 188–189). So, it is possible to safeguard what Apel calls *abstractive fallacies* (1998: 53–68); that is, stressing the importance of human beings' rational dimension at the expense of isolating or event forgetting an equally important and necessary dimension (Cortina 1990).

---

[6] For further information about the contributions made by various researchers, see Conill (2006a).

The third question has to do with the idea of limiting the task of ethics in the substantiation field. Apart from justifying rules, a developed proposal puts forward ethics whose task is to: (a) clarify the moral fact and what it consists of; (b) clarify the reasons why human beings behave morally; and (c) apply all acquired knowledge about specific areas of shared life (Cortina 1996: 119–134). Thus, there is a need to find an application method not tied to law or to strategic reason and which is coherent with these three levels of moral reflection and with civic public ethics.

One interesting and enriching, proposal in recent decades was made by Peter Ulrich (1993, 2008). He begins with the transcendental pragmatics to design an integrative proposal that includes economic ethics and allows systemic economic development to be corrected by the moral transformation of economic rationality. Therefore, firstly, it proposes implementing a continuous reflection process so economic rationality can itself discover the ethical-communicative rationality that underlies it – in other words, a type of rationality which, along with the strategic-technical and the calculative-instrumental types, shapes the skeleton of socio-economic reason with its roots in a normative background that is discursive, and not contractualistic or utilitarian. In this way, the main concern over Ulrich's integrative approach is not the technical or administrative order, but "(…) the lifeworld's communicative rationality" (Conill 2006b: 68). This is an approach from which modern economics can be reconciled with moral economics through democratic control by the affected parties to promote a social-type economics backed by normative aspects – regulatory ideas – and real aspects – feasible proposals (Ulrich 1993: 53–54).

Ulrich's integrative economic ethics is an attempt to overcome the duality of elusive and irreconcilable worlds after consolidating modern economic science: that of economic rationality and extra-economic moral reflection. Behind this interest lies the concern about "(…) the increasing problematisation of global effects for the life praxis of the system's 'unleashed' dynamics" (Ulrich 1993: 7–8), which for Ulrich, negatively affects human and social development, whose effects are worsened by separating the economic world and the moral world (Ulrich 1993: 9–10). For this reason, the integrative approach proposes transforming economic rationality so it neither excludes moral reflection, nor operates beyond the perfect neutral and autonomous economic model based on human beings' behavioural and motivational homogeneity.

According to Ulrich, the attempt made to combine the economic and moral worlds is nothing new, but has followed two very different directions throughout history. On one hand, corrective economic ethics, although this proposal does not entirely overcome the duality of worlds; and, on the other hand, functional economic ethics, which is an alternative variant of the corrective proposal but makes the mistaken attempt to lay the foundations of something moral through an emancipated reflection of all ethical influences (Ulrich 1993: 10–15).

Ulrich understands corrective economic ethics to be a series of ideas and strategies which view "(…) ethics as being a corrective of economy's failure" and, consequently, is "(…) a corrective of economic rationality" (Ulrich 1993: 10). So, this proposal attempts to apply some general principles to the economic sphere to solve problems relating to certain matters escaping the legislation currently in force

(Ulrich 1993: 11–12). This proposal is therefore seen as "(…) a premodern under-standing of ethics, (…) as a partially modernised form of the traditional model of authority of the relation between ethics and economy" (Ulrich 1993: 14), as it offers solutions that ignore both economic rationality and the economic context itself.

Ulrich understands functional economic ethics as the use of ethics as a mere fac-tor to improve the way economic systems operate. According to Ulrich, this pro-posal is a variant of the predominant model of economic rationality, as its main interest lies in showing the morals inherent to the economic praxis, which condition the possibility of a system functioning properly. So, it is an approach concerned about "(…) indicating to what extent and scope economic rationality itself already operates as a modern ethics, or can be put to good use for this purpose by means of suitable systemic parameters" (Ulrich 1993: 15). Yet, despite its application and implementation, it allows analytical science to develop for certain matters, and functional economic ethics lacks a broader framework of action as it can neither explain, nor lay the foundations of, "(…) all the normative pre-assumptions of an apt economic system to operate from a purely economic point of view" (Ulrich 1993: 28–29). This inconvenience shows the systemic limits of applying the pro-posal as a solution to bridging the open gap between economic rationality and moral reflection. This is particularly true because, as it is a purely teleological conception of ethics, it reveals a substantial deontological deficit that restricts its possibilities of being applied and developed, and also because, by adopting a preferably individu-alistic methodology, it suffers from the crucial viewpoint that allows reflections to be made about the validity of empirical proposals. Above all, it takes a merely sys-temic perspective; its view of life is incorrect or non-existent (Ulrich 1993: 29–35).

To overcome the shortcomings of corrective economic ethics –shown as a limiter of economic activity– and functional economic ethics –which reflects only on the mechanisms that best operate in satisfying a given n in economics– Ulrich proposes combining economic rationality and practical rationality to unravel "(…) the nor-mative and axiological assumptions of economic rationality itself" (Conill 2006b: 70). In other words, the intention here is to reconcile both rationalities so that they are complemented in the hard task of: (a) specifying a minimum deontological char-acter; (b) encouraging the reciprocal recognition of the communicative compe-tences of those involved or the affected parties, resolving existing conflicts through dialogue and consensus; (c) critically reflecting on the preferences that allow them to be rationally clarified and put in order so that economic rationality criticises its own normative assumptions and becomes aware of its own ethics; and (d) returning economic rationality the sense of non-systemic presuppositions by returning the economic system to the political and institutional order, and the lifeworld of con-temporary society (Ulrich 1993: 40–48). As Ulrich argues that:

> Economic rationality, as it is "known" from the history of dogmas and theory, must not be only limited, nor be applied, but be transformed ethically-philosophically, so that it is immediately located in reason. This is not disparaging about the original conception of economic rationality, but expresses only the unavoidable ethics primate (as the normative logics of people's unconditioned recognition) before the economy (as the normative logics of conditioned cooperation among individuals who act as being strictly guided by its useful-ness and success). The ethics primate is found in the essence of the "matter "and takes a general perspective of the rational economic task as rational action. (Ulrich 2008: 99)

The key therefore lies in understanding, firstly, that a regulatory idea exists, based on which rationality is guided in economic activity processes that go beyond the mere interest in personal well-being; and, secondly, its main concern is to seek the ethical minimums that allow cooperation between economic agents and, thus, the correct undertaking of economic activity. Finally, these moral minimums are neither external to economic reason itself, as they form a constitutive part of this reason, nor are they justified by their capacity to manage improvements in the results of the economic process results, but rather by the mutual recognition of the dignity we deserve as rational beings (Ulrich 1993: 45–46). For this reason, it is essential to submit the economic reason to a reflection process about its own identity and about the assumptions that constitute it. This reflection will allow it to rediscover the existence of minimum ethics which, far from having been imposed or coming from outside – extra-economic – are clearly shown to form a constituent part of society.

Accordingly, for Ulrich, the ethical transformation of economic rationality is feasible with an ethical-discursive approach based on what is moral, as in the proposal developed by Apel and Habermas. This is because, from it, it is possible to reconstruct the validity aims of rational economic activity; in other words, those pragmatic conditions of the language that enable "(…) the argumentative agreement on the legitimate hopes of all those involved in the process of creating value or those affected by it" (Ulrich 2008: 112). In this way, the rational management of scarce resources – e science – is intrinsically linked to those matters "(…) about the rational ethics treatment of the social conflicts among all those involved —legitimacy—" (Ulrich 2008: 112). Adopting this position means accepting that managing efficiency based on economic rationality devoid of a moral reflection is impossible since "(…) the rational solution of conflicts about the distribution of costs and profits (internal and external) of the economic task is a normative problem that cannot be solved in purely economic rationality categories" (Ulrich 2008: 112–113). In this way, legitimacy becomes a condition of the possibility of undertaking economic activity itself and, therefore, of society and its citizens; a moral demand which, in order to be met, requires an attempt to redesign the economic rationality that gives ethics meaning and capacity as an intrinsic part of its internal structure:

> The unconditional moral demand that seeks to be recognised as a normative condition of any rational action, is that of legitimacy (…). So, it is a matter of extending the economic rationality idea so that it includes 'rational' legitimacy as the constitutive ethical-rational condition. With it, the idea of some basic guidance for the ethical integration of economic rationality is reached. (Ulrich 2008: 112)

Since it was made, Ulrich's integrative proposal has considerably influenced the development of various currents of thought and theoretical-practical proposals of applying what is moral to the macro- and meso-economic level. However, this influence is not devoid of criticism, or of guidelines to improve its suitability and specification in the practical domain for several reasons:

Firstly, by recognising the most formal and normative Kantian position as the only possibility of achieving objectivity in the field of economics, the proposal does not put other major contributions of Kantian thought to good use (Conill 2006b: 71). For example, the emotive nature underlying the commitment of mutual respect for another person's dignity – a reciprocal recognition which is simultaneously communicative and emotive – conditions the possibility of any dialogue process between valid interlocutors whose objective is to be understood by one another in terms of worldly matters (Cortina 2010). Moreover, there is the *unsociable sociability* of human beings, a Kantian concept that "(…) expresses a historic dynamism through mankind's natural tendencies and impulses" (Conill 2006b: 206–210), which can also be applied to the economic world.

Secondly, when it comes to focusing its arguments on what is normative and formal, the integrative approach neglects to go more deeply into the level of suitability; i.e., interpreting contexts and their logic to "(…) more appropriately understand economic activity, its rationality and some notions to which Ulrich resorts to in order to interpret it in the modern world (e.g., those of freedom, the person and citizenship)" (Conill 2006b: 72).

Thirdly, because when reducing applied ethics to corrective and functional aspects in order to criticise it and censor it, the integrative proposal establishes false reasoning (through *precipitated induction*, for instance). Among other aspects, it is not true that any methodological proposal to apply ethics is built around two worlds: justification and application; it is not possible to associate all existing applied ethics proposals with a corrective or functional approach; and it is not true that the integrative proposal is an alternative to applied ethics because, in fact, it is still a specific applied type of ethics (Conill 2003a: 122–123).

Fourthly, when restricting its arguments to the normative conflict that underlies the modern economic notion – that of the duality between two normative logics – the integrative approach ends up discriminating against experiential reasoning, as opposed to the normative and formal kind, and this attitude could lead to abstractive fraud (Conill 2006b: 75).

Fifthly, because when it pays attention to *homo oeconomicus'* transformation of perfect and complete rationality through a constant process of self-criticism concerning the normative assumptions and fundamental concepts that shape it, giving it meaning and legitimacy, the integrative proposal is no longer concerned about the theoretical development of economics (Panchi 2004: 324) and the role played by feelings and emotions in rational actions and processes during economic decision-making (Calvo 2012, 2013).

Sixthly, because when focused mainly on integrating the level of the foundation and the level of the application, the integrative approach lacks any necessary reflection about the level of suitability of universal principles and norms. Here, the main task involves guaranteeing its proper application to and implementation in different areas of human activity (García-Marzá 2004: 124–128).

For these reasons, *integrative economic ethics* is an interesting, but insufficient, applied ethics proposal. In line with this, Jesús Conill (2003b, 2006b) or Domingo García-Marzá (2004), among others, consider it necessary to specify a more suitable economic ethics proposal; one that lives up to the expectations of our times. It is a proposal which, like Ulrich's, begins with the basic assumptions of ethics in the discursive sense – dialogue and a possible understanding among those involved in or affected by the norm – and one supported by a suitable method to apply what is moral, which is "(…) capable of capturing the peculiarities of the modern economy, particularly its current development stage" (Conill 2003b: 9).

In line with this, over the last two decades the Valencia School has proposed a reflexive discursive-type framework whose margins have been revised and extended to enrich and promote Apel and Habermas' original proposal. This has managed to correct some of its limitations by: (a) minimising the original proposal's excessive proceduralism; (b) extending the basic tasks of the ethics; (c) contributing proposals that allow a plausible process to be specified to apply moral knowledge based on the given contexts and cases related to all human activities, such as critical hermeneutics; and (d) including the cordiality aspect that allows theory to adapt to the behavioural and motivational reality, shown by fieldwork and laboratory experiments with strategy games, just as a *cordial community* would expect and desire. All this shapes a proposal for *cordial discursive ethics* that combines reason and emotion so it can emerge, develop and be promoted in the practical sphere.

Cordial discursive ethics proposes the hermeneutic-critical approach as a suitable method for moral considerations. This is because, among other aspects, it corrects and/or puts right the shortcomings pointed out in Ulrich's integrative approach by extending the concept of communicative reason using experiential reasoning. Experiential reasoning avoids excessive formalism and lack of interpretation and, in this way, manages to show the moral meaning of economic activity in real processes, and in economic and ethical theoretical reflection (Conill 2003a, 124).

The hermeneutic-critical method of applying moral considerations begins from the idea that only the adaptation of what is universal using a circular critical interpretation process allows the praxis to become a specific aspect that can be implemented (Conill 2000a, b, 2003a, b, 2006a, b; Cortina 2010). Among other matters, as the norm to be applied cannot be unlinked from the context of the activity that gives it meaning, we cannot claim it remains merely as conventionalism devoid of the critical character of an overall and plural reality into which it must be inserted (Cortina 2003: 31). It is therefore necessary to unravel and critically interpret the principles and the actual values of each context, for example a deepening in hermeneutic-critical terms which "(…) not only incites creating the conditions in which to apply discursive ethics (e.g., in the situation of those who hold no power in today's global jungle), but also opens out to others, to different cultures, to what is strange" (Conill 2006b, 72).

From this hermeneutic-critical perspective, applying moral considerations is not related merely to the deductive process, where attempts are made to discern the moral principles that have to guide different areas of activity, or the inductive process, where the maximum patterns of behavior are drawn and justified through empirical, even circular, observation when the meaning of both directions is combined as a whole. That makes it a matter of continuous movement which, firstly, penetrates the professional praxis itself to interpret the specific fields of activity, and to grasp the principles, norms and values that constitute the civic ethics on which they are founded, sustained and properly developed. Secondly, it is introduced into the domain of critical deliberation to seek moral justification and deal with its adaptation and the possibilities of specifying all the contexts to be applied.

Regarding the economic praxis, by interpreting the specific circumstances of economic processes and their consequences, the hermeneutic-critical discourse is concerned with discovering whether the morally justified norm can be applied. To this end, it is introduced into the reconstruction at two levels: the normative and real levels. The normative level refers to clarifying and justifying the framework that allows the harmonisation, robustness and durability of societies with a post-conventional level of moral development –basic rights that guarantee both its citizens' peaceful coexistence (Cortina 1990, 239–253)– and the coordination of action that allows common objectives to be specified and fulfilled. The real level refers to the specific contexts of action taken to unravel the action framework that modulates and guides activity (Cortina and Martínez 1996: 160–164). In this way, economic rationality emerges, along with the task of identifying not only the universal ethical principles that shape the normative framework, but also the values, virtues and strategies that allow them to develop properly (Cortina 2003: 21).

Cordial discursive ethics starts with public civic ethics of shared minimums, as in Apel and Habermas' original proposal, but goes further by including a necessary moment of cordiality that makes them human (Cortina 2007b: 191). In this way, the excessive formalism of the original proposal is avoided, and, the critical reflection process – as with the Kantian proposal – includes moral good, the reason for action, purposes, values and moral virtues, without limiting its field of action to norms. Thus, it introduces a necessary emotive element which, along with a reflective elements on norms, purposes, reasons, values and virtues, allows to be implemented and promoted in practice: *cordial reason*.

First of all, cordial reason stems from the idea that values, principles and ethical rules emerge, enrich and purify the heart of societies with a post-conventional level of moral development by means of dialogue and intersubjective agreement reached among all those affected. It is therefore a matter of paying attention to and showing respect for those minimum levels of justice shared by citizens with different good life projects "(…) that lead them to consider their coexistence as something fertile" (Cortina 1993: 196). The citizen-based, minimum and public ethics that is expressed through "(…) values of freedom, equality and solidarity, as materialised in human rights, the value of active tolerance, and the impossibility of proposing to others the ideal of life itself if it is not through dialogue and testimony" (Cortina 2000: 42).

Secondly, cordial reason understands that there is a communicative link between beings capable of talking and acting who participate in practical discourses where different worldly things are discussed through reasoning (Cortina 2007b: 214–215). This reciprocal reason of people's argumentative capacities brings about a *ligatio* that *ob-liges* internally without having to resort to the different elements external to the relationship itself, such as gifts or coercion of law, because people see one another and know that these elements are necessary to discern what is fair and true. As Cortina reasons, anyone who:

> (…) performs communicative actions and takes part in reasoning processes, when they do so, they recognise that any gifted person with a communication competence is a valid interlocutor, which is linked to a communicative bind and, therefore, to "certain duties"; (s)he discovers a *ligatio* that *ob-liges* internally, rather than from an alien proposal. (2007a: 116)

Thirdly, cordial reason understands that there is also an emotional link that predisposes people to want to relate with fellow citizens in order to fulfil interests with a mutually shared sense, to value their lives and those of others as being worthy of being preserved; to feel compassion for those who suffer and benevolence for those who need it, and so on. This is a *ligatio* that *ob-liges,* expressed through recognition of facing beings with an absolute value whose lives are originally bound. As Cortina reasons,

> (…) it is a link among human beings who recognise themselves in some way as "flesh of the same flesh" and "blood of the same blood", and should, hence, be felt and be known that they are obliged to mutually back one another in order to perform and complete projects of lives worthy of being lived. (2007b: 215)

Fourthly, cordial reason suggests that both links –communicative and emotional– complement one other, and are two sides of one coin, as one cannot be implemented without the other (Cortina 2010: 17). Knowing what is fair is of very little value if people do not appreciate the existence of fairness in the world. Likewise, estimating what is fair is of barely any value if people are not capable of participating in practice discourses in which debates take place and agreements are reached.

Fifthly, cordial reason states that the duty involved in both links – communicative and emotional– does not stem from gratitude shown for help received because this would leave all those people who were unable to respond adequately to it with no feasible link, only those who could only feel respect for the dignity discovered behind the human capacity to reason about what affects them and their own responsibility, and who can feel emotion for themselves and others (Cortina 2007b: 215–216). This dignifies the human being as an absolute value from which a series of rights and duties emanates and which *ob-liges* those who are already linked to act in a given way.

> (…) We recognise that links already exist, we realise that we are substantially linked. So "unlinking" from some or many implies having to take an active rejection position against them. It is not only a matter of us not creating a link with them, but of us actively rejecting the existing link as we deny considering those who are in some way already linked: we decline an *ob-ligation* that already exists. And *decline* is an active verb, not a passive one, and is also a transitive verb. (Cortina 2007a: 115)

In short, it is a matter of a rationality which rises to the demands of the historical moment, in which reason and emotion go hand-in-hand to create cordial links that are optimally beneficial for all the related parties, and where people fulfil their maximum happiness as regards others based on cordial reciprocity within the limits set by the minimum levels of justice in public civic ethics. Such rationality meets that observed in the fieldwork and laboratory experiments done with strategy games, and with that wished for and demanded by a cordial society with a post-conventional level of moral and emotional development.

From this perspective, including cordiality will allow economic rationality to be introduced at the right emotional and moral point, which will allow cordial relationality tending to offer maximum profits. This is particularly the case because it allows the creation and promotion of cordial goods that condition the possibility of economic, social and human development. In other words, any shared resource or collective heritage that emerges and develops thanks to the human relationships shaped by communication and emotional recognition and respect shown to human dignity based on cordial reason ethics.

Bibliography

Apel, Karl-Otto. 1998. *Teoría de la verdad y ética del discurso.* Barcelona: Paidós.
Bowles, Samuel, and Herbert Gintis. 1998. Is equality Passe? Homo Reciprocans and the future of egalitarian politics. *Boston Review* 23 (6): 1–27.
———. 2003. The origins of human cooperation. In *The Genetic and Cultural Origins of Cooperation*, ed. P. Hammerstein, 429–444. Cambridge, MA: MIT Press.
———. 2004. *Homo Economicus and Zoon Politikon: Behavioral Game Theory and Political Behavior,* 1–16. http://www.umass.edu/preferen/gintis/Homo%20Economicus%20and%20 Zoon%20Politikon.pdf. Accesed 25 Sept 2017.
———. 2006. Social Preferences, Homo Economicus and Zoon Politikon. In *Work of Contextual Political Analysis*, ed. Robert E. Goodin and Charles Tilly, 172–186. New York: Oxford University Press.
———. 2011. *A Cooperative Species. Human Reciprocity and its Evolution.* Princeton: Princeton University Press.
Calvo, Patrici. 2012. Cooperación y sentimientos morales en el enfoque de racionalidad económica de Elinor Ostrom. Una mirada crítica de la teoría de juegos. In *XIX Congrés Valencià de Filosofia*, ed. Enric Casaban, 425–441. Valencia: SFPV.
———. 2013. Neuro-racionalidad: heterogeneidad motivacional y compromiso moral. *Daimon. Revista Internacional de Filosofía* 59: 157–170.
Conill, Jesús. 2000a. Globalización y ética económica. *Papeles de ética, economía y dirección* 5: 1–8.
———. 2000b. Marco ético-económico de la empresa moderna. In *La ética de la empresa. Claves para una nueva ética empresarial*, ed. Adela Cortina, 51–74. Madrid: Trotta.
———. 2003a. El carácter ético y deliberativo de las éticas aplicadas. In *Razón pública y éticas aplicadas. Los caminos de la razón práctica en una sociedad pluralista*, ed. Adela Cortina and Domingo García-Marzá, 121–142. Madrid: Tecnos.
———. 2003b. El sentido ético de la economía en tiempos de globalización. *Revista de Filosofía* 29: 9–15.
———. 2006a. *Ética hermenéutica. Crítica desde la facticidad.* Madrid: Tecnos.
———. 2006b. *Horizontes de Economía Ética.* Madrid: Tecnos.
Cortina, Adela. 1990. *Ética sin moral.* Madrid: Tecnos.
———. 1992. *Ética mínima.* Madrid: Tecnos.
———. 1993. *Ética aplicada y democracia radical.* Madrid: Tecnos.
———. 1996. El estatuto de la ética aplicada. Hermenéutica crítica de las actividades humanas. *Isegoría. Revista de Filosofía Moral y Política* 13: 119–134.
———. 2000. Ética empresarial en el contexto de una ética cívica. In *La Ética de la empresa. Claves para una nueva Ética empresarial*, ed. Adela Cortina, 35–50. Madrid: Trotta.
———. 2003. Ética de la empresa y desarrollo económico. In *Construir confianza*, ed. Adela Cortina, 39–54. Madrid: Trotta.
———. 2007a. Ethica cordis. *Isegoría. Revista de Filosofía Moral y Política* 37: 113–126.
———. 2007b. *Ética de la razón cordial. Educar en la ciudadanía en el siglo XXI.* Nobel: Oviedo.
———. 2008. European economic ethics research a diagnosis. *Zeitschrift für Wirtschafts- und Unternehmensethik* 9 (1): 10–27.
———. 2010. *Justicia cordial.* Madrid: Trotta.

————. 2013. *¿Para qué sirve realmente… la ética?* Barcelona: Paidós Ibérica.
————. 2017. *Aporofobia, el rechazo al pobre. Un desafío para la democracia.* Barcelona: Paidós Ibérica.
Cortina, Adela, and Emilio Martínez. 1996. *Ética.* Madrid: Akal.
Diccionario de la Lengua Española. 2017. *Cordial.* http://dle.rae.es/?id=AqyMdg9. Accessed 28 Sept 2017.
García-Marzá, Domingo. 2004. *Ética empresarial: del diálogo a la confianza.* Madrid: Trotta.
Genovesi, Antonio. 1786. *Lecciones de comercio, ó bien de economía civil. Tomo III.* Trans. Victorian de Villava. Madrid.
Goffman, Erving. 1956. *The Presentation of Self in Everyday Life.* Edinburgh: University of Edinburgh.
Habermas, Jürgen. 1987 [1981]. *Teoría de la acción comunicativa. Vol. 1 & 2.* Madrid: Taurus [English version: Habermas, Jürgen. 1984. *Theory of Communicative Action Vol. 1: Reason and the Rationalization of Society.* Boston: Beacon Press; Habermas, Jürgen. 1987. *Theory of Communicative Action Vol. 2 Lifeworld and System: A Critique of Functionalist Reason.* Boston: Beacon Press].
————. 1991 [1984]. *Escritos sobre moralidad y eticidad.* Barcelona: Paidós.
————. 2001. *Justification and Application. Remarks on Discourse Ethics.* Cambridge, MA: MIT Press.
Hugo, Víctor. 1862. *Les Misérables.* Brussels: A. Lacroix, Verboeckhoven & Ce.
Kant, Immanuel. 2005. *Groundwork of the Metaphysics of Morals.* Toronto: Broadview.
Krugman, Paul. 2013, Abril 13. Correlation, causality, and casuistry. *The New York Times.* https://krugman.blogs.nytimes.com/2013/04/18/correlation-causality-and-casuistry/. Accessed 28 Sept 2017.
Olson, Mancur. 1965. *The Logic of Collective Action: Public Goods and the Theory of Groups.* Harvard: Harvard University Press.
Ortega, José y Gasset. 1960 [1929]. *The Revolt of the Masses.* New York: Norton & Co.
Ostrom, Elinor. 1990. *Governing the Commons. The Evolution of Institutions for Collective Action.* Cambridge: Cambridge University Press.
————. 1998. A behavioral approach to the rational choice theory of collective action. *American Political Science Review* 92 (1): 1–22.
————. 2000. Prefacio a la edición en español de *Governing de commons.* In *El Gobierno de los Comunes. La Evolución de las Instituciones de Acción Colectiva,* ed. Elinor Ostrom, 9–13. Mexico: Fondo Cultural de Economía.
————. 2003. Toward a behavioral theory linking trust, reciprocity, and reputation. In *Trust & Reciprocity. Interdisciplinary Lessons from Experimental Research,* ed. Elinor Ostrom and James Walker, 19–79. New York: Russell Sage Foundation.
————. 2012. Experiments combining communication with punishment options demonstrate how individuals can overcome social dilemmas. *Behavioral and Brain Sciences* 35 (1): 33–34.
Oxford English Dictionary. 2017. *Cordial.* https://en.oxforddictionaries.com/definition/monitor. Accessed 25 Sept 2017.
Panchi, Luis-Augusto. 2004. *De ética económica a economía ética. Fundamentos a partir de una racionalidad ético-interpretativa, con una aplicación al caso ecuatoriano.* Quito: Ediciones Abya-Yala.
Sen, Amartya. 1977. Rational fools. A critique of the behavioral foundations of economic theory. In Frank Hahn and Martin Hollis, ed. *Philosophy and public affairs,* 317–344. Oxford: Blackwell Publishing.
————. 1987. *On ethics and economy.* Oxford: Blackwell Publishing.
————. 2000. *Development as freedom.* New York: Anchor.
————. 2002. *Rationality and freedom.* Harvard: Harvard Belknap Press.
————. 2009. *The Idea of Justice.* Cambridge, MA: The Belknap Press of Harvard University Press.
Simon, Herbert A. 1955. Behavioral model of rational choice. *The Quarterly Journal of Economics* 69 (1): 99–118.

Stiglitz, Joseph E. 2012. *The price of inequality: How today's divided society endangers our future*. New York: W. W. Norton & Co.

Tomasello, Michael 2010. *¿Por qué cooperamos?*. Madrid: Katz. [English vertion: 2009. *Why we cooperate*. Cambridge, MA: The MIT Press].

———. 2014a. *A natural history of human thinking*. Cambridge, MA: Harvard University Press.

———. 2014b. The ultra-social animal. *European Journal of Social Psychology* 44: 187–194.

Tuomela, Raimo. 2007. *The philosophy of sociality: The shared point of view*. New York: Oxford University Press.

Ulrich, Peter. 1993. *Bases para una ética económica crítica*. Alcalá de Henares: Instituto de Dirección y Organización de Empresas/Universidad de Alcalá.

———. 2008. *Ética Económica Integrativa: Fundamentos de una economía al servicio de la vida*. Quito: Ediciones Adya-Yala.

Vaish, Amrisha, Malinda Carpenter, and MIchael Tomasello. 2010. Young children selectively avoid helping people with harmful intentions. *Child Development* 81 (6): 1661–1669.

Warneken, Felix, and Michael Tomasello. 2006. Altruistic helping in human infants and young Chimpanzees. *Science* 311 (5765): 1301–1303.

Chapter 8
Cordial Goods: The Role of Intangibles in Economics

Abstract Extending the margins of economic rationality in an effective and ethical-critical sense through cordiality opens the door to the possibility of managing and promoting the intangible capital which, just like reciprocity, trust, affinity or reputation, is a condition of the possibility of economic progress. This is because, among other things, these allow the establishment and development of the relational processes, like cooperation, that allow it but with an underlying emotional and communicative dimension, which cannot be duly managed through merely strategic-technical and calculative-instrumental rationality. It is also because these assets are a both a means and an end for the economy as they are an essential element to deal with managing common good and are, at the same time, a special kind of common good. The aim of this chapter is to show the role, characteristics and cordial dimension that underlie the common goods that are so important for the economic domain, such as reciprocity, trust or reputation, through the works of Elinor Ostrom, Pierpaolo Donati, Amartya Sen or Domingo García-Marzá, among others.

The conclusions drawn from *Global Human Capital Trends 2016* by Deloitte reveal the role that some intangible goods, such as commitment, trust, care, affinity, reputation, identity, recognition, compassion, reciprocity and others can play in economic, social and human development. Among other relevant things, this annual report analyses and shares the data of more than 7000 surveys conducted with professionals – mainly business and human resources leaders – from 130 countries. It also suggests the lack of sense and interest shown by employees in what they do, which generates a disincentive that has a strong negative effect on their commitment and involvement with the organisation, and therefore affects their professional careers and self-fulfilment, as well as the organisation's productivity and profits. Given this fact, the report offers some guidelines on how to properly manage these intangible, but necessary, goods for the good health of the organisation and human capital involved. It also indicates that happiness and commitment, for instance, do not combine well with salary bonuses, recreational rooms and picturesque offices. Meanwhile, it reveals that feeling at ease in one's workplace helps to: promote freedom and autonomy; create a shared culture; improve internal communication; reinforce recognition; design working atmospheres that imply; and involve people in

© Springer International Publishing AG, part of Springer Nature 2018   127
P. Calvo, *The Cordial Economy - Ethics, Recognition and Reciprocity*,
Ethical Economy 55, https://doi.org/10.1007/978-3-319-90784-0_8

different business projects; devise training plans where it is the professional who decides; and promote participation and the implementation of a leadership model based on team management, among other aspects (Deloitte 2016: 4–5). There are therefore reasons of the heart and the head lying behind the proper management of these goods.

Other studies, like *State of the Global Workplace: Employee Engagement Insights for Business Leaders Worldwide*, by Gallup and *the Edelman Trust Barometer Executive Summary. Annual Global Study*, have since 2003 given a good account of the economic impact of deficient management of some of these intangible goods indicated by *Global Human Capital Trends 2016*. Firstly, in theory the Gallup report on the consequences of commitment in economy estimates that annual losses through employees' lack of commitment would be around 450–550 billion US dollars, about 112–138 billion euros in Germany, and some 52–70 billion pounds sterling in the UK (Gallup 2013: 7). Secondly, the Edelman barometer on the trust civil society shows in economic institutions, organisations and business reflects a constant drop in its levels since the crisis began; a causal relationship between increased mistrust and dissatisfaction with business objectives; and general expectations among most of the people surveyed: economic institutions, organisations and business should not only consider maximising economic profits if they wish to gain civil society's trust, they will also have to worry about environmental respect and social and human development through specific actions in matters of education and training, health and well-being, the natural environment, human rights, equalities, and so on.

As these studies have proliferated, it is not surprising that economics institutions, organisations and business are more concerned about the possibility of managing these goods practically. Among other matters, it is increasingly difficult to ignore the necessary character of such goods as a condition to enable better economic activity development and better working towards business objectives. However, they are goods whose specificity – their common and emancipatory nature, their relational and communicative structure, and their coordinating and self-fulfilling capacity – demands suitable treatment that matches the expectations that come into play. This is especially so because they are goods that do not combine well with their merely instrumental and strategic use, which complicates their emergence and promotion in a domain like the economic one, where the predominant economic theory encourages strategic-instrumental rationality and penalises all complementary or alternative behaviour, despite providing better results in practice.

In spite of such diatribes and impediments, they are goods with considerable historic and long-standing tradition within the economic and social theory. At least since the Classical period, these goods have been worked on from numerous viewpoints. Although many have been marginalised by current neoclassical thought given their intangible nature and the apparent impossibility of measuring and quantifying their genuine impact on activity, nowadays they still form part of the important and enriching alternative socio-economic proposals and not to the conventional theoretical model.

The objective of this chapter is to elucidate the role, characteristics and, above all, the possible management of assets such as reciprocity, trust or reputation, with an underlying strategic-technical and calculative-instrumental dimension, which is also ethical-cordial. Therefore, the role that civil society and institutions play in managing the common good is analysed with the works of Ostrom. Secondly, the contributions made from the economy and relational sociology to manage the common good are considered with the works of authors like Zamagni and Pierpaolo Donati. Third and finally, the communicative and affective dimension that underlies intangible assets like reciprocity, trust and reputation is shown, with the works of Sen, and mainly those of García-Marzá.

8.1 Common Goods: Intangibles As Essential Assets for the Economy

Concern for common goods dates back to Classical Greece and continues in our world today. Plato, Aristotle, Saint Thomas Aquinas, Machiavelli, Erasmus of Rotterdam, Hobbes, Antonio Genovesi, John Stuart Mill, Ostrom, Zamagni and Donati are some of the thinkers who have reflected on this throughout history, in connection with economic development, governance, public happiness, law, peace, morale, excellence, social and human progress, species survival, cooperation, social cohesion and natural resources, among other things. In this way, common goods have been related to tangible and intangible resources that are shared, enjoyed and managed by community members, and whose coexistence, coordination and progress depend on them to a greater or lesser extent.[1]

Nevertheless, with the current of neoclassical thought appearing and its influence on human activities in any area in the twentieth and twenty-first centuries, on one hand, intangible common goods like commitment, trust or reputation were marginalised and disparaged while, on the other hand, tangible common goods, for example, natural resources in forests, rivers or seas, were subject to the logic of the efficiency and coercion of law. In other words, from this point in time, the management of the latter was left to governments after they became public goods, or profit-making organisations after they became private goods, or governments and organisations at the same time after becoming a type of public-private good, owned by the State and managed by profit-making organisations.[2]

This change in mentality about the best way to manage common goods properly was strongly influenced by the 1968 publication entitled "The Tragedy of the Commons" by Garrett Hardin.[3] This pessimistic and depressing work metaphorically

---

[1] For an in-depth study of the historical and conceptual development of common goods, see Álvaro Ramis (2017) and Zamagni (2007a, b, 2014, 2016).

[2] The first-time common goods were considered "(…) in economic terms goes back to 1911, when the American economist Katharine Coman published her study 'Some unsettled problems of irrigation', in the *American Economic Review*" (Zamagni 2014: 8).

[3] As Zamagni (2014: 8) points out, "William Lloyd was the first author to describe the phenomenon that would later become known as "the tragedy of commons", in two lectures given at Oxford University in 1832".

discerned the destiny of common goods if their management continued to be entrusted to civil society: they would disappear. Hardin's thesis began with human beings' natural tendency to maximise their own benefit no matter what the cost. Applying this axiom to the exploitation processes of common goods allowed Hardin to forecast the point of no return based on common sense which all processes of collective action reach if not coordinated by an external institution with the capacity to generate binding rules of compelling strength: a limited resource being overexploited that can, therefore, disappear. In this way, Hardin stressed two worrying and unsolvable issues that demanded having to leave the management of a common good with governments and private organisations. Firstly, any attempt made by civil society to coordinate action to manage a given tangible good or resource of a collective heritage kind, be it a forest, a river basin, grazing land, a sea or an urban setting, proves futile and counterproductive without the help of external coercion that forces the parties to stick to any agreements reached. Secondly, trusting agents' capacities to cooperate and coordinate action is an entelechy that inevitably leads to the disappearance of the managed common good or resource.

For Hardin, human incapacity to be able to materialise shared objectives, and to cooperate and coordinate action to seek their satisfaction for their natural tendency towards selfishness, is an unbridgeable gap and any attempt to clear it ends up inexorably becoming fatal for humanity. Human beings maximise their own interests, and anyone who allows access to the common good will take as much advantage as possible of it to exhaust it.

> Therein is the tragedy. Each man is locked into a system that compels him to increase his herd without limit – in a world that is limited. Ruin is the destination toward which all men rush, each pursuing his own best interest in a society that believes in the freedom of the commons. Freedom in a common space brings ruin to all. (Hardin 1968: 1244)

In this way Hardin suggests that the main problem in managing common goods lies in the impossibility that those involved will cooperate in seeking a mutually beneficial purpose on which their activity, survival and/or development depends; for instance, efficiently managing a limited resource. Hence Hardin defended its transformation into a private, a public or a public-private good as the sole possibility of avoiding its predictable and tragic end:

1. *Private good*: it is a matter of privatising the common good by selling it to a profit-making organisation. Those organisations, controlled by efficiency logics, could control its overexploitation and avoid tragedy. Hardin recognises that transforming the good into privately-owned property is not a fair solution, but between a lack of justice and such a necessary resource disappearing, opting for the former is preferable (1968: 1247).
2. *Public good*: this is when the State is in charge of managing the common good. As an institution that guarantees everything that is public, it has the necessary means to control access to the common good and ensures its efficient management by guaranteeing its sustainability and survival in time (1968: 1245). Hardin understands that converting it into a public good would inhibit the freedom of its

use, which he justifies by arguing that establishing some "(…) alternative to common goods does not have to be perfectly fair to be preferable" (1968: 1247).

3. *Public-private good*: this is a mixed solution in which the State becomes the owner and guarantees the good, and a private business or organisation becomes its manager and usufructuary. So, the State will maintain its rights and control over the common good, but will transfer its management and exploitation to a private organisation governed by efficiency logic (1968: 1247–1248).

The three solutions offered by Hardin reveal his complete mistrust of civil society's own capacities and resources to be able to properly manage those common goods on which the survival and the development of its good life projects depend. Then there is the merely economistic and mercantilist sense of common goods, linked only to natural and tangible resources with a market value, whose exploitation can generate a sustained economic benefit.

Since it was published in 1968, Hardin's article has acted as a guide for preparing and implementing government policies on managing common goods which, based on one or more of these three solutions, has ignored civil society. Even today, although Ostrom showed in 1990 that transforming a common good into a private, public or private-public good further worsens the overexploitation of natural ecosystems and, therefore, makes them inefficient and likely to disappear, most States still mistrust civil society's capacity to manage goods or resources of collective heritage in a sustained and sustainable way. The same applies even to transnational common goods that can be made universal, like air quality, exploiting oceans, preserving biodiversity, defending human rights, managing scientific knowledge and universal public health, among many other matters.

A practical case is found in biological resource centres (BRCs), also known as biobanks. These specific common goods or resources are defined by Spanish legislation (*Law 14/2007, of 3 July, on Biomedical Research*) as any "(…) public or private non-profit-making establishment that includes a collection of biological samples offered for diagnosis or biomedical research purposes, and organised as a technical unit with quality, order and fate criteria" (Jefatura del Estado 2007: 28830). Thus, all civil society's possible initiatives are excluded or limited through the creation of institutions or organisations of collective action, which could be more efficient and sustainable in the medium and long term; or through participatory processes based on citizen commitment to preserve and improve an inheritance of great human and transgenerational value.

The same occurs with common goods that are neither natural nor have a market price. Available immaterial goods, such as trust, care, reciprocity, reputation, affinity, participation and commitment that emerge from not merely self-interested relations, depend on mutual expectations of technical, strategic, emotional and moral questions, and sustain the correct, efficient and capable management of other tangible and natural common goods, regardless of whether or not they are relational. So, they are goods which, despite having been marginalised by the predominant economic theory for over a century, are now starting to be perceived as something that cannot be waived to carry out any human activity, even economic activity.

Without trust, reciprocity and reputation, for example, it is very hard for suppliers to supply, customers to purchase products or services, stakeholders to invest their money in a business project, the media to publish news about the activity undertaken, workers to form part of the personnel and to get completely involved in accomplishing business performance, and so on. Similarly, if there is no active commitment, the necessary social change, with all its potential, is unlikely to take place or spread.

Raising awareness about the value of such matters has returned an interest in common goods in a broad sense, and not only in tangible and natural goods. Accordingly, political scientists Ostrom and Carole J. Uhlaner, economists Zamagni, Oliver E. Williamson and Benedetto Gui, sociologists Donati, Renate Mayntz and Wolgang Hofkirchner, and philosophers like Jacques Maritain and Martha Nussbaum have worked on their conceptualisation, the role they play in the economy and society, their potential, sustainability and survival, and their management and implementation in various areas of human activity.

Among other important matters, their studies stress the need to extend the concept by unlinking it from its merely economistic and tangible sense to open the way for those goods which, like citizen participation, reciprocity or commitment, play a key role in the development of societies, economics and politics. Civil society can also be included in the management of the common good because it is necessary, firstly, to specify what a society's common good is. Legitimising it socially and morally does not depend on governments or experts, but on the intersubjective agreement of all those affected by it (Cortina 2007b). This is secondly, because managing the common good efficiently, sustainably and constantly requires the collective actions of institutions, organisations and the citizens of society, as shown by various case studies throughout history and conducted worldwide (Cárdenas and Ostrom 2004; Ostrom 1990, 2003; Ostrom and Nagendra 2010). All this underlies the notion that the efficient, sustainable and optimally beneficial management of a society's material or immaterial common goods is possible and promotes, but does not exclude, limit or control civil society's participation, through the collective action of institutions, organisations and initiatives, just as different practical cases have demonstrated worldwide and throughout history (Ostrom 1990, 1999).

In line with this, it is worth highlighting that promoting relationships shaped by reciprocity in a cordial sense could help to generate and develop these intangible common goods in various areas of human activity, such as the economic sphere, and to also manage and develop all other tangible goods, such as common, public or private natural resources. This means implementing relational, reflexive and emotional reason according to what has been empirically observed in laboratory experiments and fieldwork, and what is expected and desired by a cordial society whose citizens know they are capable of entering into a dialogue about what affects and interest them. They feel capable of feeling emotion for themselves and for others, and being committed to their practical performance. Accordingly, some theoretical proposals, like relational goods and moral resources, help to relate reciprocity to managing and promoting common goods, and to reconstruct the conditions making their generation and development possible in a competitive area of activity like economics.

8.2 Relational Goods: The Potential of Common Goods for Transformation and Realisation

In the 1980s, various thought currents from human and social sciences mainly showed an interest in the relational dimension of the human being after verifying its involvement in constructing meaning, in correctly developing different areas of human activity, and in specifying the transformation processes of reality and social morphogenesis (Archer 1982, 1987, 1988, 1995; Donati 1986, 2011, 2013). From then on, the progress made in this field gradually resulted in abandoning these interpretations which, consolidated in self-interested behaviours and merely welfare structural effects, ignored, on the one hand, the transforming potential that civil society amasses through the committed participation of its institutions, organisations and associations and promoted, on the other hand, an atomised society made up of isolated, calculating, homogeneous, heteronomous, disembodied individuals incapable of specifying common objectives, and implementing and coordinating the collective actions that make their satisfaction possible. This is how a new paradigm for human and social sciences came about, focusing on the relational value of human beings. One view allowed more accurate observation, analysis, description and interpretation of the complexity of the human being's social and moral reality, underlying the idea of society going through a constant changing process thanks to the reciprocal relationships its citizens establish and develop based on autonomy and commitment. In the words of Sen (2000), these citizens have good reasons to appreciate and estimate anything as being valuable, regardless of whether it has a market price.

The studies conducted from this new relational paradigm allowed the discovery, or better still the rediscovery, of one of the mechanisms of cohesion and coordination of action most widely used by, and relevant for, civil society: *relational goods*, a kind of intangible – transforming and self-fulfilling – common good[4] whose different forms "(...) provide democracy with substance in all its social, cultural, economic and political dimensions" (Donati 2013: 155). Along these lines, and as stated by Donati, a pioneer along with Carole J. Uhlaner in rediscovery, conceptualisation, development and application of relational goods in practice:

> Empirical studies show how widespread they really are. These are goods that are invisible to the naked eye (they are *intangible goods* and are continually sought out by people), but they come into existence only under particular conditions. As examples we could think of goods such as the following: trust between people or families in difficulty who are willing to help one another; a collaborative and serene climate in a company; the feeling of safety among the residents of a neighborhood; a social or health service able to improve the quality of relations between parents and offspring; the spirit of collaboration in a sports team; cooperation among members of an orchestra; an internet site that receives and gives useful information to a group of people interested in that service; and so on (Donati 2014: 21).

---

[4] All relational goods are common, but not all common goods are relational. As Donati argues (2014: 33), "Relational goods are the subset of common goods that can only be generated together: no one who takes part in them can be excluded from them; they cannot be subdivided and are not the sum of individual goods".

The term relational goods was coined by Nussbaum in *The Fragility of Goodness: Luck and Ethics in Greek Tragedy and Philosophy* (1986). Like her reinterpretation of Aristotle's texts about goodness, Nussbaum identified the concept with those shared experiences where the really important point is the relationship constituted, and not its outcome. This is mainly because this relationship is shown as a condition to enable the generation and promotion of the resources implied in the eudaemonia of related agents, such as friendship, trust, reciprocity, identity, commitment, love, participation, compassion or care.[5] These resources are born and die with the established relationship, whose appearance allows stable and humanly enriching interactions to be established for all participants.

From here, several researchers collected and developed the concept from its various areas of knowledge to adapt it to today's context of modern societies, for example, sociologist Donati, economists Benedetto Gui, Bruni, Sugden and Zamagni or political scientist Uhlaner.[6] Certain issues underlie their research works which give them specificity and their own character: (a) they emerge from autonomous, symmetrical and committed interpersonal relationships; (b) they disappear when instrumentalised; (c) they are enriched with use and become poorer with disuse; (d) they allow participants to establish robust, stable cooperative actions, capable of satisfying common interests; (e) they are generated and enjoyed in company; (f) they are democratic and public; (h) they offer relational value, that which is involved in developing human self-fulfilment.[7] When faced with such important questions for human life, it is not surprising that, as Donati argues, "Our life is a continual search for relational goods, but we have a very limited awareness of what they are and how they can be generated and regenerated" (2014: 21).

From all these previous considerations, and following different works in line with them,[8] it is possible to identify certain basic traits that define relational goods and confer them with autonomy as opposed to private goods and public goods especially, for instance, incompatibility with the individualist and the merely self-interested dimension that is the basis of conventional economic theory:

(i) *Identity-like*: these goods are constructed from the alterity of the related parties. Identity is therefore a condition to allow them to be generated and strengthened.

---

[5] From the relational goods perspective, caring has been recently dealt with by economist Cristina Carrasco (2014). Her contributions help to understand necessary aspects to consider in "(…) preparing indicators of time as a measure of care as a relational good" (Carrasco 2014: 49).

[6] The first works that collected and developed the concept were *Relational Goods* and "Participation. Incorporating Sociability into a Theory of Rational Action" (Uhlaner 1989) and "La cultura della vita. Dalla società tradizionale a quella post-moderna" (Donati, 1989).

[7] For further details of relational goods, see Donati (2013, 2015); Donati and Solci (2011) and Uhlaner (2014).

[8] Bruni (2008: 93–95, 2005: 554–557); Bruni and Zamagni (2007: 237–242); Donati (1989, 1991, 2008, 2013, 2014); Gui (2000); Uhlaner (1989: 254, 2014); Zamagni (2006: 57–61, 2008: 480–485, 2009: 11–16, 2010a:72–73, 2010b: 87–89).

(ii) *Reciprocal*: these goods emerge and develop through two-way interpersonal actions. So, they are conditioned to a particular response, in terms of quantity or quality of the bound or bindable parties, whether or not this is known.

(iii) *Fragile*: these goods are based on reciprocal expectations of behaviour between bound or bindable parties. They therefore do not allow any possible external coercion forcing a response to any help received. Freedom is, therefore, the foundation of all reciprocal relations allowing them to emerge and develop.

(iv) *Valuable*: these are goods that are not a good match with instrumentalisation. Their use is merely a mechanism to fulfil a given private objective, as their value is independent of either the social or market function they have.

(v) *Emotional*: these are goods that proliferate from the shared emotions and feelings encouraging the behavioural response of related agents, like gratitude or compassion.

(vi) *Simultaneous*: these are goods used at the same time as they are generated; in other words, where related agents simultaneously *co-produce* and *co-enjoy* the co-generated good. It is therefore not possible to separate the profit made by the agent through its use from the value obtained by all the other agents who participate in the relationship established.

(vii) *Communicative*: these are goods that maintain a communicative dimension as they require understanding to establish a suitable relationship allowing and developing them. So, it is not possible to separate the production process and enjoyment of these goods from generating sense as relationality demands understanding among the involved subjects or those affected by things, actions and decisions.

(viii) *Growing*: these are goods that offer a growing marginal utility, as their value rises with use and falls with disuse. Thus, their behaviour differs from that of other types of goods[9] because the more time and effort invested in producing and enjoying them, the greater the satisfaction experienced by the bound parties.

(ix) Self-fulfilling: these are goods involved in people's self-fulfilment – in meeting maximum levels of happiness – but only if related with others.

(x) Regenerative: these are the goods that make the enrichment and transformation of society and its various areas of human activity possible thanks to the relational processes of social morphogenesis that they enable.

As Donati states, (2014), in this way relational goods become visible when members of society realise that certain goods exist which have no (or can have no),

---

[9] According to Becchetti et al. (2010: 102–104), the law on marginal utility indicates that the satisfaction that a certain good contributes to an individual tends to decrease when used over a long period. This means that, for instance, the experienced utility value when a meal begins starts to fall as the individual feels full, and can even enter a negative phase if eating goes on. So, the value of a given good is measured by its marginal utility rather than its objective utility. Yet this decreasing marginal utility is not applicable to relational goods, as they work in the opposite way to standard goods: the more they are used, the more satisfaction they provide.

owner; do not (or cannot) belong to a group; and are not (or cannot be) accessible individually or indiscriminately, which occurs with private and public goods, depending on the case. These resources are (and form) part of human sociability, of their relational nature, without which societies could not exist, develop and survive. Consequently, "If these goods are ignored dismissed, or repressed, the entire social fabric is impoverished, mutilated and deprived of life blood with serious harm caused to people and the overall social organisation" (Donati 2014: 23).

This relational capital is therefore perceived as a feasible possibility to offer a plausible response to the new challenges of the twenty-first century. Among them, the establishment of a society which, far from the traditional dichotomy between the State and a market encouraging individualism and fomenting dislike among citizens, is capable of appreciating how to participate and being committed to everything that affects it and that it is fighting for. So, it is necessary to orientate reciprocal behaviours towards a moral horizon – one that allows relational processes to materialise that generate relational goods and prevent relational evils from flourishing (Donati 2014: 24). Hence two basic traits underlying the conceptualisation of relational, emotional and communicative goods offer some clues about what their horizon of meaning may be, as there are two dimensions to relational goods that take them closer to cordial reason ethics. Beginning with cordiality, goods would emerge, be enriched and justified, and would be dealt with based on the reciprocal relationships shaped from the mutual recognition of communicative capacities for entering dialogue and reaching agreements about different worldly matters, from emotional competences to feeling emotions for oneself and others, whether or not they are known, based on the respect and dignity that any human being deserves given his/ her absolute value.

8.3 Cordial Goods: The Communicative and Emotive Potential of Common Goods

Different experimental studies with strategy games in evolutionary economy (Bicchieri et al. 2004; Henrich et al. 2001), neuroeconomics (Kosfeld et al. 2005; Fehr et al. 2002) and neuropolitics (Fehr et al. 2013) have empirically verified what many theorists have upheld in at least the last four decades in sociology, philosophy, economy and politics: what underlies failure or success in cooperation are emerging, relational, communicative and emotional goods like trust, reciprocity, commitment, reputation, credibility or legitimacy. This is mainly because a rise in the levels of trust, reputation, reciprocity and commitment, among other things, leads to the taking of greater risks when it comes to cooperating; the establishment of commonly beneficial objectives for all related parties; cutting the transaction costs originating from any business exchange[10]; and creating strong, long-lasting links that

---

[10] For further information about the notion of transaction costs, see North (1994: 359–368).

minimise uncertainty, improve mid- and long-term profit expectations and provide other benefits.

Along these lines, Sen stated that trust is an intangible resource (2000, 2003). However, this is necessary for the economy to develop correctly, which is closely linked to the related parties' level of commitment to certain implicit and explicit rules, of which some are moral:

> Successful operation of an exchange economy depends on mutual trust and the use of norms –explicit and implicit. When these behavioral modes are plentiful, it is ease to over-look their role. But when they have to be cultivated, that lacuna can be a major barrier to economic success. (Sen 2000: 263)

Ostrom also believes trust is an intangible resource that plays a very important role in the economic sphere, but she also considers that other relevant relational goods exist for the economy and its institutions, organisations and agents to develop properly, and also for trust to appear and be reinforced among the related parties. For Ostrom, a resource like trust can be complemented and enriched with other resources that have similar characteristics, like reputation and reciprocity (Ostrom 2003: 19–79). From this viewpoint, guiding behaviour for reciprocity allow institutions, organisations and economic agents to acquire or finance their reputation. Depending on its level of development they are considered *worthy of trust* by others, and may or may not be able to form part of relational processes that are highly beneficial for all those involved. Consequently, for Ostrom, these three intangible resources are related and complement each other, which allow them to go beyond the traditional suboptimum balances of the preponderant economic theory, based on the rationality of *homo oeconomicus*, and to accomplish optimum (or almost optimum) economic performance through relationality that is not merely self-interested.

García-Marzá (2004, 2005, 2007) expresses similar views to Ostrom. He understands that trust is a fundamental, but insufficient, resource for performing economic activity.[11] He believes trust has to be complemented with other intangible goods to allow economic development and the appearance and development of trust itself, like reciprocity and reputation, but also responsibility, recognition and commitment. García-Marzá also coincides with Sen in that a close link exists between trust in and commitment with those legitimate expectations of behaviour that bound or bindable parties expect in different areas of human activity. Indeed García-Marzá specifies that trust is a mechanism that enables and improves economic relationships, whose development is linked to expectations of: (a) experience and knowledge about the continuity of the natural and social order; (b) the competition and technical skills and capacities of the agents, and of the linked institutions, organisations and companies; (c) considerations of the interests at risk of the affected people. These three characteristics warn that, behind trust, there is an underlying rationality linked to technical and strategic factors but also moral ones.

---

[11] For a comparison of the theoretical proposals put forward by Sen and García-Marzá, see Reyes (2008: 153–172).

(...) that trust has a rational basis means that we have good reasons to place our trust in a product, a person or a company. The ethical perspective and, with it, the ethical bases of trust, clearly appear when we notice the series of reasons that support our conviction, which are not limited to the technical and strategic domain (expectations and competition), but also refer to a moral dimension (rights and responsibilities). (García-Marzá 2004: 76)

From this perspective, after reconstructing the conditions of the possibility underlying any interpersonal relationship, this resource and other relational, emerging, communicative and intangible resources, which are just as important for economic activity, like reputation, reciprocity, responsibility and commitment, emerge as moral resources.[12] In other words, they are resources because they allow different actions to be performed because they partly allow cooperation between agents and the coordination of different action plans, regardless of whether these are individual, group or general plans, that are to be developed and reinforced with others' action plans. They are also moral because not only are they influenced by what is conventional – the beliefs, values and rules shared by a given community – but, and above all other things, for the practical reason – the capacity of humans to guide their actions and decisions with moral judgements about what they consider to be fair or unfair, correct or incorrect (García-Marzá 2004: 67–68).

Sen follows the same idea when he suggested that "(...) capitalism works effectively thought a system of ethics that provides the vision and the trust needed for successful use of the market mechanism and related institutions" (Sen 2000: 263). This is confirmed by constant evidence that people often act from commitment to something with good reasons to be valued but which goes against the objectives they recognise and ultimately wish to maximise. This tends to happen even though no intrinsic importance is attached to these behavioural rules (Sen 1977, 1987). This suggests that paying attention only to motivation based on self-interest is a mistake, as the reasons underlying commitments intrinsically linked to judgements made about what is fair or right ought to be taken into account. These are sound reasons bringing meaning to certain behaviours and attitudes, and they are worthy of consideration and respect from those affected to be built into a *motivating force for action*. They emerge by reciprocally recognising that those involved or affected are *worthy of equal dignity and respect* (García-Marzá 2004: 47).

From this perspective, moral resources are seen as economic assets (García-Marzá 2004: 67–68), firstly, given their strategic value, as their use allows business objectives to be met and maximises profits. Above all, though, given their communicative value, this is because their generation and reinforcement underlies the credibility and legitimacy of the economic institution or organisation's actions and decisions – its capacity to act in accordance with the legitimate expectations of its stakeholders (Cortina 2000: 85). An economic institution or organisation worthy

---

[12] The term moral resource was coined by economist Albert O. Hirschman in "Against parsimony: three easy ways of complicating some categories of economic discourse" (1984: 11–84), and has been conceptually worked by Hirschman himself, by sociologists Claus Offe and Ulrich K. Preuss in "Democratic Institutions and Moral Resources" (1991), and mainly by philosopher García-Marzá in *Ética emrpesarial: del diálogo a la confianza* (2004).

of the reciprocity, reputation, trust and commitment of its stakeholders means that the intersubjective agreement reached about the actions and decisions that legitimise it remains in force.

Thus, it is a special kind of social capital needed to optimally achieve business objectives. Intangible resources and the emerging effect[13] allowing relationality in contexts of human activity with an underlying rational-communicative dimension, for which proper management is the condition allowing it to be generated and constantly developed.[14] Trust, reciprocity, responsibility, commitment, legitimacy, and the credibility or reputation of the institution, organisation or company, for instance, depend on the agreement it reaches with its valid interlocutors, and this agreement is communicatively generated; that is, intersubjectively through a dialogue process which: (a) includes all the people affected by their actions and the decisions they make; (b) is structured around certain logic rules; (c) is justified and enriched by good reasons; (d) stems from any possible non-argumentative coercion. So, an institution, organization or company that wishes to generate and reinforce these so that activity can be undertaken correctly must bear in mind their technical and strategic, but also moral, dimension. This is accessible only through dialogue with those involved or affected by their actions and the decisions they make; in other words, based on the legitimacy and credibility offered by a feasible intersubjective agreement with all its valid interlocutors, which is reached without breaching the principles of communication, inclusion, equality and reciprocity.

What all this suggests is communicative goods. First of all, they represent a value in themselves, regardless of their economic function, the results that can be accomplished or their market value. Secondly, they reveal a relational and communicative structure, which is the condition of it being generated and developed. Thirdly, they are an emergent effect of the relational link established, as they are born and die in the same relationship and cannot, consequently, be generated and enjoyed either individually or collectively, but socially. In short, they are goods that are constructed, fed and justified relationally and with dialogue, and they produce a strategic and, above all, a communicative value for the company.

These characteristics of communicative goods, however, mean it is necessary to take another step forward and introduce a third dimension, the emotional dimension. This is because, as argued in relational goods theory (Donati 2013; Donati and Calvo 2014a) and also from neurosciences (Calvo 2013: 162–166; Calvo and González-Esteban 2013: 93–116; Cortina 2011, 2012, 2013a; Medina-Vicent 2016; Pallarés-Dominguez 2016), the relational link requires feelings and emotions in order to emerge and be constructed, and humans are biologically capable, socially

---

[13] As Donati explains, "Saying that it is an emergent effect means that it requires a certain combination (not a simple aggregation) of factors, elements, or components as discussed above; its emergent character accents the fact that the relational good is a 'third' entity that exceeds the involved subjects' contributions and that, in certain cases, may not have been foreseen or thought of as the initial intention" (2014: 31).

[14] To learn other perspectives of the value of such intangible resources in the economy, see Donati and Calvo (2014b) and Donati (2014).

willing and morally committed to feel emotions for themselves and for others, whether or not they know them. This has been stated by Cortina (2013b: 126):

> (…) it is not just a matter of mutually recognising ourselves as valid interlocutors of the dialogues that constitute us because we are capable of language. It is also a matter of internally recognising the dignity to which we have a right through our internal value. And it is also a matter of cordial recognition that our lives are originally linked, which is why it is important to live them from compassion.

After considering this emotional dimension underlying communicative goods, these goods can be considered to be associated with cordiality, and they become cordial goods. Firstly, we find the resources maintaining a structure based on the complementarity of two areas of reflection, as revealed by communicative goods: the strategic-technical and the moral. Secondly, there are resources whose moral space is arranged around three complementary moments, as cordial reason ethics, such as those proposed and developed by Cortina in her most recent works (2007b, 2010, 2013b, 2017), suggest: the hermeneutic-critical moment, the communicative moment and the cordial and compassionate moment. From this viewpoint, a cordial good can be understood as the collective heritage that emerges and develops from relationships being built on the reciprocal recognition of human dignity, and on participants' communicative and emotional capacities to criticise both knowledge and action affecting them and for which they are responsible. It is also based on establishing links with others to meet commonly desirable objectives – relationships shaped from the foundations of *etica cordis* extended to what is expected in the present (Cortina 2007a, b, 2010, 2013a, b, 2017).

The role played by cordial goods in economic development, but also in social and human development, opens the door to a need to reconsider, improve and/or change the fundamental concepts of the predominant economic theory and, from this stage, to begin considering another economic approach coherent with the observations from fieldwork and laboratory experiments, and with what can be morally expected and is desirable for a cordial society with a level of moral and emotional maturity in accordance with the requirements of the historical moment. In other words, a relational economy shaped from dignity, bindability and justice through a strategic-instrumental and, above all, cordial rationality that is communicative, compassionate, bindable and dignifying.

Bibliography

Archer, Margaret. 1982. Morphogenesis versus structuration: On combining structure and action. *The British Journal of Sociology* 33 (4): 455–483.
———. 1987. Resisting the revival of relativism. *International Sociology* 2 (3): 235–250.
———. 1988. *Culture and Agency: The Place of Culture in Social Theory*. Cambridge: Cambridge University Press.
———. 1995. *Realist Social Theory: The Morphogenetic Approach*. Cambridge: Cambridge University Press.

Becchetti, Leonardo, Luigino Bruni, and Stefano Zamagni. 2010. *Microeconomia. Scelte, Relazione, Economia Civile*. Bologna: Il Mulino.

Bicchieri, Cristina, John Duffy, and Gil Tolle. 2004. Trust among Strangers. *Philosophy of Science* 71 (3): 286–319.

Bruni, Luigino. 2005. Felicità, Economia e Beni Relazionali. *Nuova Umanità* 27 (159–160): 543–565.

———. 2008 [2006]. *Il Prezzo Della Gratuità*. Madrid: Ciudad Nueva.

Bruni, Luigino, and Stefano Zamagni. 2007 [2004]. *Civil Economy: Efficiency, Equity, Public Happiness*. New York: Peter Lang.

Calvo, Patrici. 2013. Neuro-racionalidad: Heterogeneidad motivacional y comportamiento moral. *Daimon. Revista Internacional de Filosofía* 59: 157–170.

Calvo, Patrici, and Elsa González-Esteban. 2013. Neuroeconomía, ¿un saber práctico? In *Ética y neurociencias: la aportación a la política, la economía y la educación*, ed. Domingo García-Marzá and Ramón A. Feenstra, 93–116. Castellón de la Plana: Publicacions de la Universitat Jaume I.

Cárdenas, Juan-Camilo, and Elinor Ostrom. 2004. What do people bring into the game? Experiments in the field about cooperation in the commons. *Agricultural Systems* 82: 307–326.

Carrasco, Cristina. 2014. El cuidado como bien relacional: hacia posibles indicadores. *Papeles de relaciones ecosociales y cambio global* 128: 49–60.

Cortina, Adela. 2000. Ética empresarial en el contexto de una ética cívica. In *La ética de la empresa. Claves para una nueva ética empresarial*, ed. Adela Cortina, 35–50. Madrid: Trotta.

———. 2007a. Ethica cordis. *Isegoría. Revista de Filosofía Moral y Política* 37: 113–126.

———. 2007b. *Ética de la razón cordial. Educar en la ciudadanía en el siglo XXI*. Oviedo: Nobel.

———. 2010. *Justicia cordial*. Madrid: Trotta.

———. 2011. *Neuroética y Neuropolítica. Sugerencias para la Educación Moral*. Madrid: Tecnos.

———. 2012. Neuroética, presente y futuro. In *Neurofilosofía práctica*, ed. Adela Cortina, 9–38. Comares: Granada.

———. 2013a. Ética del discurso: ¿un marco filosófico para la neuroética? *Isegoría. Revista de Filosofía Moral y Política* 48: 127–148.

———. 2013b. ¿Para qué sirve realmente... la ética? Barcelona: Paidós Ibérica.

———. 2017. *Aporofobia, el rechazo al pobre. Un desafío para la democracia*. Barcelona: Paidós Ibérica.

del Estado, Jefatura. 2007. Ley 14/2007, de 3 de julio, de Investigación bi- omédica [*Biomedical Research Act 14/2007, of 3 July*]. *Boletín Oficial del Estado* 159: 28826-28846. http://www.isciii.es/ISCIII/es/contenidos/fdinvestigacion/Ley_In-vestigacion_Biomedica.pdf. Accessed 25 Sept 2017.

Deloitte. 2016. *Global Human Capital Trends 2016. The New Organization: Different by Design*. Deloitte University Press.

Donati, Pierpaolo. 1986. *Introduzione alla sociologia relazionale*. Milan: Francine.

———. 1989. *La cultura della vita. Dalla società tradizionale a quella postmoderna*. Milan: FrancoAngeli.

———. 1991. *Teoria relazionale della società*. Milan: FrancoAngeli.

———. 2008. Discovering the relational character of the common good. In *Pursuing the Common Good: How Solidarity and Subsidiarity Can Work Together*, ed. Margaret Archer and Pierpaolo Donati, 659–683. Vatican City: The Pontifical Academy Social Sciences.

———. 2011. Modernization and relational reflexivity. *International Review of Sociology. Revue Internationale de Sociologie* 21 (1): 21–39.

———. 2013. *Sociologia relazionale. Come cambia la società*. Brescia: Editrice La Scuola.

———. 2014. Relational goods and their subjects: The ferment of a new civil society and civil democracy. *Recerca. Revista de Pensament i Anàlisi* 14: 19–46.

———. 2015. *L'enigma della relazione*. Milan: Mimesis.

Donati, Pierpaolo, and Patrici Calvo. 2014a. New insight into relational goods. In *New Insight into Relational Goods*, ed. Pierpaolo Donati and Patrici Calvo, 7–17. Castellón: Publicacions de la Universitat Jaume I.

————. 2014b. *New Insight into Relational Goods*. Castellón de la Plana: Publicacions de la Universitat Jaume I.

Donati, Pierpaolo, and Riccardo Solci. 2011. *I beni relazionali. Che cosa sono e quali effetti producono*. Turin: Bollati Boringhieri.

Edelman Berland. 2003–2016. *Edelman Trust Barometer Executive Summary. Annual Global Study*. Edelman Berland.

Fehr, Ernst, Urs Fischbacher, and Simon Gächter. 2002. Strong reciprocity, human cooperation and the enforcement of social norms. *Human Nature* 13 (1): 1–25.

Fehr, Ernst, Holger Herz, and Tom Wilkening. 2013. The lure of authority: Motivation and incentive effects of power. *American Economic Review* 103 (4): 1325–1359.

Gallup. 2013. *State of the Global Workplace: Employee Engagement Insights for Business Leaders Worldwide*. Washington, DC: Gallup Inc.

García-Marzá, Domingo. 2004. *Ética empresarial: del diálogo a la confianza*. Madrid: Trotta.

————. 2005. Diálogo y responsabilidad: bases éticas de la confianza en la empresa. *Revista Icade* 64: 91–108.

————. 2007. Responsabilidad social de la empresa: una aproximación desde la ética empresarial. *Veritas* 2 (17): 183–204.

Gui, Benedetto. 2000. Behind transaction: On interpersonal dimension of economic reality. *Annals of Public and Cooperative Economics* 71 (1): 139–169.

Hardin, Garrett. 1968. The tragedy of the commons. *Science* 162 (1): 1243–1248.

Hirschman, Albert O. 1984. Against parsimony: Three easy ways of complicating some categories of economic discourse. *Bulletin of the American Academy of Arts and Sciences* 37 (8): 11–84.

Henrich, Josep, Robert Boyd, Samuel Bowles, Colin Camerer, Ernst Fehr, Herbert Gintis, and Richard McElreath. 2001. In search of Homo Economicus: Behavioral experiments in 15 small-scale societies. *American Economic Review* 91 (2): 73–78.

Kosfeld, Michael, Markus Heinrichs, Paul J. Zak, Urs Fischbacher, and Ernst Fehr. 2005. Oxytocin increases trust in humans. *Nature* 435 (1): 637–677.

Medina-Vicent, Maria. 2016. Neurociencia y teoría política feminista. La inestabilidad sexo-género-sexualidad a través de la obra de Paul B. Preciado. *Pensamiento. Revista de Investigación e Información Filosófica* 72 (273): 981–996.

North, Douglass C. 1994. Performance through time. *The American Economic Review* 84 (3): 359–368.

Nussbaum, Martha. 1986. *The Fragility of Goodness: Luck and Ethics in Greek Tragedy and Philosophy*. Cambridge: Cambridge University Press.

Offe, Claus, and Ulrich K. Preuss. 1991. Democratic institutions and moral resources. In *Political Theory Today*, ed. David Held, 143–171. Stanford: Stanford University Press.

Ostrom, Elinor. 1990. *Governing the Commons. The Evolution of Institutions for Collective Action*. Cambridge: Cambridge University Press.

————. 1999. *Design Principles and Threats to Sustainable Organizations that Manage Commons [Workshop on Political Theory and Policy Analysis]*. Indianapolis: Center for the Study of Institutions, Population, and Environmental Change, Indiana University. http://beyondostrom. blog.rosalux.de/files/2013/05/Design-Principles-and-Threats-to-Sustainable-Organizations-That-Manage-Commons.pdf. Accessed 25 Sept 2017.

————. 2003. Toward a behavioral theory linking trust, reciprocity, and reputation. In *Trust & Reciprocity. Interdisciplinary Lessons from Experimental Research*, ed. Elinor Ostrom and James Walker, 19–79. New York: Russell Sage Foundation.

Ostrom, Elinor, and Harini Nagendra. 2010. Governing the commons in the new millennium: A diversity of institutions for natural resource management. In *Re-inventing construction*, ed. Ilca Rudy and Andreas Ruby, 380–387. Rudy Press: Berlin.

Pallarés-Domínguez, Daniel. 2016. Neuroeducación en diálogo: neuromitos en el proceso de enseñanza-aprendizaje y en la educación moral. *Pensamiento. Revista de Investigación e Información Filosófica* 72 (273): 941–958.

Ramis, Álvaro. 2017. *Bienes comunes y democracia. Crítica del individualismo posesivo*. Santiago de Chile: LOM ediciones.

Reyes, Agustín. 2008. El Enfoque de las Capacidades, la Agencia Cognitiva y los Recursos Morales. *Recerca. Revista de Pensament i Anàlisi* 8: 153–172.

Sen, Amartya. 1977. Rational fools. A critique of the behavioral foundations of economic theory. In *Philosophy and Public Affairs*, ed. Frank Hahn and Martin Hollis, 317–344. Oxford: Blackwell Publishing.

———. 1987. *On Ethics and Economy*. Oxford: Blackwell Publishing.

———. 2000. *Development as Freedom*. New York: Anchor.

———. 2003. Ética de la empresa y desarrollo económico. In *Construir confianza*, ed. Adela Cortina, 39–54. Madrid: Trotta.

Uhlaner, Carole. 1989. Participation. Incorporating sociability into a theory of rational action. *Public Choice* 62 (3): 253–285.

———. 2014. Relational goods and resolving the paradox of political participation. *Recerca. Revista de Pensament i Anàlisi* 14: 47–72.

Zamagni, Stefano. 2006. *Heterogeneidad motivacional y comportamiento económico. La perspectiva de la economía civil*. Madrid: Unión Editorial.

———. 2007a. El bien común en la sociedad posmoderna: propuestas para la acción político-económica. *Revista Cultural Económica* 25 (79): 23–43.

———. 2007b. *L'economia del bene comune*. Rome: Città Nuova.

———. 2008. La Economía civil y los bienes relacionales. In *Las nuevas economías. De la economía evolucionista a la economía cognitivista: más allá de las fallas de la teoría neoclásica*, ed. Riccardo Viale, 169–186. Flacso México: Mexico.

———. 2009. Fraternity, gifts and reciprocity in Cáritas in Veritate. *Revista Cultural Económica* 27 (75–76): 11–29.

———. 2010a. Catholic social thought, civil economy, and the spirit of capitalism. In *The True Wealth of Nations*, ed. Daniel K. Finn, 63–93. Oxford: Oxford University Press.

———. 2010b. Globalization: Guidance from Franciscan economic thought and caritas in veritate. *Faith & Economics* 56: 81–109.

———. 2014. Bienes communes y economía civil. *Revista Cultura Económica XXXII* 87: 8–25.

———. 2016. Il bene comune come berillo intellettuale in economia. *Archivio di filosofia* 84 (1–2): 161–176.

Chapter 9
Cordial Economics: The Participation of Civil Society in the Economy

Abstract As previous chapters have shown, no single source of motivation lies behind economic behaviour, which is more likely the result of many causes, most importantly maximising one's own benefit, as well as prosocial feelings, and moral principles and values. These questions promote more critical reflection on the possibility of finding an alternative economic model that is more human, efficient and beneficial for all the parties affected by activity. From a civil perspective – like the one developed by Stefano Zamagni – and a cordial one – like that developed by Adela Cortina – the aim of this chapter is to propose guidelines to design an economy that measures up to the requirements of the historical moment through institutions, organisations and businesses, whose designs include such important aspects as compassion, care, reciprocity, commitment, and the active and committed participation of civil society.

The Big Short (Adam McKay 2015), a film adaptation of Michael Lewis's novel *The Big Short: Inside the Doomsday Machine* (2010), offers a critical reflection on the causes leading to the bankruptcy of the American property sector which, in 2008, resulted in possibly the greatest economic crisis in history. Through the true stories of four characters who independently discover 3 years after the financial collapse of 2008 the failures of the mortgage market due to derivatives – financial contracts – the film tells how connivance between big financial corporations, well-known academic experts and important media outlets as well as the refusal of the American government and most important economic institutions to accept the bankruptcy of the system and to act consequently at a global level for the financial system, the economy and society in general.

Despite the devastating effects of the crisis, Alan Greenspan, former president of the Fed (Federal Reserve) and one of the greatest defenders of the liberalisation of financial derivatives, continues to defend the benefits of the market deregulation and management by the economic institutions prior to the collapse. As he stresses in his autobiography, *The Age of Turbulence. Adventures in a New Wold* (2008), for Greenspan, reputation and confidence are essential aspects of the capitalist system as the laws intended to regulate them "(…) at best can prescribe only a small frac-

© Springer International Publishing AG, part of Springer Nature 2018   145
P. Calvo, *The Cordial Economy - Ethics, Recognition and Reciprocity*,
Ethical Economy 55, https://doi.org/10.1007/978-3-319-90784-0_9

tion of the day-by-day activities in the marketplace" (Greenspan 2008: 256). Wealth creation, therefore, requires people to take calculated risks based on the reputation of the parties. Because, as Greenspan argues:

(…) the greater our trust in the people with whom we trade, the greater the accumulation of wealth. In the market system based on trust, reputation will have a significant economic value. Reputation, capitalised formally as "goodwill" on business balance sheets or otherwise, is an important contributor to the market value of a company. (2008: 256)

In this way, Greenspan releases the system from responsibility for the financial disturbances of the twenty-first century and blames the entire crisis on the cowardice and lack of ethics and integrity of some investors and banking and business professionals. It is not the model, but rather the behaviour of some people who have generated a loss of confidence in the sector that has notably damaged the capacity of people to create wealth through business. However, despite championing the freedom of the market under self-regulation, Greenspan defends the bank rescues carried out by the States during the recent crises in order to safeguard the system (2008: 182–205).

Greenspan arguments in this respect, however, rather evoke the famous passage from Saint Augustine of Hippo in *The Confessions* (1864), in which he recalls how, as an immature adolescent, he prayed to God to give him "(…) chastity and continency, only not yet. For I feared lest Thou shouldest hear me soon, and soon cure me of the disease of concupiscence, which I wished to have satisfied, rather than extinguished" (Saint Augustine 1864: 161). Greenspan defends market self-regulation and sets himself against any kind of State control or intervention despite what has happened over the past 20 years. But not now. When the cyclical crises reproduced by the system are so devastating that they shake its foundations, the Greenspan sees State intervention to rescue the financial corporations that have acted irresponsibly and maliciously as a lesser evil to safeguard high-risk investments made by cowardly speculators (Greenspan 2008: 182–205). Based on this and as has already been mentioned, Deaton considers that the crises appear to be "(…) designed to benefit the rich, as, thanks to them, it is easier to rewrite the rules. This is why education reform makes no progress in the US, because children go to private universities. The same thing happens with health. In crises, these things always get worse" (Díaz, 27 May 2012).

On the other hand, Greenspan is right when he states that confidence and reputation are two key assets for the economy. He also correctly says that the crisis has a great deal to do with the deficit of ethics and excess of cowardice in the economic sphere. Both these factors have undermined the rational basis for confidence and reputation, particularly their communicative and affective dimension. However, it is not true that economic agents are the only ones responsible for the crisis. The deficit of ethics and excess of cowardice also guided the behaviour, actions and decisions of many businesses, organisations and economic institutions during the years before the crisis. For example, the liberalisation of the mortgage market so strongly promoted and defended by institutions like the American government and the Federal Reserve through laws, reports and predictive models was greatly abused by many large corporations via derivatives such as subprime mortgages. Rather than fairness and prudence, this had a great deal to do with excessive cowardice with regard to the suffering and social costs it generated. All this was largely due to the design principles configured by the institutions, organisations and businesses. These are largely principles from economics which, like the maximisation of business profits, efficiency, competitiveness and individualism, modulate the private and collective behaviour of professionals and guide the decision-making processes of institutions, organisations and businesses.

But to eradicate or ameliorate the deficit of ethics and excess of cowardice destroying reputation, confidence and other goods involved in the proper development and promotion of the economy, it is necessary to specify an adequate framework of values and principles capable of rationally guiding the behaviour, actions and decisions both of the agents involved, such as the institutions, organisations and businesses making it up. And this is precisely where a cordial and relational perspective like the one proposed in this work can offer ideas, patterns and guidelines to achieve a fairer, more efficient economy creating greater happiness by encouraging institutions, organisations and businesses to include in their designs aspects as important for generating reputation and confidence as reciprocity, recognition, commitment, credibility, affectiveness and cooperation. A cordial economy matching both what is empirically observed in laboratory experiments and field studies and that expected and desired by a plural society with a post-conventional level of moral development and emotional maturity.

The objective of this chapter is to offer guidelines to design an economic proposal that measures up to the requirements of the historical moment. For this purpose, the institutional design is firstly examined to show the basic traits that allow the necessary cordial point of view to be included in the economy. Secondly, we take a close look at organisational and business designs that are capable of providing information about their actions and decisions, and of duly managing the motivational and behavioural heterogeneity that underlies them. Thirdly and finally, both the place that civil society occupies and the role it plays in the cordial economy proposal are shown as guidelines to promote and encourage its moral and emotionally committed participation.

9.1   Cordial Institutions: Cordiality As a Principle of Institutional Design

During the decades that work has been conducted on the role of institutions in various areas of human activity, especially economic areas, where laboratory experiments were complemented with fieldwork,[1] Ostrom showed how efficiently

---

[1] Ostrom complements her laboratory experiments with fieldwork on case studies. These included irrigation systems, like the Benacher and Faitar canals in Valencia, the Tibi dam in Alicante, the Segura River in Murcia and Orihuela (Ostrom 1990: 69–81) or small plots in Nepal (Ostrom

managing scarce resources requires the complementary contributions of different types of institutions – public, private and civil society – for citizens to get involved and for collective action processes to materialise.

> As an institutionalist, studying empirical phenomena, I presume that individuals try to solve problems as effectively as they can. That assumption imposes discipline on me. Instead of presuming that some individuals are incompetent, evil or irrational, and others are omni-scient, I presume that individuals have very similar limited capacities to reason and figure out the structure of complex environments. (Ostrom 1990: 25)

Ostrom's proposal was outlined after observing economic institutions all over the world which had managed to defy the passage of time by coping with different and constant structural, cultural, socio-political, ideological and environmental changes. These collective action institutions were created by civil society to manage certain common, but scarce, goods, such as irrigation basins, forests, rivers, seas, etcetera, which, in many cases, had survived and remained sustainable for over 750 years.[2]

After an in-depth study of how and why these institutions had been able to sur-vive for such a long time, and had helped with the survival of managed common goods, Ostrom reached the conclusion that an institution is actually a specific form of social capital. In other words, it is a series of rules and rules of use created and developed by citizens[3] to coordinate action in various areas of human activity in order to efficiently manage different scarce goods or resources, which may be eco-nomic, political, health-related, etc., thanks to reciprocity, participation, commit-ment and trust. Among other things (Ostrom 1986: 19; 1990), institutions determine who is entitled to take part in decision-making processes; which actions are allowed; which affiliation rules are used; which procedures must be followed; what informa-tion must be available; what punishment must be received when rules are breached; and how achievements are distributed.

> (…) we discuss the value of institutions as a form of social capital formed through diverse processes involving the development of trust, norms of reciprocity, and networks of civic engagement, including the rules and laws within and between levels of organisations. Each condition affects the expectations that individuals have about patterns of interactions that groups of individuals bring to a recurrent activity at local or larger levels. Thus, we reassert the heuristic usefulness of the concept, not as defined within a single level, but representing the value of social networks in mediating shared interests at the levels of the individual, communities, and society as a whole. (Brondizio et al. 2009: 261–262)

1999a, 2001); prairies and mountain forests, like the Zanjeras in the Philippines, Törbel in Switzerland, and the Hirano, Nagaike and Yamanoka in Japan (Ostrom 1990: 61–102), and the mangroves of Colombia (Cárdenas and Ostrom 2004); fisheries like the lobster industry on the Maine River in the USA (Schlager and Ostrom 1992) and the fishing towns on the Turkish coast of the Aegean Sea (Ostrom 1990: 144–146), among others.

[2] Today's *Fishers Community of El Palmar*, successor of the *Comú de peixcadors de la Ciutat de Valencia*, is a civil society institution which has managed fishing on the Albufera Lagoon of Valencia since 1250 (Ramón-Fernández 2001: 21).

[3] Ostrom understands rules to be human creations which, subject to intervention and change by humans, allow the structure of the incentives of a given situation to be modified (Ostrom 1986: 5–6), and rules of us to be the rules addressing whether or not rules are followed.

In line with this perspective of the institution as social capital developed by Ostrom, there are relevant underlying issues that should be considered. Firstly, institutions require suitable citizen participation for them to emerge, develop and be sustainable. This does not depend on an elite group of intellectuals and experts – for instance, economists or political scientists – but on everyone involved or affected by the activity which is intended to be efficiently and effectively coordinated. Secondly, the rules constituting an institution are not hermetic and unquestionable, but are open to review, improvement and amendment in order to adapt them whenever necessary to the constant, different cultural, political, social and environmental changes that take place, attacking their integrity, continuity and survival. Thirdly, institutions can be created by the public and private spheres, but also in the social sphere, as there is evidence for three cases of this in history around the world. Fourthly, managing scarce resources requires the complementation of different institutions because in civil society institutions there is the kind of collective action that has provided much more efficient management than the public, private or public/private management of tangible common goods.

Ostrom therefore concludes that there is no-one better to sustainably manage a common good or resource than those involved in/affected by it (1995a: 40), provided they have available sufficient mechanisms, resources and incentives to do so. So she opts for an alternative way of resolving the drama (rather than the tragedy) of common resources: their transformation into a civil good in terms of their management by civil society. In line with most of Ostrom's works (1990, 1995a, b, 1997, 1998, 1999b, 2001, 2003, 2012a), this third form may be feasible provided three essential tasks are performed: extending the economic rationality framework so it can encourage and promote the collective action of the people involved or affected; empowering economic agents' capacities to be linked to seeking objectives that are commonly beneficial for everyone; and promoting the civil society institution's autonomy through complementary help from other institutions, for example, public ones.

Thanks to her laboratory experiments and fieldwork with strategy games, Ostrom managed to draw the attention of experts to the fact that the economic sphere does not operate well when left in public and private hands. Civil society also plays a relevant role in managing scarce resources, and ignoring or disparaging their capacities may prove counterproductive for the economy and society due to loss of irreplaceable resources. It is precisely this idea of Ostrom's that is found in the civil economy proposal developed by Zamagni in the last 25 years, suggesting an economy shaped around three spheres – market, State and civil society – and its different logics – efficiency, equity and reciprocity – and private, public and civil institutions, organisations and businesses.

The original civil economy proposal was devised by Genovesi in the second half of the eighteenth century in two volumes of his work *Delle lezione di commercio o sia d'economia civile* (1765 & 1767), a treatise that was written with the intention of offering an economic model capable of responding to the need for justice and happiness of society at that time (Genovesi 1785a: 3). Genovesi grounded himself in civil society, civil virtues, reciprocity, *paideia*, public happiness, interpersonal relationality and mainly common goods to design an alternative theory of the individualistic paradigm that was consolidated in Europe during the Age of Enlightenment. According to Genovesi, this was in particular because he could not provide an heuristic response to people's different good life projects as these are achieved through goods such as friendship, love, legitimacy or mutual trust, which are not generated and enjoyed individually, but rather in relation with others (Genovesi 1785a: 10–35).

In this way, and after Genovesi put forward this theoretical proposal, the idea of a civil and civilising market emerged whose correct operation was a condition of the possibility of a fairer and, above all, a happier society. As it requires suitable places to establish interpersonal relations, commerce offers the necessary conditions for people to fulfil their requirements and live a fully humane life through interpersonal relations. Among other aspects, this is because it entails having to promote peace and freedom among people, societies and nations (Genovesi 1785a: 5, 57, 1785b: 8, 18–19), which offers those involved the chance to develop properly. Here Genovesi was very critical about the idea of promoting economics where the only possible motivation was self-interest, as it encourages vices and scorns virtues (Genovesi 1785a: 134–135) and, consequently, limits the possibilities of achieving complete happiness which, in his view, was public, civil and relational (1785b: 27).

In the 1990s, Zamagni retrieved and developed Genovesi's original idea to offer a feasible response to the socio-economic problems of the twenty-first-century society as a result of a social structure arranged around two fundamental institutions – the market and the State – whose main objective is to ensure that their two main regulatory principles are correctly implemented: efficiency and equity. In other words, by guaranteeing an exchange-of-equivalence activity through the efficiency principle, the market allows wealth for society to be generated unintentionally, while the State ensures that any possible drawbacks in the distribution of this unintentional wealth generated by market activity are corrected in order to guarantee action with solidarity based on a principle of equity (Bruni and Zamagni 2007: 21).

However, Zamagni understands that both institutions are necessary, but not sufficient, to respond to the interests involved in the twenty-first-century society, especially that bound to fulfilling various good life projects. As the *happiness paradox* put forward by Richard A. Easterlin in "Does Economic Growth Improve the Human Lot? Some Empirical Evidence" (1974) shows, after analysing the work of psychologists Philip Brickman and Donald T. Campbell, "Hedonic Relativism and Planning the Good Society" (1971), reaching a certain level of income and improving people's objective conditions do not appear to have real effects on their happiness, and can even reverse the process. In 2010, Daniel Kahneman and Deaton also put forward some arguments along these lines in their study "High income improves evaluation of life, but not emotional well-being". Their work concluded that beyond the $75,000 annual income threshold, no proportional improvement exists in people's emotional levels of well-being, only in the feeling of being a success. So, neither higher earnings nor being more successful are synonyms for happiness:

> More money does not necessarily buy more happiness, but less money is associated with emotional pain. Perhaps $75,000 is a threshold beyond which further increases in income

no longer improve individuals' ability to do what matters most to their emotional well-being, such as spending time with people they like, avoiding pain and disease, and enjoying leisure. (Kahneman and Deaton 2010: 16492)

From this perspective, for Zamagni, today's problem of socio-economic development has nothing to do with available resources, but instead corresponds to scarceness of relationality (Zamagni 2018). Firstly, because this fact does not go beyond the suboptimum equilibrium balance barrier imposed by axiological individualism, as several laboratory experiments and pieces of fieldwork using strategy games have suggested (Zamagni 2006). Secondly, because in this way it is hard finding a way to make economic activity as profitable and sustainable as possible (Zamagni 1999). Thirdly, because the generation and development of these goods depends on it, like friendship, trust, participation and care or alterity, which are involved in market-society cohesion, managing talent capital and people's self-fulfilment (Zamagni 2010).

To overcome the lack of relationality in today's economy and its harmful effects on the complete development of that society, of societies and people, Zamagni proposes introducing a third logic, reciprocity, through civil society. In this way, the economy would correspond to all three different and complementary spheres – market, State and civil society – and each would contribute rules to its design in relation to the logics of efficiency, equity and reciprocity through its institutions.

In this way, the independent proposals by Ostrom and Zamagni uphold an economy with the active presence of civil society, reciprocity and prosocial sentiments to provide a suitable response not merely through self-interested relational processes to the interests of justice and happiness of twenty-first-century societies. These three aspects allow the cordial viewpoint to begin to be introduced into economy through a process of institutional change and by redesigning the rules of economic institutions – private, public and civil – to adapt them to those required by the economic, social and human context. Such institutional redesign must take into account at least six important aspects which allow economy to rise to the observed, expected and demanded standards:

(a) Cordial civil ethics: in order to introduce the cordial viewpoint into economics, an institutional design based on the public civil ethics framework is absolutely necessary, based on those minimums of justice which, shared by a society with moral pluralism and expressed through values of freedom, equality and solidarity, human rights and active tolerance, "(…) and as the impossibility of proposing to others what is ideal in life if it is not through dialogue and testimony" (Cortina 2000: 42). This is public ethics of minimums and citizens that is civil and neither State-based nor private, as it belongs to society rather than the State. It is also cordial, as it emerges for the purpose of contributing to develop a fairer and happier society. It is therefore ¡ a common, relational and cordial good that "(…) must be respected and embodied by States and markets" (Cortina 2010). These minimums of justice must form part of an all-embracing framework of the rules and rules of use that constitute the design of institutions, "(…) below which it is impossible to fall without suffering inhumanity" (Cortina 2010: 31).

(b) Cordial recognition: in order to integrate the cordial viewpoint into economics, the whole relational process must start from the cordial recognition of the communicative and emotional capacities of all the related or potentially related parties to debate and reach agreements about the rules that must constitute the design of the institutions involved, as well as their truth and moral validity. This is based on the prior emotional and moral link between them, whether or not this is known, and on the respect and care that all human beings deserve as absolute goods with a value, but not a price, to which it is worth being committed while undertaking common projects and which may or may not quantitatively respond to any help received. From such cordial recognition arise expectations that can establish cooperation that seeks a maximum profit for all related parties.

(c) Cordial reciprocity: in order to include the cordial viewpoint in economics, institutional design must promote and encourage reciprocity, especially cordial reciprocity, as it allows the mutual recognition of beings able to dialogue, assess, feel emotional, act and be committed in any area of activity. Reciprocity allows these relational processes to be implemented, addressing both the materialisation and fulfilment of objectives that are commonly beneficial for related parties, and critical reviews and an intersubjective agreement on the sense of the different types of rules that must constitute the design of the institutions involved. These constitute reciprocal relationships cordially constituted where related parties mutually and unconditionally recognise the communicative and affective capacities, and the absolute value to which human beings are entitled.

(d) Cordial dimension: in order to constitute the cordial viewpoint in economics, institutional design must be concerned about the communicative and emotional dimension that underlies it. On one hand, acquiring and developing emotional capacities among related agents must be promoted. These include gratitude, esteem, appreciation, empathy, love, dignity and, above all, compassion about what belongs to one and what does not, because this help for all other feelings and emotions becomes suitable *moral collaboration* (Cortina 2013: 122–126). On the other hand, institutional design must encourage and promote areas of relationality and communication where those affected by activity and the rules and rules of use that coordinate it can reach agreements about its moral validity. Proper management of this cordial, communicative and emotional dimension of economics allows optimum balances to be struck, leading to the best possible socio-economic, self-fulfillment and moral results.

(e) Cordial goods: in order to establish the cordial viewpoint in economics, institutional value must appropriately evaluate the appearance and enrichment of cordial goods, as well as public and private goods. It is not a matter of considering them to be replaceable goods that come into play in a case of need when private or public goods fail. Instead these are complementary elements that cannot be ignored, conditioning the possibility of socio-economic and human development, such as legitimacy or trust.

(f) Cordial responsibility: in order to establish the cordial viewpoint in economics, institutions must be responsible for their actions and decisions. In other words, they must respond to the legitimate interests that come into play and provide an explanation to those affected by their actions and decisions relating to economic, social and environmental issues. For instance, how communicative and emotional recognition is present in different decision-making processes; how to obtain maximum profit from a cordial civic ethics frame; what allows the underlying communicative and emotional dimension to be duly managed; and how are decisions made on what measures are to be taken to implement certain values in practice, such as equality, sustainability, active respect, participation, and so on.

By covering these six aspects at least, an economy constituted in the market-State-civil society sphere, like that proposed by Zamagni and Ostrom, can introduce the cordial viewpoint it needs from its institutions, which both meet the challenge of the empirical observations of fieldwork and laboratory experiments carried out with strategy games and constitute something desired and required by a cordial, moral and emotionally committed, capable and mature society. This is because, as Gintis argues, ceasing to favour the *homo oeconomicus* perspective allows the appreciation of the coexistence of different types of *homo* in the economy and the institutions, organisations and businesses that comprise it: *oeconomicus, parachius, egualis* and *reciprocans*, among others (Gintis 2000: 252). This is precisely what explains the series of observable conducts in economic contexts. Also, thanks to this, inherited structures can be amended to opt for an economy model representing greater, negative and positive freedom for human beings, ultimately including all possibilities of human action and interaction. Where this freedom is found, it is possible to apply and implement cordial organisational and business models that make economic profits by producing quality services and goods within the limits of minimum justice, and without ignoring the full development of societies and their citizens' lives.

9.2   Cordial Organisations and Businesses: Cordiality As a Horizon for Action

The economy that are equal to the requirements of the historical moment not only needs to be structured around cordial institutions that are equal to the demands of the historical moment and to what is observed, expected and desired by a plural society with a post-conventional level of moral development and emotional maturity. Organisations and businesses must also be capable of accounting for their actions and decisions, and of duly managing the underlying motivational and behavioural heterogeneity. Neoclassical thought, however, has focused its concerns on an organisation and company model based on the logic of efficiency, whose motivational strength arises only from maximising a particular short-term profit. States, meanwhile, have opted for a public organisational model based on the logic of equity, whose main motivation is society's common good through managing public goods or applying inclusive politics that avoid economically excluding a certain part of society. So, for Zamagni it is necessary to promote the appearance of organisations that are governed by the logics of reciprocity, and therefore allow relationality that permits the cordial goods needed for economy and social and human development to operate correctly so that these can be produced (Zamagni 2007: 32).

Accordingly, Zamagni's civil proposal of economy indicates the key role of civil society in generating and developing this type of organisations that allow reciprocity to be introduced into economic activity. Along these lines, Zamagni describes three civil society organisation types. Some are based on horizontal subsidiarity, others on vertical subsidiarity, and others on the restitution principle. Although each one carries out an outstanding task within the economy and society, they do not generate relational processes in the same way:

(a) *Civil organisation*: such an organisation is not for profit and people freely and willingly relate to one another to carry out common projects in accordance with the idea of fulfilling shared interests. In other words, they are not individual and cannot be made universal. This model emerged with the civil humanism movement of the fifteenth century and is based on horizontal subsidiarity – organisations based on civic virtues and guided by reciprocity logic that acts by applying the horizontal subsidiarity principle, "(…) the duty of helping, emphasising what is social to someone's service" (Zamagni 2007: 33).

(b) *Subsidiary organisation*: a subsidiary-type organisation is a model of non-profit organisations in which people confer a share of sovereignty so they can work on improving an area or activity and on protecting those involved or affected by them, such as trade unions, residents' associations, BSPI,[4] and so on. Such an organisation emerged in the nineteenth century to support the public sphere and is based on the principle of vertical subsidiarity: the duty of intervening in a given activity or area to improve it and to protect those involved in or affected by it.

(c) *Social organisation*: a social organisation is a non-profit organisation that meets social requirements thanks to sponsoring, patronage or social action, like foundations, professorial chairs, and so on. This kind of organisation emerged in the twentieth century thanks to the restitution principle being applied; in other words, private organisations and businesses, aware that they partly make profits thanks to society and, therefore, set up non-profit foundations or organisations that fulfil social requirements through social action, patronage or sponsorship projects.

With these three types of civil society organisations, Zamagni opts for the civil models as these organisations generate relational processes that manage to produce

---

[4] BSPI are *Bank Savings Prorection Institutes*, created to protect bank accounts, mainly of small and medium savers, and to solve banks' solvency problems. Set up in Mexico, the aim of such a decentralized public administration organization is to contribute to the stability of the banking system and to safeguarding the payments system (Solís 2002)

(a) a strategic value and economic profit, efficacy, cohesion, effectiveness, etcetera, and also a self-fulfilled value – relational goods, and (b) *empowering capital*, a type of social capital whose objective is not to merely help, but to extend areas of freedom that promote relationality to empower related parties.

Civil organisations supported on the horizontal subsidiarity principle could solve the problem of today's economy, which, converted into an efficient mechanism for producing consumer goods, is incapable of promoting interactions of reciprocity that also produce the relational goods that allow their sustainability, and which also lie behind fulfilling the different good life projects of related parties. Non-profit organisations of this kind combine both issues. On one hand, they produce service goods by observing efficiency and efficacy; on the other, they are constituted as a relationality area thanks to the regulatory framework supporting them, whose main guidelines lie in reciprocity.

Civil organisations enable the empowering social capital of related parties to emerge and develop. Although Robert Putnam described two types of social capital in *Democracy Work: Civic Traditions in Modern Italy* (1993), with the words *link* and *bridge,* Zamagni understands that civil organisations generate different kinds of social capital that is fundamental for the economy to operate properly. The first of these is *empowerment-type social capital,* which is involved in the generation and expansion of the areas of freedom that allow relationality, empowerment, and will be related with giving in order to empower. This is understood as the series of relationships created among civil society organisations, such as different NGOs, foundations, non-profit associations or organisations, and central, regional or local political-administrative institutions, in order to materialise actions which, in themselves, could not be carried out. So, the regulatory principle does not lie in particular or generalised trust, but in vertical subsidiarity (Zamagni 2007: 36; 2011: 13–60), whose objective is to extend citizen's spaces of freedom (Zamagni 2007: 32; 2015: 222–225).

However, Zamagni's proposal focuses on a relationality proposal for economics through non-profit civil organisations governed by the logic of reciprocity. Yet there are other possibilities, as private, public or civil society economic organisations and businesses are governed by other logic, e.g. solidarity, efficiency or justice, which allow other logics, such as reciprocity, in order to be sustainable and supported in establishing stable and enriching relationships from which relational goods, like friendship, trust, reciprocity, commitment, reputation, and others are produced in order to make and maximise profits appropriately. For instance, an NGO is governed by the logic of solidarity, but it also needs to be concerned about efficiency as it works with scarce resources, whose poor management could delay it from correctly performing its activity, limit its potential, or even make it disappear. Likewise, a private company is controlled by the logic of efficiency but also needs to be concerned about reciprocity to generate stable mutually beneficial relations that allow cordial goods like legitimacy, credibility, trust, and so on to be managed.

So, based on an unconditioned type of reciprocity like cordial reciprocity, and seeking maximum economic profits based on recognising the communicative capacities of the bound or bindable parties to make sense of different worldly matters based on dialogue and intersubjective agreement; emotional competences in feeling emotional concerning oneself and for others; and the pre-existing link that produces an emotional and moral *ligatio* that *ob-liges* people to relate to one another and also the respect and dignity that human beings deserve as an absolute value – different non-profit or profit-making business and organisation models can establish reciprocal relationships based on one or several forms of observable reciprocity. This might include reciprocal altruism, strong reciprocity, institutional reciprocity, solidarity reciprocity, transitive reciprocity, indirect reciprocity, social reciprocity, inclusive reciprocity and others. Any reciprocal relationship stems from the mutual recognition of the bound or bindable parties and, thus, from a previous and unconditioned reciprocity that enables it. The difference lies in the recognition it stems from: the instrumental reciprocity from which the others are valid means to fulfil a particular purpose, or cordial recognition in relation to beings that are able to talk, act and become emotional, with an internal and absolute value that makes them worthy of respect and dignity.

So, among the new challenges faced by economic organisations and businesses, either public, private or from civil society, there is the management of those cordial goods. They are communicative and emotional at the same time and condition the possibility of their proper development and sustainability, which demands creating and maintaining reciprocal relationships within a framework of cordiality through one or several reciprocity models. This is especially true as the historical moment requires going beyond its technical and strategical dimension and is also concerned about the moral and affective side underlying them, a division accessible only by using cordial rationality supported by the mutual recognition of communicative capacities – to speak and reach agreements about something in the world – and emotional capacities – to do it for oneself and for others – supported by dignity.

There are different communication mechanisms that help build areas of dialogue capable of allowing the *cordial participation*[5] of civil society in an economic business or organisation, such as codes of ethics and conduct, ethics and social responsibility reports, ethics and social responsibility audits, ethics and social responsibility lines[6] (Bestratén and Pujol 2005, 2006; García-Marzá 2004). These five possible communication mechanisms are independent of each other, but also necessarily complement each other as a whole. When applied and correctly implemented, minimum bases are established to create areas of dialogue that allow economic organisations and businesses to seek an understanding with their stakeholders and, thus, a possible agreement that confers their activity credibility and legitimacy. As García-Marzá argues, only by integrating these mechanisms "(…) is it possible to confer consistency the goodwill that underlies trusting relations" (2004: 239).

---

[5] Cordial participation is understood as interpersonal relationality which, shaped by rationality in a cordial sense, like that proposed by Cortina, which is both reflexive and emotional at the same time, also seeks to understand something about the world and it happening in a practical domain.

[6] In the last two decades, García-Marzá has been working on adapting and systematising it, a task that has been reflected in the design of an *all-round ethics management system* for institutions, organisations and businesses (2004: 229–240).

Managing the communicative dimension, however, is not easy for economic institutions, organisations and businesses, regardless of whether they are the private, public or civil society type. This is particularly the case because implementing these or other possible communication mechanisms needs civil society's committed participation to be implemented. The proliferation of scandals in the economic domain, through corruption, nepotism, misappropriation of public funds, money laundering, business cartels, hiding properties and profits, monopolies, non-justified excesses that correspond to government organs, and many bad practices, all feed civil society's discontent and its hostility to participatory processes which are key to legitimising the behaviours performed and the decisions made by economic institutions, organisations and businesses. So, it is necessary to also consider the emotional dimension that underlies them; that is, seek areas of relationality to generate and promote the positive emotional form required to retrieve civil society's commitment and, in this way, its participation in the communication areas that lead to an agreement about worldly matters.

9.3   Cordial Civil Society: From Participatory Disaffection to Active Commitment

One of the main consequences of the different globalisation processes – economic, political, social, cultural and so on – provided and encouraged by the new information and communication technologies has been the rediscovery of civil society and, with him, the leading role of the different public and private organisations making it up. As suggested by different studies, (Beck 2005; Crouch 2004; Feenstra 2015; Feenstra et al., 2017; Kaldor 2003), although it is true that management of power takes place in the political domain, it is also true that part of this power is generated and developed in the domain of civil society. It is here in this domain where, for example, a cordial good like legitimacy occurs, making possible the relationality involved in the development of different areas of human activity, including the political and economic spheres. As previously mentioned, these goods have a rational base linked to technical-strategical aspects, but especially to moral-emotional ones, and these prosocial minimums of justice and emotions do not correspond to States, but rather to citizens and their relationships. Thus, civil society's involvement in their appearance and promotion is fundamental. Hence most of the theories on social change (Donati 2013), governance and institutional, organisational and business design in recent decades (García-Marzá 2004, 2017; González-Esteban 2013; Ostrom 1990, 2005, 2012b, c) have seen that the promotion and empowerment of a strong, active and committed civil society is a key factor in generating social innovation processes that favour a fair social order, more legitimate and enriched economic and political institutions, organisations and businesses promoting society and innovation and a more fulfilled and happier society. As John Keane argues in the monitory democracy proposal,[7] where an able and motivated civil society is promoted to monitor different institutions, organisations and business in various activity areas:

> (...) we still live in the age of the put-on. The combination of monitory democracy and communicative abundance nevertheless produces permanent flux, an unending restlessness driven by complex combinations of different interacting players and institutions, permanently pushing and pulling, heaving and straining, sometimes working together, at other times in opposition to one another. Elected and unelected representatives routinely strive to define and to determine who gets what, when and how, but the represented, taking advantage of various power-scrutinising devices, keep tabs on their representatives – sometimes with surprising success. (Keane 2013: 176)

Today's crisis context, however, represents an important challenge for maintaining the cordial dimension of economic institutions, organisations and businesses. Today's hostility in civil society's to everything concerned with politics and economics becomes lack of concern or demotivation for anything related to their management and development. The main problem in the economic world for such hostility lies in the fact that the number and impetus of civil society's legitimate expectations have increased, given today's precarious situation affecting most of society, especially that of the more vulnerable groups. The paradox lies in the fact that it receives constant news about political corruption, business lobbies that pressurise political institutions to legislate against the common good, financial scandals related with public administrations, misappropriation of public money, tax amnesties for tax evaders, business cartels where the price, the distribution and even the characteristics of products are agreed on, distribution of dividends among directors of businesses saved with public funds, the increase in pollution and destruction of the environment caused by predatory activity and an uncaring, irresponsible culture, and so on. As Keane indicates, these scandals involve problems that underlie democratic societies: "(...) there is no shortage of organised efforts by the powerful to manipulate people beneath them; and hence the political dirty business of dragging power from the shadows and flinging it into the blazing halogen of publicity remains fundamentally important" (Keane 2013: 176).

This fact has led to civil society feeling more distrust towards economic institutions, organisations and businesses, and considerably more hostility to anything that has to do with economics, although paradoxically it knows this and feels affected (Dekker and Feenstra 2015: 7–13). So it is not surprising that civil society feels demoralised, and such demoralisation has negative consequences for it and for institutions, organisations and businesses, given the rise in costs of managing cordial goods, especially credibility and legitimacy, which need to be related to their stakeholders. It is therefore difficult for them to sell their products and services, to be properly supplied, to have human and financial capital to grow and develop, and so on.

For all these reasons, new communication mechanisms and channels are sought that better allow processes to include civil society in the tasks of the institutions,

---

[7] For further information about monitory democracy and its practical development, see Feenstra (2012) and Feenstra et al. (2017).

organisations and businesses making up the different spheres of human activity to make maximum profits in both economic and self-fulfilment terms from dialogue and intersubjective understanding. In other words, they generate and promote cordial goods which, like legitimacy, are behind economic, social and human development.[8] Above all, however, ways to generate and promote emotions and positive feelings are explored to allow civil society to be committed to participation in commonly valued fulfilment, beneficial for all related parties.

Thus, one possibility would entail designing and implementing internal and external relationality areas in institutions, organisations and businesses to allow the feelings and emotions involved in various areas of activity to freely and willingly emerge. In other words, to create and promote areas where people or groups can freely relate to one another and make the underlying emotional dimension, and the components that make it up, visible. In this way, the institution, organisation or business can, in this way, find out which feelings and emotions allow common projects that are highly beneficial for all related parties if they are established and fulfilled; give themselves valid arguments to explain their use and enrich them through dialogue with their stakeholders; criticise them when they fall below the minimums levels the justice from cordial civil ethics; adapt them to each specific context depending on their logics and objectives; and promote and encourage them to empower cooperation to move towards maximum economic profits without turning against social and human development.

From this perspective, managing civil society's committed participation in the economy could be achieved in at least four steps:

(a) Firstly, the institution, organisation and business should encourage the use of cordial reciprocity in relationships with and among civil society to avoid the merely strategic use of human cooperation. In other words, reciprocal relationships should be sought tending to fulfil an own, collective or universal objective always based on cordiality, active recognition of communicative and affective capacities, and respecting the absolute value of related parties.

(b) Secondly, the institution, organisation and business should work on the appearance and empowerment of cordial recognition, based on which minimum expectations arise allowing relationality between people or groups based on the mutual recognition of communicative and affective capacities of related parties, the respect that they deserve and the internal value humans possess.

(c) Thirdly, the institution, organisation and business should design and implement areas of cordiality to manage the emotional and communicative dimension underlying it, which allows its committed participation in its design and activity. In other words, communication areas which should be able to criticise and make sense of the institution's, organisation's or business's actions and decisions through dialogue and an intersubjective agreement with all those affected, and relationality areas where the emotions and feelings involved in materialis-

---

[8] For specific proposals of the new communication mechanisms and channels between civil society and institutions and organizations, see Feenstra (2012) and Feenstra et al. (2017).

ing and fulfilling objectives commonly valued and beneficial for all related parties can emerge and be promoted.

(d) Fourthly, the institution, organisation and business should promote civil society's cordial participation in relational and communicative spaces, participation which is involved in the appearance, justification and enrichment of the goods required to carry out its activity. In other words, promoting the communicative participation of civil society actors moving towards intersubjective agreement on the meaning of the activity, and is also relational, tending to generate an emotional basis to allow evaluations to be made when what is fair and correct takes place in the practical domain. From this, it is possible to think about the appearance and development of intangible and necessary goods.

(e) Fifthly, the institution, organisation or business should be concerned with cordial goods, as these condition the possibility of them developing and surviving. Put another way, it should work on the communicative and emotional dimension of those goods, like legitimacy, trust, commitment, compassion, affection or affinity, which form the basis of its relations and enable cordially beneficial activity for all related parties where, in short, things are evaluated for their cordial and not merely strategic-instrumental benefit, and on achievement striving for what is economical, social and moral.

To conclude, it is cordial economics concerned about properly feeding the underlying technical-strategic dimension, the communicative dimension and the emotional dimension to live up to the expectations of the historical moment, and in agreement and harmony with that observed in fieldwork and laboratory experiments done with strategy games, and with that desired and expected by a cordial society which is morally mature and respectful, emotionally intelligent, committed and bound.

Bibliography

Beck, Ulrich. 2005. *Power in the Global Age*. Cambridge: Polity Press.

Bestratén, Manuel, and Luis Pujol. 2005. Ética empresarial y condiciones de trabajo. *Seguridad y salud en el trabajo* 42: 6–17.

———. 2006. *NTP 693: Condiciones de trabajo y códigos de conducta*. Barcelona: Centro Nacional de Condiciones de Trabajo, INSHT.

Brickman, Philip, and Donald T. Campbell. 1971. Hedonic relativism and planning the good society. In *Adaptation Level Theory: A Symposium*, ed. Mortimer H. Appley. New York: Academic.

Brondizio, Eduardo S., Elinor Ostrom, and Oran R. Young. 2009. Connectivity and the governance of multilevel social-ecological systems: The role of social capital. *The Annual Review of Environment and Resources* 34 (1–3): 253–278.

Bruni, Luigino, and Stefano Zamagni. 2007 [2004]. *Civil Economy: Efficiency, Equity, Public Happiness*. New York: Peter Lang.

Cárdenas, Juan-Camilo, and Elinor Ostrom. 2004. What do people bring into the game? Experiments in the field about cooperation in the commons. *Agricultural Systems* 82: 307–326.

Cortina, Adela. 2000. Ética empresarial en el contexto de una ética cívica. In *La ética de la empresa. Claves para una nueva ética empresarial*, ed. Adela Cortina, 35–50. Madrid: Trotta.

————. 2010. *Justicia cordial.* Madrid: Trotta.

————. 2013. *¿Para qué sirve realmente... la ética?* Barcelona: Paidós Ibérica.

Crouch, Colin. 2004. *Post-democracy.* Cambridge: Polity Press.

Dekker, Paul, and Ramón A. Feenstra. 2015. Activism and civil society: Broadening participation and deepening democracy. *Recerca. Revista de Pensament i Anàlisi* 17: 7–13.

Díaz, Ixone. 2012, May 27. Angus Deaton: "Las Crisis Están Creadas Para Beneficiar a Los Ricos". *El País, XL Semanal.*

Donati, Pierpaolo. 2013. *Sociologia relazionale. Come cambia la società.* Brescia: Editrice La Scuola.

Easterlin, Richard A. 1974. Does economic growth improve the human lot? Some empirical evidence. In *Nations and Households in Economic Growth: Essays in Honor of Moses Abramovitz,* ed. Paul A. David and Melvin W. Reder, 89–125. New York: Academic.

Feenstra, Ramón A. 2012. *Democracia monitorizada en la era de la nueva galaxia mediática. La propuesta de John Keane.* Barcelona: Icaria.

————. 2015. Activist and citizen political repertoire in Spain: A reflection based on civil society theory and different logics of political participation. *Journal of Civil Society* 11 (3): 242–258.

Feenstra, Ramón A., Simon Tormey, Andreu Casero-Ripollés, and John Keane. 2017. *Refiguring Democracy: The Spanish Political Laboratory.* New York: Routledge.

García-Marzá, Domingo. 2004. *Ética empresarial: del diálogo a la confianza.* Madrid: Trotta.

————. 2017. From ethical codes to ethical auditing: An ethical infraestructura for social responsibility communication. *El profesional de la información* 26 (2): 268–276.

Genovesi, Antonio. 1765–1767. *Delle lezioni di commercio, o sia di economia civile,* 2 vols. Naples: Fratelli Simone.

————. 1785a. *Lecciones de comercio, ó bien de economía civil, Tomo I.* Trans. Victorián de Villava. Madrid.

————. 1785b. *Lecciones de comercio, ó bien de economía civil, Tomo II.* Trans. Victorián de Villava. Madrid.

Gintis, Hebert. 2000. *Game Theory Evolving: A Problem-Centered Introduction to Modeling Strategic Interaction.* Princeton: Princeton University Press.

González-Esteban, Elsa, ed. 2013. *Ética y gobernanza: un cosmopolitismo para el siglo XXI.* Granada: Comares.

Greenspan, Alan. 2008. *The Age of Turbulence. Adventures in a New Wold.* London: Penguin.

Kahneman, Daniel, and Angus Deaton. 2010. High income improves evaluation of life, but not emotional well-being. *Proceedings of the National Academy of Sciences of the United States of America* 107 (38): 16489–16493.

Kaldor, Mary. 2003. *Global Civil Society: An Answer to War.* Cambridge, MA: Polity Press.

Keane, John. 2013. ¿Democracracia monitorizada? La historia secreta de la democracia desde 1945. In *Ética y gobernanza: un cosmopolitismo para el siglo XXI,* ed. Elsa González-Esteban, 149–181. Granada: Comares.

Lewis, Michael. 2010. *The Big Short: Inside the Doomsday Machine.* New York: W.W. Norton & Company.

McKay, Adam. 2015. *The Big Short.* Paramount Pictures.

Ostrom, Elinor. 1986. An agenda for the study of institutions. *Public Choice* 48 (1): 3–25.

————. 1990. *Governing the Commons. The Evolution of Institutions for Collective Action.* Cambridge: Cambridge University Press.

————. 1995a. Designing complexity to govern complexity. In *Property Rights and the Environment. Social and Ecological Issues,* ed. Susan Hanna and Mohan Munasinghe, 33–46. Washington, DC: The Beijer International Institute of Ecological Economic and the World Bank.

————. 1995b. Self-organization and social capital. *Industrial and Corporate Change* 4 (1): 131–159.

————. 1997. Esquemas institucionales para el manejo exitoso de recursos comunes. *Gaceta Ecológica* 45: 32–48.

———. 1998. Self-governance of common-pool resources. In *The New Palgrave Dictionary of Economics and the Law*, ed. Peter Newman, vol. 3, 424–433. London: Macmillan Press.

———. 1999a. *Design Principles and Threats to Sustainable Organizations that Manage Commons [Workshop in Political Theory and Policy Analysis]*. Indianapolis: Center for the Study of Institutions, Population, and Environmental Change, Indiana University. http://beyondostrom.blog.rosalux.de/files/2013/05/Design-Principles-and-Threats-to-Sustainable-Organizations-That-Manage-Commons.pdf. Accessed 25 Sept 2017.

———. 1999b. Social capital: A fad or a fundamental concept. In *Social capital: A multifaceted perspective*, ed. Partha Dasgupta and Ismail Serageldin, 172–214. Washington, DC: World Bank.

———. 2001. Reformulating the commons. In *Protecting the Commons: A Framework for Resource Management in the Americas*, ed. Joanna Burger, Elinor Ostrom, Richard B. Norgaard, David Policansky, and Bernard D. Goldstein, 17–41. Washington, DC: Island Press.

———. 2003. Toward a behavioral theory. Linking trust, reciprocity, and reputation. In *Trust & Reciprocity. Interdisciplinary Lessons from Experimental Research*, ed. Elinor Ostrom and James Walker, 19–79. New York: Russell Sage Foundation.

———. 2005. *Understanding Institutional Diversity*. Princeton: Princeton University Press.

———. 2012a. Experiments combining communication with punishment options demonstrate how individuals can overcome social dilemmas. *Behavioral and Brain Sciences* 35 (1): 33–34.

———. 2012b. Nested externalities and polycentric institutions: Must we wait for global solutions to climate change before taking actions at other scales? *Journal of Economic Theory* 49 (2): 353–369.

———. 2012c. Why do we need to protect institutional diversity? *European Political Science* 11 (1): 128–147.

Putnam, Robert D., Roberto Leonardi, and Raffaella Nanetti. 1993. *Making Democracy Work: Civic Traditions in Modern Italy*. Princeton: Princeton University Press.

Ramón-Fernández, Francisca. 2001. *El ingreso de la Comunidad de Pescadores de El Palmar en la transmisión hereditaria del "Redolí"*. Valencia: Publicacions de la Universitat de València.

Saint Augustine of Hippo. 1864. *The Confessions of S. Agustine*. Oxford: John Henry and James Parker.

Schlager, Edella, and Elinor Ostrom. 1992. Property-rights regimes and natural resources: A conceptual analysis. *Land Economics* 68 (3): 249–262.

Solís, Ricardo. 2002. *Del Fobaproa al IPAB. Testimonios, Análisis y Propuestas*. México: Plaza y Valdés.

Zamagni, Stefano. 1999. Social paradoxes of growth and civil economy. In *Economic Theory and Social Justice*, ed. Giancarlo Gandalfo and Ferrucio Marzano, 212–136. London: MacMillan Press.

———. 2006. *Heterogeneidad motivacional y comportamiento económico. La perspectiva de la economía civil*. Madrid: Unión Editorial.

———. 2007. El bien común en la sociedad posmoderna: propuestas para la acción político-económica. *Revista Cultural Económica* 25 (79): 23–43.

———. 2010. Reciprocidad y fraternidad. El papel de los sentimientos en la economía. In *XXI Seminario Étnor de Ética y Economía. ¿Lecciones Aprendidas? Nuevos Caminos para el Crecimiento y Nuevas Formas de Vida Ética en las Estrategias Empresariales del Siglo XXI*, ed. Jesús Conill, 55–66. Valencia: Fundación Étnor.

———. 2011. Slegare il Terzo Settore. In *Libro Bianco sul Terzo Settore*, ed. Stefano Zamagni, 13–60. Bologna: Il Mulino.

———. 2015. El reto de la responsabilidad civil de la empresa. *Mediterráneo Económico* 26: 209–225.

———. 2018. Le bien commun dans le discours èconomique actuel. *Transversalitès. Défis économiques et propositions chrétiennes*, 144 (1): 7–33

Chapter 10
Cordial Big Data: Managing the Cordial Dimension of a Business

Abstract The big data era represents a challenge for businesses, but also a great opportunity for them. Big Data, and increasingly advanced, versatile and accessible data analysis tools, offer businesses the chance to develop and systemise extraordinary quantities of data from many and varied sources, as well as providing their stakeholders with relevant information based on it. This is opening up new prospects for the management of cordial goods. Among other things, it allows businesses to develop new communication channels capable of collecting specific, detailed, continuously updated information on their economic, social and environmental impacts; the legitimate interests and expectations at stake; on the level of trust, reputation and affinity they arouse among their stakeholders; and on the affective factors stimulated by their actions and decisions, among many other things. The purpose of this chapter is to propose guidelines for designing a monitoring system which, based on the communication, storage and processing of big data and the committed participation of stakeholders, offers businesses the possibility of inspecting their underlying dimensions of morality, emotions and responsibility.

Over the last few years, the *Edelman Trust Barometer*, which compiles and systemises the data from more than 34,000, carried out in 28 countries, has highlighted several important issues which invite reflection. Firstly, there is the intrinsic relationship between trust and business profits. The majority of these surveyed refuse to buy products or services from companies that do not deserve their trust (68%) and they even advise their friends, acquaintances and family members against them (58%). On the other hand, they do buy products and services from companies that deserve trust (80%) and they recommend them to their friends, acquaintances and family members. Meanwhile, there is the social role of businesses. The majority of those surveyed (80%) believe that a business can and should play an important role in solving social problems through actions which, at the same time, increase its profits. This is an important detail, as those surveyed are not asking for altruistic actions. They understand companies' logic and ask them to seek business profits by choosing actions that also have positive repercussions on their social and environmental surroundings (Edelman Berland 2016). Finally, a resource like communication makes it possible to manage intangibles as important for the survival of companies and increasing business profits as trust.

© Springer International Publishing AG, part of Springer Nature 2018   163
P. Calvo, *The Cordial Economy - Ethics, Recognition and Reciprocity*,
Ethical Economy 55, https://doi.org/10.1007/978-3-319-90784-0_10

The general results change notably when the responses given by the *informed public* – those with education or who bother to find out about the economic situation on different levels – are separated from those of the *mass*, who do not care or prefer not to think about the current economic situation and what is being done or could be done to improve it. The trust of the informed public in institutions, organisations, leaders, media and companies is up to 15 points higher than the trust of the *mass* public (Edelman Berland 2016, 2017).

The conclusion of the results of the Edelman Trust Barometer over the last few years is that businesses need to begin to recognise that their survival and development depend on the proper management of intangibles, and that this management requires fluid, open, continuing dialogue with stakeholders to find out what interests are at stake, give information about how they are responding to these interests and find out the stakeholders' level of satisfaction (Edelman Berland 2015, 2016, 2017).

Considering this, the aim of this chapter is to propose guidelines for designing a system for monitoring the emotional and moral dimension of businesses that helps to generate and promote cordial goods, making it possible for them to carry out their activities correctly. To do this, we will first show that social responsibility offers a method of approaching the radical reality of the company in an elegant, intelligent, mature way. The possibility of monitoring the cordial dimension of businesses using new Big Data and big data analytics technologies will then be demonstrated. Finally, a system of monitoring and complying with ethics and social responsibility will be shown, based on open big data, a communication mechanism through which companies can provide open information and big data analysis tools to all their stakeholders with the main aim of empowering them and increasing the size of the *informed population*. This makes it possible to manage and promote trust, reputation, responsibility, affinity and other intangible goods that are a condition of its activity. Underlying these is a dimension that is at once emotional and moral.

10.1   The Intelligent Business: Managing ethics and Social Responsibility

As Diego Gracia argues (2015), human beings are the most inadequate animal in existence. We need only look at our vulnerable situation at birth or deficient immunological system to see this. Had the survival of humans depended on their capacity to adapt, they would have disappeared as a species thousands of years ago. However, we have managed to survive thanks to a capacity not accessible to other animals, at least to the same degree: intelligence. This capacity allows us to think about and design better possible worlds. Because of this, unlike other animals, human beings do not adapt to the environment. We transform it, inverting the process, so it is adapted for us and not the other way round, leading to human-controlled evolution. This is why, while animals live in the environment, human beings live in culture, in the context of a planned world.

Similarly, for José Ortega y Gasset (1960, 1967), people are creatures predisposed to take charge of their own lives. They cannot not do so, as their free existence forces them to choose between different possibilities, and their capacity to prefer the preferable requires them to think about and plan the *best of all possible worlds* (Roldán 2015). In other words, "Living means constantly deciding what we are going to be" (Ortega y Gasset 1958: 234), not opting for just anything, but deciding elegantly and intelligently between the different possibilities, particularly those making it possible to overcome circumstances, in order to plan a fully human life.

> Caprice is to be avoided. Caprice signifies doing anything among the many things that can be done. Its opposite is the act and habit of *choosing* from among many things precisely the one that demands to be done. This act habit of choosing selectively was at first designated as *elegentia* by the Latins, and then *elegantia*. This term possibly the origin of our word intelligentia. In any event, elegance would have been an apter name for what we instead awkwardly categorise as ethics; since the latter is the art of choosing the best conduct, it is the science of what has to be done. (...) Elegant is the man who neither does nor says any old thing, but instead does what should be done and says what should be said (Ortega y Gasset 1967: 13–14)

What this best possible world is for a moral and emotionally mature society was specified on 25 September 2015 in the 17 Sustainable Development Goals (SDG) as the signatories were urged to make joint efforts to minimise inequalities, generate sustainable economic growth, eradicate hunger and poverty and consume responsibly, among many other things. Now the aim is to design it, seeking to bring it into being in practice. And this is where businesses play a fundamental role because of the power they have to transform the social situation (Zamagni 2013, 2014, 2017). This is particularly the case for businesses that are concerned and take care to promote and develop a cordial nature. In other words, they have a plan for life and, within the scope of their freedom, they carry it out intelligently, taking into account both their own strategic dimension and the moral and emotional dimensions underlying them. Properly managing these makes it possible to enjoy maximum business profits by generating and promoting goods including reciprocity, trust, reputation, affinity and legitimacy.

In this process of projection towards the future in the context of the planned world, social responsibility can play an important role for a company, as it offers tools, guidelines and orientations to avoid adverse circumstances and face its radical reality elegantly and intelligently. Among many other things, social responsibility allows a company to find out its strengths, weaknesses, opportunities and threats so it can adapt more quickly and better to legal, social, economic and environmental changes, minimise transaction costs and maximise business profits. This is also because it promotes the construction of a suitable employment climate, the eradication of poverty and inequalities, respect for human rights, the inclusion of the most disadvantaged groups, environmental sustainability, managing intangibles involved in the proper development and promotion of its activity, and so on. In other words, social responsibility helps companies maximise business profits while at the same time contributing to achieving the SDG. However, it requires social responsibility not only concerned with improving the strategic management of the company but, above all, promoting a business culture and a form of existence linked to moral and affective aspects. This is social responsibility which, in the context of citizen ethics, goes beyond merely strategic use by promoting processes of dialogue with its stakeholders justifying and legitimising the company's actions and decisions and relationship processes that generate the motivation required for fair and responsible actions.

In this sense, although there are precedents related to philanthropy and sponsorship, the specialised literature begins with social responsibility in the 1950s, when American society began to demand that businesses should justify the use being made of their power of influence in economic, social, political, cultural and other areas of human activity (González-Esteban 2001).

The specific concept of social responsibility began in 1953, linked to intelligence, the art of choosing well and preferring the preferable. As Howard R. Bowen states in his book *Social Responsibilities of the Businessman*, this new way of looking at business is related "(…) to the obligations of businessmen to pursue those policies, to make those decisions, or to follow those lines of action which are desirable in terms of the objectives and values of our society" (Bowen 1953: 6). Bowen was drawing attention to two models of business and their circumstances in his age that did not seem to fit these new times very well, so that they could be overcome with proper planning: the neoclassical approach, as an anachronism, and the democratic one, as insufficient. The former, based on economic marginalism, considered only the individual interests of the businessman or shareholder, while the latter, based on industrial democracy, went beyond the mere individual interest of the owner to also include the collective expectations of employees. For Bowen, however, corporate social responsibility has nothing to do with what "(…) businessmen want or consider to be good" or with the possibility of achieving balances between internal groups with different interests. Instead it concerns what society understands as preferable. For this reason, when companies carry out actions to generate profits, they must do so taking into account above all society's general interest in them carrying out their activity, both in terms of the interests at stake and the applicable rules.

> The modern businessman cannot be locked upon as an absolute monarch ruling by divine right and interpreting his social responsibilities as the carrying out of his own decisions as to what is "good" for the people. The businessman, rather, is subject to the standards of the community and to the pressures exerted by various interest groups (Bowen 1953: 120).

During the 1960s and 1970s, Keith Davis took the main ideas from Bowen's work and developed them. Through what he called the *Iron law of social responsibility*, Davis put aside the philanthropic meaning of social responsibility to focus on the intrinsic relationship between power and responsibility in the business world.

Like Bowen, Davis initially focused his attention on the owner's responsibility rather than the company's, suggesting, in *Can Business Afford to Ignore Social Responsibilities?* (1960) that the owner's power and responsibility go hand-in-hand and require proportionality in both senses:

> To the extent that businessmen or any other group have social power, the lessons of history suggest that their social responsibility should be equated with it. Stated in the form of a general relationship, it can be said that *social responsibilities of businessmen need to be commensurate with their social power*. (Davis 1960: 71)

However, Davis later looked at this idea in greater depth in the book *Business and its Environment* published in 1966 together with Robert L. Blomstrom, and made a first approach to what he called the Iron Law of Responsibility:

> If power and responsibility tend towards a state of balance in the long run, *then the avoidance of social responsibility leads to gradual erosion of social power.* This is the Iron Law of Responsibility: Those who do not take for their power ultimately shall lose it. (Davis and Blomstrom 1966: 174)

Finally, Davis developed and extended the Iron Law of Responsibility in the article "The Case for and against Business Assumption of Social Responsibilities", published in 1973, focusing his attention on the business and not the businessman and above all taking an interest in reconstructing the conditions of the possibility of power: "Society grants legitimacy and power to business. In the long run, those who do not use power in a manner which society considers responsible will tend to lose it" (Davis 1973: 314).

So, through the ideas of Bowen, Davis and other mid-twentieth-century thinkers, social responsibility was disentangled from philanthropic actions and business sponsorship – the *what* – to begin to be seen as the justification of businesses' management of the power granted by society to be able to carry out their activity and maximise profits. In this way, the *what* was superseded by the *how*, which became the main focus of attention in social responsibility (Davis 1975: 19–24). From this point onwards, a socially responsible company began to be seen as one managing to justify to society *how* it has managed to generate its profits rather than having anything to do with *what* a businessman does with his portion of the profits.

From the 1980s onwards, there began to be a change of paradigm in business management. Firstly, stakeholder theory, put forward by R. Edward Freeman in 1984, showed that to approach the radical reality of a business properly it was necessary to take on a diverse set of interests at stake involving many groups to different degrees, depending on the specific nature of the business. These groups, which Freeman called *stakeholders* and related to "(…) all of those groups and individuals that can affect, or are affected by, the accomplishment of organizational purpose" (Freeman 1984: 25), were responsible to some degree for the power of the business, so the way in which that power was being used needed to be justified to them. Secondly, the triple bottom line suggested by John Elkington in *Towards the Sustainable Corporation: Win-Win-Win Strategies for Sustainable Development* (1994) and later developed in *Cannibals With Forks: The Triple Bottom Line of Twenty-First-Century Business* (1997), in which, basing himself on the *Brundtland Report* which the UN had drawn up in 1987, urged businesses to base their strategy on sustainability, seeking economic benefits at the same time as social development and environmental quality. Thirdly and finally, the development of the discourse of stakeholder theory during the 1990s stated that, as Freeman suggested, coexisting with the set of business interests at stake were the individual and collective strategic expectations of stakeholders. Satisfying these makes it possible to improve strategic business management. Above all, though, what specifies and defines the content of social responsibility – making it possible to legitimise the way the business uses its power – is dialogue and possible agreement between all those affected by the business's actions and decisions: in other words, meeting the legitimate expectations that are common to all of them (González-Esteban 1999, 2001, 2002, 2007, 2012).

This discursively revised stakeholder theory opened the door to a new business paradigm, the plural business. This model of business is conceived as a set of reciprocal relationships whose credibility and legitimacy refers to the intersubjective dialogue and agreement of all internal and external stakeholders on meeting the legitimate economic, social and environmental expectations at stake (García-Marzá 2004: 161).

Both social responsibility and this new model of plural business began to be consolidated in 2001, when the European Commission decided that the most intelligent way to achieve the strategic goal set at the Lisbon European Council in 2000, "(…) to become the most competitive and dynamic knowledge-based economy in the world capable of sustainable economic growth with more and better jobs and greater social cohesion" (Lisbon European Council 2000) was by promoting social responsibility in the business sphere (COM 366 Final 2001). This meant encouraging the voluntary inclusion by businesses of social and environmental concerns, together with economic ones, as well as establishing processes of dialogue with their stakeholders.[1]

From this point, work began to specify the processes and communication mechanisms allowing committed participation by stakeholders in the possible intersubjective agreement between the business's actions and decisions. Currently most important among these are ethical codes of conduct; ethics and social responsibility committees; sustainability reports; ethical and social responsibility audits; and lines of compliance, developed and systemised by García-Marzá from an ethical and discursive point of view in his proposed *Integrated System for Managing Ethics and Social Responsibility* (García-Marzá 1994, 2004, 2017).

Codes of ethics and conduct are formal documents in which the company informs its stakeholders about its nature; its predisposition to do and say things in a particular way in accordance with specific moral values, as well as the rules governing its activity; and the commitments it is prepared to make to implement them (García-Marzá 2004, 2017; Lozano 2004, 2007). These codes were drawn up for the first time in the sixteenth century to guide medical practice,[2] and they have now become a fundamental tool for dealing with issues as important as internal cohesion, behavioural consistency, the construction of identity, the establishment of business culture, market differentiation, and so on, in any area of activity.

Ethics and Social responsibility committees are the forum for dialogue and deliberation by the company's stakeholders. These committees emerged in the health sphere during the second half of the twentieth century when, in 1953, the

---

[1] The Green Paper (COM 366 Final 2001) offers an idea of social responsibility for the twenty-first century based on four basic issues: voluntary nature, triple accountability, dialogue with stakeholders and co-responsibility.

[2] The Royal College of Physicians' *Code of Medical Ethics* is considered to be the first in history (Brown et al. 2007: 128).

National Institute of Health required all research on human subjects carried out at its facilities to have the prior approval of a committee of experts overseeing its protection, known as the Institutional Review Boards.[3] The committees have now been extended to different areas of activity, including the economic sphere (Cortina 1996), a communication tool whose main function is to advise and make reports on issues relating to social responsibility; manage the notification of alerts, reports of misconduct, suggestions and improvement proposals received; cooperate in resolving disputes; raise awareness of the need to be economically, socially and environmentally sustainable; train internal stakeholders on the code of ethics; promote the business's culture; and supervise social responsibility reports, among other things.

Ethics and social responsibility reports are formal documents in which the business publishes its impacts in terms of economic, social and environmental sustainability. Beginning during the 1980s and 1990s and jointly promoted by UNEP (United Nations Environmental Programme) and CERES (Coalition for Environmentally Responsible Economies) since 1997, social responsibility reports are a tool for communication between businesses and the stakeholders whose main function is to generate added value: transparency, reputation, trust, affinity, self-knowledge, improvement, structural adjustment, visualisation of potential and weaknesses, control and prevention of conflicts, improvement of job satisfaction, rapid adaptation to new challenges, good brand image, minimisation of transaction costs, and so on. There are currently different methodologies for drawing up reports, including most importantly the Global Reporting Initiative, because it is most commonly used, updated more regularly and clearer. It has indicators for measuring and publishing social responsibility indicators concerning businesses and making them accountable in this respect.

Ethics and Social responsibility audits are a process for evaluating and communicating the level of compliance with commitments made by businesses concerning social responsibility. Their main function is to certify the consistency between what is said and what is done. Or, as García-Marzá argues, "(…) to show that the organisation 'means it', that social responsibility is not a mere strategy but forms part of its ethics" – in other words its character and its form of existence and action (2017: 274). To implement them,[4] García-Marzá suggests a methodology based on Habermas's theory of communicative action and discursive ethics in which the observer's and participant's perspectives coexist to provide objective data and perceptions of business reality (García-Marzá 2017: 274). From this dual perspective, María Pilar Rodríguez et al. (2006) developed and applied an ethics and social

---

[3] In the health sphere, there are other kinds of committee, the Healthcare Bioethics Committees, which began in 1968 when the Harvard Medical Faculty (US) set up an *ad hoc* committee to clarify the circumstances of brain death (Post and Blustein 2015: 133), and the national bioethics committees which began in the seventies in countries like France, Italy and Portugal to draw up reports, proposals and recommendations from the public authorities (Cortina 1996).

[4] Other relevant studies of methodology and implementation of ethical audits are Rodríguez et al. (2006) and Lozano (2007).

responsibility audit model based on general variables; specific, measurable indicators; and different audit phases and stages (preparation, fieldwork and final report).

Ethics and social responsibility lines are the different communication channels established by the business so that stakeholders can give opinions and warnings, report misconduct and provide solutions and/or suggestions on its standards of morality and responsibility (García-Marzá 2017). Based on the whistleblowing systems that have emerged since 1971 and become consolidated in 2002 with the Sarbanes-Oxley (SOX) Act approved by the US Congress as a prevention and control measure for quoted companies (Sarbanes-Oxley Act, 30 July 2002), their main function is to systemise all notifications and warnings about breaches of the company's commitments and requirements concerning social responsibility. They also collect information on the proposals of stakeholders related to the applicability of the code of ethics and conduct; the review of social responsibility policies; the adaptation of the mechanisms allowing their implementation and proper development; the truthfulness and quality of the social responsibility report; and the improvement and proper operation of the line of social responsibility itself, among other things (García-Marzá 2017; Calvo 2015a, b, 2016a, b).

These communication management mechanisms or tools, duly complemented, (García-Marzá 2017) allow the business to fulfil its responsibility to generate and promote the intangible goods necessary for its proper development, such as reputation, affinity or trust. Nowadays, though, the current big data revolution poses a challenge to businesses because of at least three issues. Firstly, the information gap opening up between those facing up to this new situation and those turning their backs on it is going to be the most distorting element in the economy over the next few years. Secondly, the management of intangibles like trust, reputation or affinity depends largely on the management of both the strategic and the moral and emotional dimensions of the company, and nil or inadequate monitoring is becoming a disruptive factor. Above all, though monitoring is not only within reach of businesses, which can use big data analytics to get a better picture of the impacts caused by its activity and needs, expectations, interests and motivations of its stakeholders. The stakeholders themselves, thanks to increasingly accessible, free technologies and the emergency of business advisor websites, are starting to oversee businesses so that they can make much fairer, more prudent and more beneficial decisions.

10.2   The Monitored Business: Whistleblowing in the Big Data Era

During the Conference on Professional Responsibility held in Washington D.C. on 30 January 1971, the political activist Ralph Nader made a "call to the responsibility" to the different professionals from the world of economics to monitor businesses and give warnings when they had evidence of destructive, immoral practices that could damage the health of either the businesses or society. This warning was the starting point for the term whistleblowing, a neologism coined by Nader himself to define and highlight the committed, responsible attitudes of management and employees who put the general interest of society before the particular interest of the public or private institution, company or organisation where they carry on their activities (Boffey 1971: 549–551), as well as preventing these people being linked with pejorative terms such as "grass" or "informer" (Nader et al. 1972).

After almost half a century of conceptual and practical theorising,[5] whistleblowing has managed to arouse the interest of businesses thanks to support and promotion in national and international regulations, codes and directives, particularly those linked with social responsibility.[6] These include the ISO 26000 standard on social responsibility, which, in its section *6.3.6 Human rights issue 4: resolving grievances* and *4.4 Ethical behaviour* promote "(…) establishing and maintaining mechanisms to facilitate the reporting of unethical behaviour without fear of reprisal" (International Organization for Standardization 2010). Also, the *Global Reporting Initiative G.4*, which, through its indicators G.4–49, G.4–57 and G.4–58, urges businesses to report on the compliance systems they use to achieve social responsibility goals.

However, these regulations, guidelines and standards have tended towards a biased, inadequate and, we might even say disappointing, implementation of whistleblowing in business. In particular, this is because they call for efforts to be made to implement channels for warnings and reporting ethical/legal irregularities, but say nothing on the need to develop and implement monitoring systems to allow proactive, constant surveillance of expected behaviour through the opening of communication channels between businesses and their stakeholders. With this, they downgrade their potential as an element for transforming the economic and social situation as well as their capacity to manage the intangible resources needed to carry out economic activity, such as trust, reputation, affinity and responsibility, which have an underlying cordial dimension.

In a narrow sense, to monitor means "Observe and check the progress or quality of (something) over a period of time; keep under systematic review" (Oxford 2017). However, in a broad sense, as suggested by Nader and other whistleblowing theorists, monitoring covers legal, social, environmental and moral aspects. For example, examination of the degree to which the legitimate expectations at stake have been met; the economic, social and environmental impacts of the company's activity; the affective factors concerning stakeholders; the level of trust, affinity and reputation achieved; the prevention of illegal practices, and so on. This means monitoring as an action to protect, respect and remedy, as suggested by Marco Ruggie's guidelines, and carrying on business activities in the context of the Sustainable Development Goals (SDG), as urged by the United Nations (United Nations 2011, 2015).

---

[5] For a study of the process of conceptual theorising and the practice of whistleblowing, see Calvo (2016a, b).

[6] To look at the relationship between whistleblowing and social responsibility in depth, Win Vandekerckhove (2006).

In the past, the lack of interest of monitoring regulations, guidelines and standards could have been due to the complexity or lack of technological resources to cope with monitoring responsibility in business management with real guarantees. Today, however, the possibility of storing large volumes of data – Big Data; the development of big data analytics; and the rapid advance of the Internet of Things, which provides much more precise information about trends, demands, interests, expectations, behaviours, motivations and emotions of internal and external stakeholders (Yager and Espada 2017; Kocovic et al. 2017; Tascón and Coullaut 2016) have meant monitoring is not only possible but also necessary and required in order to carry on economic activities efficiently, effectively and responsibly. Ultimately it is a matter of being prepared for the requirements of the historical moment.

Big Data and the increasingly advanced, versatile and accessible data analysis tools offer businesses the chance to develop and systemise extraordinary quantities of data from many and varied sources, as well as providing their stakeholders with relevant information based on this data. This is a challenge for businesses because of at least two issues. Firstly, the information gap opening up between those facing up to this new situation and those turning their backs on it is going to be the most distorting element in the economy over the next few years. Another factor is that the management of intangibles such as trust, reputation and affinity largely depends on management of the strategic, moral and emotional dimensions of the company. If monitoring does not exist or is inadequate, it is a disruptive factor.

Concerning social responsibility big data, there are diverse, versatile tools for big data analysis that can be used by businesses for monitoring overall or specific aspects of this. Some of them are easy to access and even cost very little. For example, for analysing documents, legislation and reports relating to social responsibility, there is *BigQuery* from Google, an online data storage platform that constitutes a big data analysis tool. To analyse stakeholders' levels of commitment, there is *Kaushik*, which uses a metric based on identifying the motivations, emotions and feelings behind trust, reputation, affinity and cohesion. To analyse corporate reputation, there is *Asomo*, which combines semantic analysis and crowdsourcing techniques; *Socialmention*, which calculates the company's reputation in social media; and *BlogPulse*, which monitors the content of all the blogs in the world to discover the company's image. For the internal and external analysis of emotions and feelings related to the company and the activity it carries out, there are *Klout* and *PeerIndex*, which trawl data from millions of external spaces and the company's own information, and *Ciao, Swotti* and *TwitsObserver*, which carry out *opinion mining* to extract relevant information from the comments made by stakeholders on forums, websites, blogs, social media, and so on. Finally, to carry out research and control (monitoring) concerning the attitudes of an institution, business or economic organisation and their stakeholders, there are *Socialmention, Google Insights, Social affairs Contango, Twitter Search*, and *Sysomos*, among many others.

All these tools allow proper comprehension and management of a business's responsibility and the motivations underlying it. Meanwhile, their systematic use allows the company to find out about the interests at stake in real time, as well as the economic, social and environmental conflicts and their material nature. They also make it possible to think of a new concept of social responsibility report, a new way for businesses to be accountable for their economic, social and environmental impacts. Big data analysis tools promote *reportingapps* or *triplebottomapps,* applications offering real-time information about the economic, social and environmental impacts of the company by processing internal and external data and turning it into bubble charts, cartograms, maps, node trees, Sankey diagrams, chord wheels, matrices, and so on. This means, the reports will be much more up to date, complete and comprehensible but, above all, participatory, as the company and its stakeholders will share, to different degrees, the leading role and responsibility for drawing up the report. In other words, the company is responsible for designing and offering an open 3.0 platform for collecting, processing and communicating data so that both it and its stakeholders contribute to the contents of the report via relevant information they upload to the platform, in the case of the company, or through news, opinions and notifications which they place in newspapers, websites, forums, blogs, social media, channels of social responsibility and so on, in the case of stakeholders.

This new conception of social responsibility reports as open and participatory makes it possible to see, quickly, clearly and in real time, the efforts that have been made or are being made by the company to put right deficiencies, failings or mistaken actions and decisions; the level of satisfaction of the interests at stake; what affective factors it arouses among stakeholders; and what new conflicts are arising, among many other things. But it also makes it possible to check the truthfulness of the information the company publishes in the report thanks to the analysis of information from external sources, such as business advisors; websites that compile and process information provided directly by companies' own employees. Among many of these, we should highlight *Glassdoor*, which provides data going far beyond how stakeholders value the company, looking at internal trust, affinity, reciprocity, justice and responsibility. Among other important issues, Glassdoor provides interesting information about opportunities, wages, work-life balance, culture, quality and the companies values, as well as how strongly employees would recommend working at the company to a friend. Other similar business advisors, although currently less developed, are beginning to collect and process opinions from customers, suppliers, civil society organisations and other stakeholders, offering valuable information about issues related to satisfying the company's economic, social and environmental interests.

All these issues have awakened the effective interest of big companies in Big Data, as well as the latent interest of small and medium-sized enterprises and stakeholders, which now have reasons to expect a new inclusive, accessible technology allowing them to participate in companies' expectations and profits. However, the current use of Big Data in business is a long way from being adequate.

In terms of the monitoring of businesses using the Big Data they directly and indirectly produce, it is currently far from the horizon of meaning suggested by Nader and many other whistleblowing theorists of the last 50 years, as its use is one-way, exclusive and instrumental. Businesses with enough power to use it are, firstly, applying mechanisms for controlling big data –information governance– that limit, twist and distort the information available for their own benefit and, secondly, using big data analysis as a behaviour prediction model allowing them to optimise profits by controlling free will or simply taking advantage of the matrices of opinion of stakeholders, particularly customers. Both approaches bias and pervert the meaning underlying monitoring (Feenstra 2012, 2015b; Feenstra et al. 2017), generating suspicion among competitors, making the business world more opaque and promoting distrust among stakeholders. This undermines its potential an instrument not merely for adaptation but also transforming the social situation (Feenstra 2015a, b) and its capacity to manage the intangible resources needed to carry out economic activity, such as trust, reputation, affinity and reciprocity, which have an underlying cordial dimension (Calvo 2016b, c).

Concerning the Internet of Things (IoT), the continuing cases of bad practice related to the improper compilation and use of data, the behavioural relativism of algorithms, tactics of fragmentation, disaggregation and depersonalisation of the responsibility of a company for its actions and decisions and, especially, *human obsolescence* underlying the *technological absolutism* and *algorithmic dictatorship* – as predicted by Günther Anders (1980) – is generating an intense debate on the conflicts, limits and consequences of the current trend towards the almost total computerisation of all business processes –production, decision-making, communication and relational– to optimise the business and improve its competitiveness.[7] This is the source of a new philosophical discipline: the *Ethics of Things* (EoT). A new field of research whose main task consists of explaining the normative assumptions of the Internet of Things (IoT) and criticising, based both on argument and dialogue, both the design and the knowledge and behaviour of platforms, cyberphysical ecosystems, smart machines, algorithms or devices collecting information and fed by big data relevant information and applicable knowledge to make decisions that affect us and are competitive. Ethics requiring responsibility, transparency, autonomy and monitoring to prevent the negative effects of *Smart Business*.[8] Because, among other things, algorithms are a double-edged sword which, without public control or scrutiny, can cause unfair, rather irresponsible situations with very little benefit for the parties in a relationship.

For this and other reasons, it is necessary to work on the design and application of monitoring and compliance systems which, in the context of ethics and social responsibility and through compliance with big data analytics tools and other communication instruments, such as codes of ethics and conduct and social responsibility committees, channels, audits and reports, allow companies both to use big data properly and include stakeholders in the scrutiny of the behaviour of the business, the proper operation of the system and the truthfulness of the information available, as well as content creation.

---

[7] All this is leading to the emergence of new concepts and fields of study, such as algorithmic ethics, the ethics of data, algorithmic government or the governance of algorithms, among other things, as well as a requirement for proper monitoring to prevent possible resulting damage. To find out more about all these issues, Monasterio (2017) and Calvo (2017).

[8] For an in-depth study of this new discipline of knowledge, Calvo (2017).

10.3 Monitoring and Compliance Systems: Public Control and Scrutiny of Business Behaviour

The big data revolution represents an unavoidable challenge for businesses. Used intelligently, big data analytics offers companies the chance to monitor the impacts of its activity, the conflicts involved and the interests and effects of their stakeholders. This provides the business with valuable information to, firstly, carry out its activity to the standard required by the historical moment and, secondly, to make more rational and responsible decisions and, finally, to manage and promote the goods necessary for carrying out its activity efficiently and sustainably, such as reputation, trust and affinity.

However, one of the dangers of monitoring big data is that it can encourage businesses to leave their present or future course in the hands of technological chance and the improper or irresponsible use of the information available (Suárez-Gonzalo 2017; Tascón and Coullaut 2016). To prevent this, it is necessary for businesses to take control of this by designing a monitoring system capable of getting the most from big data through effective, efficient and responsible management. In accordance with different international directives and standards, as well as the specialised literature,[9] this monitoring and compliance system must contain at least six steps:

1. *Management and action protocol*: this is the guideline document including all the information relating to the processes and actions of the system. It includes the resources available; the structure of the system; the basic management and action plan for the system; the plan to roll out and implement the system (Communication Plan, Social Responsibility Plan, Process Plan, etc.); business, industry and international rules, codes and standards that constitute the regulatory environment for the system (the values, principles and regulations of the profession and the sector; the ISO26000 standard concerning Social Responsibility; the Social Responsibility Act; the Data Protection Act, the company's social responsibility policy; Marco Ruggie's governing principles; the sustainable development goals, etc.); a document describing the structure, instruments and scope of the monitoring system; a training programme for promoting and raising awareness of the system and its benefits, and other relevant issues relating to the proper application, implementation and development of the social responsibility monitoring processes.
2. Communication mechanisms: this concerns the different communication tools a business uses to show the way it acts and the economic, social and environmental

---

[9] In this respect, in the field of international directives, we would highlight the recommendations of the European Council via *Dictamen 1/2006 drawn up by the Article 29 Working Group on Data Protection* (2006) and the standards contained in the *BSi Whistleblowing Arrangements Code of Practice* (2008), *ECS2000: A Guidance Document for the Implementation of the Ethics Compliance Standard 2000* (1999) and *Australian Standard AS8000* (Standards Australia International Committee 2003). In the field of specialised literature, the works by García-Marzá (2017), Calvo (2015a, b, 2016a, b), Miceli et al. (2013) and Vandekerckove (2006), among others, are outstanding.

impacts caused by its activity and the commitments it is capable of taking on. These include the ethical code, in which a company shows stakeholders the values guiding the way it acts and the commitments it can take on for implementing it in practice. Also, the social responsibility report which, as well as informing stakeholders about economic, social and environmental impacts through measurable and comparable indicators, is now being postulated as a communication platform for the results of monitoring. Finally, other communication mechanisms helping to open channels for information and dialogue with stakeholders.

3. Big data analytics tools: this is a set of big data analytics tools selected for monitoring specific and general aspects of corporate social responsibility. For example, as has already been explained, data analysis tools related to social responsibility legislation and reports; to the level of commitment and affectivity (motivations, emotions, feelings and passions) of stakeholders; to the level of trust, reputation, affinity and cohesion transmitted by the business; to the interests and expectations at stake; to the impacts caused by the business's economic, social and environmental activity; to existing and/or latent conflicts; to expectations, and so on.

4. Management and compliance tools: this concerns the design and establishment of three independent but complementary and necessary management and compliance mechanisms for monitoring (control, truthfulness and alerts) social responsibility: the social responsibility committee, the social responsibility audit and the compliance mechanism (García-Marzá 2017). The social responsibility committee, as a forum for the company's stakeholders to participate and deliberate, is concerned with ensuring the proper operation of the system; monitoring suggestions, alerts and reports received via the compliance mechanism; drawing up reports and improvement proposals for the monitoring system and compliance with social responsibility; advising the company on resolving disputes related to social responsibility, and so on. The audit is in charge of revising the system and all its elements as well as the quality and truthfulness of the information compiled, analysed and published. The compliance mechanism is concerned with systemising alerts, reports, suggestions and proposals for reviewing and improving the social responsibility monitoring system.

5. Training programme: this concerns designing and implementing a training programme to promote the monitoring system among stakeholders and encourage their committed participation in the process of compiling, scrutinising and publicising information. This stimulates the growth of the informed public and, as a result, the trust, reputation and affinity of stakeholders.

6. Person responsible for monitoring and compliance: this involves appointing a person principally responsible for the monitoring and management of the monitoring and compliance system.

As a result, big data and its analytic tools mean the monitoring of ethics and social responsibility is beginning to be perceived by businesses as a possible and necessary tool for meeting the standards of stakeholders' legitimate expectations; making intelligent decisions; and managing and making the most of the intangible goods on which the possibility of carrying out its activity properly depends. But stakeholders are also beginning to perceive the potential of big data and monitoring as an instrument for scrutinising and being well informed about the business's impacts and actions and making intelligent, elegant, autonomous decisions based on the strategic, moral, emotional and responsible benefits. Based on this, both demand open data and access not limited to tools for scrutinising, compiling and analysing data –*open big data*– in order to enjoy its benefits and prevent or minimise the negative effects of the information gap, the exclusion and the instrumentalisation that can be generated by the irresponsible use of big data.

In conclusion, as Tirole there are many forms of business management but very few of them are chosen (2017: 175). Ethics and social responsibility are an intelligent solution, as they offer businesses different but complementary and necessary mechanisms for autonomous communication. This allows them to seek intersubjective agreement with stakeholders, allowing the company to develop properly, survive and maximise business profits while generating and promoting prosocial emotions that can be practically implemented and creating a business culture to meet the requirements of the historical moment. Today, however, the big data revolution opens up the possibility of going a step further and designing new communication mechanisms capable of monitoring the moral and emotional dimension underlying the business, both in its decision-making processes and its relations with stakeholders.

A monitored business is an intelligent company ready for whatever the historical moment requires. The process means it is concerned with introducing into its design aspects like compassion, dialogue, care, reciprocity, ethical commitment and the active and committed participation of civil society by specifying and promoting both the right business culture and the prosocial emotions that allow its implementation, as well as establishing the mechanisms for control and public scrutiny to improve its transparency and credibility. It is a cordial business which, ultimately, chooses from the different options which, in the context of this planned world, makes it possible to maximise the benefits for all its stakeholders.

Bibliography

Anders, Günther. 1980. *Die Antiquiertheit des Menschen 2. Über die Zerstörung des Lebens im Zeitalter der dritten industriellen Revolution.* Munich: C. H. Beck [English vertion: Anders, Günther. 1980. *The Obsolescence of Man, Volume II: On the Destruction of Life in the Epoch of the Third Industrial Revolution*].

Boffey, Philipp M. 1971. Nader and the scientists: A call for responsibility. *Science* 171 (3971): 549–551.

Bowen, Howard R. 1953. *Social Responsibilities of Businessman.* New York: Harper and Row.

British Standards Institute. 2008. *BSi Whistleblowing Arrangements Code of Practice.* http://wbhelpline.org.uk/wp-content/uploads/2012/07/PAS1998_Whistleblowing1.pdf. Accessed 25 Sept 2017.

Brown, S. Lori, Roselie A. Bright, and Dale R. Tavris, eds. 2007. *Medical Device Epidemiology and Surveillance.* Chichester: Wiley.

Calvo, Patrici. 2015a. Economía ética hermenéutica-crítica y su gestión en las organizaciones. *Revista Venezolana de Gerencia* 20 (71): 534–553.

———. 2015b. Responsabilidad social ético-discursiva: el papel del *whistleblowing* en la emergencia y desarrollo de los bienes cordiales. *Neumann Business Review* 1 (2): 1–22.

———. 2016a. Economía con sentido moral. Un sistema de monitorización y gestión de la ética para las empresas y organizaciones. *Tópicos, Revista de Filosofía* 50: 211–248.

———. 2016b. *Whistleblowing* ante la miseria moral de instituciones y organizaciones. In *Empresa, Derechos Humanos y RSC. Una mirada holística desde las Ciencias Sociales y Jurídicas*, ed. J. Víctor Meseguer and Manuela Avilés, 135–153. Cizur Menor: Aranzadi Thomson Reuters.

———. 2016c. Hacía una economía cordial. *Veritas. Revista de Filosofía y Teología* 35: 29–56.

———. 2017. Ética de las cosas ante el desafío de la Industria 4.0. *Corresponsables*. http://www.corresponsables.com/actualidad/etica-en-la-industria. Accessed 14 Dec 2017.

COM 366 Final. 2001. *Green Paper. Promoting a European framework for Corporate Social Responsibility*. Brussels: European Commission.

Cortina, Adela. 1996. Comités de ética. In *Cuestiones morales*, ed. Osvaldo Guariglia, vol. 2, 291–306. Madrid: Trotta.

Davis, Keith. 1960. Can business afford to ignore social responsibilities? *California Management Review* 2 (3): 70–76.

———. 1973. The case for and against business assumption of social responsibilities. *The Academy of Management Journal* 16 (2): 312–322.

———. 1975. Five propositions for social responsibility. *Business Horizons* 18 (75): 19–24.

Davis, Keith, and Robert L. Blomstrom. 1966. *Business and Its Environment*. New York: McGraw-Hill.

Edelman Berland. 2015. *Trust Barometer 2015. Global Annual Study*. Edelman Berlan. http://www.edelman.com/insights/intellectual-property/2015-edelman-trust-barometer/. Accessed 25 Sept 2017.

———. 2016. *Trust Barometer 2016. Global Annual Study*. Edelman Berland. http://www.edelman.com/insights/intellectual-property/2016-edelman-trust-barometer/. Accessed 25 Sept 2017.

———. 2017. *Trust Barometer 2017. Global Annual Study*. Edelman Berland. http://www.edelman.com/trust2017/. Accessed 25 Sept 2017.

Elkington, John. 1994. Towards the sustainable corporation: Win-win-win strategies for sustainable development. *California Management Review* 36 (2): 90–100.

———. 1997. *Cannibals with Forks: The Triple Bottom Line of 21st Century Business*. London: Wiley.

European Council. 2000. *Lisbon European Council. Presidency Conclusions*. http://www.europarl.europa.eu/summits/lis1_en.htm?textMode=on. Accessed 25 Sept 2017.

Feenstra, Ramón A. 2012. *Democracia monitorizada en la era de la nueva galaxia mediática. La propuesta de John Keane*. Barcelona: Icaria.

———. 2015a. Activist and citizen political repertoire in Spain: A reflection based on civil society theory and different logics of political participation. *Journal of Civil Society* 11 (3): 242–258.

———. 2015b. El potencial transformador de la democracia monitorizada a debate: contextualización teórica y diálogo con John Keane. *Revista Teknokultura* 13 (2): 639–654.

Feenstra, Ramón A., Simon Tormey, Andreu Casero-Ripollés, and John Keane. 2017. *Refiguring Democracy: The Spanish Political Laboratory*. New York: Routledge.

Freeman, R. Edward. 1984. *Strategic Management: A Stakeholders Approach*. Boston: Pitman.

García-Marzá, Domingo. 1994. Asesoría Ética En La Empresa: Hacia Un Nuevo Concepto de Empresa. In *Ética de La Empresa*, ed. Adela Cortina, 123–144. Madrid: Trotta.

———. 2004. *Ética empresarial: del diálogo a la confianza*. Madrid: Trotta.

———. 2017. From ethical codes to ethical auditing: An ethical infraestructura for social responsibility communication. *El profesional de la información* 26 (2): 268–276.

Global Reporting Initiative. 2014. *G4 Sustainability Reporting Guidelines*. https://www.globalreporting.org/resourcelibrary/GRIG4-Part1-Reporting-Principles-and-Standard-Disclosures.pdf. Accessed 25 Sept 2017.

González-Esteban, Elsa. 1999. La empresa ante sus grupos de intereses: Una aproximación desde la literatura del análisis de los stakeholders. *Papeles de Etica, Economía y Dirección* 4: 1–13.

———. 2001. *La responsabilidad moral de la empresa. Una revisión de la teoría de Stakeholder desde la ética discursiva*. Castellón de la Plana: Universitat Jaume I.

———. 2002. Defining a post-conventional corporate moral responsibility. *Journal of Business Ethics* 39: 101–108.

———. 2007. La teoría de los Stakeholders. Un puente para el desarrollo práctico de la ética empresarial y de la responsabilidad social corporativa. *Veritas. Revista de Filosofía y Teología* 2 (17): 205–224.

———. 2012. Perspectiva de los grupos de interés en la RSE. In *Responsabilidad Social Empresarial*. México: Pearson.

Gracia, Diego. 2015. Mejoramiento humano ¿de qué estamos hablando? In *El mejoramiento humano: avances, investigaciones y reflexiones ética y políticas*, ed. César Ortega, Andrés Richard, Víctor Páramo, and Christian Ruíz, 20–30. Granada: Comares.

Grupo de Trabajo del Artículo 29 sobre Protección de Datos. 2006. *Dictamen 1/2006 elaborado por el Grupo de Trabajo del Artículo 29 sobre Protección de Datos (EUWP)*. https://www.agpd.es/portalwebAGPD/canaldocumentacion/docu_grupo_trabajo/wp29/2006/common/pdfs/WP-117-sarbanes-ES.pdf. Accessed 25 Sept 2017.

International Organization for Standardization. 2010. *Norma ISO 26000: 2010*. Genova: ISO.

Kocovic, Petar, Reinhold Behringer, Muthu Ramachandran, and Radomir Mihajlovic, eds. 2017. *Emerging Trends and Applications of the Internet of Things*. Hershey: IGI Global.

Lozano, José Félix. 2004. *Códigos éticos para el mundo empresarial*. Madrid: Trotta.

———. 2007. Códigos éticos y auditorías éticas. *Veritas. Revista de Filosofía y Teología* 2 (17): 225–221.

Miceli, Marcia P., Janet P. Near, and Terry Morehead-Dworkin. 2013. *Whistle-Blowing in Organizations*. New York: Routledge.

Monasterio, Aníbal. 2017. Ética Algorítmica: Implicaciones Éticas de Una Sociedad Cada Vez Más Gobernada Por Algoritmos. *Dilemata. Revista Internacional de Éticas Aplicadas* 24: 185–217.

Nader, Ralph, Peter Petkas, and Kate Blackwell, eds. 1972. *Whistle Blowing*. New York: Bantam.

Ortega, José y Gasset. 1958. *¿Qué es la filosofía?* Madrid: El Arquero. *Revista de Occidente*.

———. 1960. *Origen y epílogo de la filosofía*. Madrid: El Arquero. *Revista de Occidente*.

———. 1967. *The Origin of Philosophy*. New York: Northon & Company.

Oxford English Dictionary. 2017. *Cordial*. https://en.oxforddictionaries.com/definition/monitor. Accessed 25 Sept 2017.

Post, Linda F., and Jefrey Blustein. 2015. *Handbook for Health Care Ethics Committees*. 2nd ed. Baltimore: John Hopkins University Press.

Reitaku University Business Ethics and Compliance Research (R-bec). 1999. *A Guidance Document for the Implementation of the Ethics Compliance Standard 2000 (ECS2000 V1.2)*. http://www.consumer.go.jp/seisaku/shingikai/iinkai2/ecsguide(i).pdf. Accessed 25 Sept 2017.

Rodríguez, María P., Carlos F. Castaño, Valentina Osorio, Héctor F. Zuluaga, and Verónica Duque. 2006. La auditoría ética: herramienta para fortalecer la integridad del carácter organizacional. *Innovar. Revista de Ciencias Administrativas y Sociales* 16 (27): 25–46.

Roldán, Concha. 2015. *Leibniz. En el mejor de los mundos posibles*. Barcelona: Bonalletra Alcompas.

Sarbanes-Oxley Act. 2002. Public Law. No. 107–204, 116 Stat. 745 (July 30, 2002). USA.

Standards Australia International Committee. 2003. *Australian Standard AS8000*. Sydney: SAIC.

Suárez-Gonzalo, Sara. 2017. Big social data: límites del modelo *notice* and *choice* para la protección de la privacidad. *El profesional de la información* 26 (2): 283–292.

Tascón, Mario, and Arantza Coullaut. 2016. *Big Data y el Internet de las cosas*. Madrid: Catarata.

Tirole, Jean. 2017. *Economics for the Common Good*. Trans. S. Rendall. Princeton: Princeton University Press.

United Nations. 2011. *UN Guiding Principles on Business and Human Rights*. New York/Geneva: United Nations.

———. 2015. Resolution adopted by the General Assembly on 25 September 2015. http://www.un.org/ga/search/view_doc.asp?symbol=A/RES/70/1&Lang=E. Accessed 25 Sept 2017.

Vandekerckhove, Win. 2006. *Whistleblowing and Organizational Social Responsibility: A Global Assessment*. Farnham: Ashgate Publishing Ltd.

Yager, Ronald R., and Jordán-Pascual Espada, eds. 2017. *New Advances in the Internet of Things*. New York: Springer.

Zamagni, Stefano. 2013. *Impresa responsabile e mercato civile*. Il Mulino: Bologna.

———. 2014. El reto de la responsabilidad civil de la empresa. *Mediterráneo Económico* 26: 209–225.

———. 2017. Economics as if ethics mattered. In *Economics as a moral science*, ed. Peter Rona and Laszlo Zsolnai. Belind: Springer.

Index

Printed by Printforce, the Netherlands